Praise for *Running in Heels*

"I honestly believed Nicholas Sparks was the only author who would make me cry . . . but along came *Running in Heels* that within a few pages had tears running down my cheeks. I literally devoured this book." *-Silvia Martinez*

"A universal tale written with clarity and elegance. An honest, open and blameless account that is highly recommended for book groups and faith groups." *-Charli Mills*

"This story stays with you long after you turn the last page." *-K. Nelson*

"You cannot simply read this book; it must be gobbled. It should be required reading for high school students. Drug and alcohol abuse harms not only the addict and the people who love them, but also the little lives they bring into the world." *- KAN*

"The end of story irony blew me away. Who could be that forgiving? Mary could! From the depths to the triumphs, Mary A. Pérez had me from hello." *-Lynne Gregg*

"Stunning! Riveting. Raw. The story will break open your heart with Mary's vulnerability and strength. There are few people that could come out of the darkness like she did. The fact that this isn't fiction is mind blowing. This is a life preserver for anyone experiencing similar circumstances." *-Boymama*

"Mary's book is exceptionally well written, never allowing for boredom! It's a classic, must-read story of redemption for women and teenage girls who wish to avoid or recover from similar heartache. Well done, Mary Perez!" *-Rhonda Tarver*

"The moment I started it, I had echoes of *The Glass Castle*. This is recommended for anyone who loved Walls' memoirs, as they have some strong parallels." -*Kath Cross*

"This book was my book club's read this month. Wonderful story about determination, forgiveness, spirituality, and fulfillment. I purchased two more copies as gifts." -*Amazon Customer*

"This could have been anyone's story. It's relatable, emotional, and raw." -*KGR*

"Cunning and deeply profound tale of strength and hardship. The reader will see Mary's pain and struggles while taking a seedy tour of America's history. Generally well-written and soulful, this is a raw and colorful piece of art." -*Celia*

"Gripping story and superb writing. This book will make you grateful for the life you have as you walk through the pain and heartbreak that Mary went through. You will be moved." -*Howard Partridge, CEO Phenomenal Products, motivational speaker & business coach*

"Enthralling. I found myself staying up late into the night because I just had to know what the next page would bring. You feel the heartbreak of a little girl, the turmoil of a troubled young woman, and the peace and beauty of the woman she grows into." -*LoveBug1987*

"A lesson of dignity! An engrossing story with a gutsy protagonist who battles adversity." -*Penelope James*

"A heart-wrenching testament to perseverance in the face of constant physical and emotional violence. An honest portrait of abuse within two generations, chronicling the author's long and often painful journey to recover her life and her faith within a most difficult legacy." -*Rita M. Gardner, author of "THE COCONUT LATITUDES: Secrets, Storms and Survival in the Caribbean"*

"If you want to learn about love, read this book. If you need hope, read this book. If you want a lesson on forgiveness, read this book. If you are a wife, a daughter, or a mother, read this book. I promise that you will be inspired!"
-*Tina R. Allen*

"Powerful, riveting story! Mary's vivid descriptions of her life made me feel like I was right there with her."
-*Darryl Rodgers, A Life Half Lived: A True Story of Love, Addiction, Tragedy, and Hope*

"Loved the Sparish words and phrases sprinkled throughout. This is a beautiful book about God's love and care, even when we run from Him." -*Carrie Smith*

"Painfully parallel to my own life. Thank you, Mary for being so open with us." -*Karin Lynn Hill*

"Her writing captured my attention and heart, intriguing me every step along the way, keeping me turning pages as fast as I could. I was in awe." -*Daphne*

"This book will tear your heart out and then put it back in."
-*R.L.*

"I didn't want to put it down. Mary has an interesting way of writing and it kept me interested in what was going to happen next. I loved waiting to see what tidbit of my history she would add, the history I lived." -*Susie Winn, www.bedandbreakfastwoodville.com*

"The writing is first rate, cohesive, and tightly woven, no gaps to leave the reader wondering. Some of the narrative was disturbing, yes, but the reader in me kept pushing on to find the end I hoped for. Mary A. Perez delivers!" –*Anonymous*

"Let me say that the Grace of God was fully manifested in the life of this woman. Truly a book for the day and hour we are now in. Amazing love, amazing book!" –*Judy Harwell*

"The transparency of the author's ups and downs shows so much vulnerability, and she really paints vivid pictures with her words while we look through a window at her life's events. How wonderful for Jesus to arrive at the scene of a woman's tragedies and bring so much healing and fruit! Bravo, Mary! Don't ever stop writing!" –*Cat Ello*

"Very moving and highly inspirational. For those who grew up in a loving and stable environs, it is difficult to image what home life would be like if it were filled with drunkenness, shouting matches, and abuse. Yet the latter description captures only a portion of Perez's dysfunctional past. Written in three parts, Mary Perez' memoir delves into the spiritual healing of one woman who was once caught in the vicious cycle of codependency."
–*Anita Lock, Story Circle Book Reviews*

"A memoir of trials, tribulations, forgiveness and perseverance. It is well-written and certainly illustrates the horrors and consequences of alcoholism and co-dependency." -*Dania R. Nasca*

"This book is a 10! It can definitely change a life and save a life." -*Jenavia Powell*

"For anyone who needs a lift-me-up because they are either dealing with hardships or struggling with a tough childhood. It truly teaches one about survival, courage and strength." -*Aura Martinez*

"The fact that truth is stranger than fiction is made evident in this memoir, which makes this book a compelling, page turner! This is an excellent read and I promise the reader will find it difficult to lay this book down!" -*Deborah J. Hulen*

"Such a beautiful blend of raw honesty and humor gives permission to readers to courageously look at and accept the messy glory of each of our unique lives and enter into our own liberty of forgiveness — received and given. And to view our past through the lens of humor!" -*Jenny Welz*

"An inspiring memoir that illustrates God's hand on our lives despite the circumstances we see around us. Mary shares a simply told account of her journey that was by no means simple to live out." -*Mary Hare*

"Riveting and heartbreaking . . . This is really a book about hope! Mary has overcome and brings encouragement to wounded souls." -*Cynthia Watts*

"Could not put this book down. Had me crying, sad, and happy at times." *-Kathleen Molloy*

"This story should inspire anyone who has suffered abuse and neglect or lived with alcoholism, as well as anyone who has lost their way and feels their faith floundering." *-Dorrie Dobbs*

"Mary's story of overcoming repeated sufferings will inspire those who have also endured hunger, abandonment, prejudice, and heartbreak and will motivate us all to keep believing that there is hope for good to enter our lives at last."
-L. Faneca

"Mary Perez has opened wide the door to her life and welcomed us all in without fear of recrimination. Written in clear and precise language, Mary's youthful awareness, tinged with humor and adult intelligence, allows her to see life for what it is." *-Sally G. Cronin*

"A memoir of struggle and perseverance, resulting in tremendous growth. It was heartwarming and tragic, yet beautifully inspiring. It left me with a powerful sense of accomplishment and triumph. Mary gives us a glimpse into a world, which is foreign to many, yet so relatable to others."
-Daphne

"Running In Heels is a story of survival, hope, faith, and an amazing Godly forgiveness, which is truly inspiring. I had no high expectations so I was surprised at what a page-turner it was. It is a beautifully written narrative, and I could not put it down." *-Teresa Churcher*

Running in Heels

A Memoir of Grit and Grace

by Mary A. Pérez

RUNNING IN HEELS: A MEMOIR OF GRIT AND GRACE.
Copyright © 2016 by Mary Ann McNulty

Published by Stellar Communications Houston

This book is protected under the copyright laws of the United States of America. Any reproduction or other unauthorized use of the material herein is prohibited without the express written permission of the author. For information, contact Stellar Communications at www.stellarwriter.com. The author has endeavored to recreate events, locales and conversations from her memories of them. Some names and identifying details have been changed to protect the privacy of individuals.

First edition: February 24, 2015, by Chart House Press.
Second edition: May 1, 2016, by Stellar Communications Houston.

Published in the United States of America.

Running in Heels: A Memoir of Grit and Grace/by Mary A. Pérez

Join the conversation at www.maryaperez.com.

Paperback 978-1-944952-03-7
Ebook 978-1-944952-04-4
Hardcover 978-1-944952-05-1

Stellar Communications Houston
www.stellarwriter.com
281.804.7089

Preparation for publication by Thea Autry and
Ella Hearrean Ritchie
Cover design by Ashlie Cook
Interior design by Megan LaFollett & Lindsey Cousins

To Mama

In wanting to be better, do better, and become wiser, I realized that I had a lot to learn and am not without my own share of flaws. You did the best you knew to do. It can't be all bad—just look at me now. I love you then, I love you now. Forever your little girl.

ACKNOWLEDGEMENTS

My heartfelt thanks go to everyone who has been a part of my life's writing journey:

Ella Hearrean Ritchie with Stellar Communications Houston: for the smooth transition in welcoming me on her team. I look forward with great anticipation on our newfound journey together to building our working relationship.

Jeff Hastings, president of Chart House Press: for lending me your ear and believing in my work. Megan LaFollett, my multi-talented editor, patient advisor and friend: It was no accident the day we met. Adorable Aurelia: you went above and beyond, as you willingly allowed mud to be slathered over your legs in modeling for that perfect shot for my book cover. Ashlie Cook: your brilliant cover design and photography captured my story's theme. Thea Autry: you painstakingly and beautifully structured my sentences.

My beta-readers, Liane Faneca and Mike Wilson: your willingness in taking time out of your busy schedules to read my manuscript cover-to-cover, hold personal conversations and give insightful inputs.

To all who supported me emotionally and financially through the process of writing this book: to my pastors and church congregation, thank you for blessing *me*! Howard and

Denise Partridge: you both exude such caring and genuine hearts of pure gold. Sandy Brockhausen: from day one you never stopped supporting me and being my cheerleader. To all the numerous writers and authors in my writers group and in the Houston Writers Guild: your knowledge, critiques and guidance made all the difference in bringing life across on the printed pages. A special thanks to all my co-workers, fellow bloggers, and friends, who shared my vision and encouraged me to keep on writing.

To Mark, my husband, confidante, and best friend: you believed in me before I believed in myself. Without your love and support I would have quit long ago.

To Anna, my lovely and social media-savvy daughter: you shared my vision from the beginning. Your commitment and drive pushed me forward.

To Angela, my bubbly and beautiful inquisitive daughter: you finally get to know who killed the family cat—just kidding.

To Daniel, my one and only handsome son: you carried the voice of reason. Thank you for your support and encouragement.

To all my loving family across the miles: I thank you for being my biggest fans.

To my dear parents: thank you for the incredible stories—some stranger than fiction.

To my Lord and Savior Jesus Christ: You made a difference in my life. You taught me forgiveness and have made my tomorrow better than my yesterday.

Contents

Prologue	1
Chapter 1: Humble Beginnings	3
Chapter 2: Heaven, Hell or Hoboken	15
Chapter 3: To Abuela's House We Go	31
Chapter 4: The Little Green Dress	43
Chapter 5: Bump in the Night	49
Chapter 6: The Crux of the Matter	55
Chapter 7: Big Brother	71
Chapter 8: My Daddy's House	75
Chapter 9: Growing Pains	83
Chapter 10: A Rock and a Hard Place	89
Chapter 11: To Live Again	105
Chapter 12: My Dark and Shining Knight	119
Chapter 13: Pipe Dreams	127
Chapter 14: Colorado's Bicentennial Adventure	135
Chapter 15: Combustion	141
Chapter 16: Motherhood	147
Chapter 17: Letters From Home	155
Chapter 18: A Day of Reckoning	167
Chapter 19: My Two Cents	171
Chapter 20: New York, New York!	177
Chapter 21: My Guardian Angel	185
Chapter 22: Texas or Bust	189
Chapter 23: Let Go and Let God	197
Chapter 24: It's Official!	205
Chapter 25: And Then There Were Four	209
Chapter 26: Good as Gold	215
Chapter 27: No Guts, No Glory	221
Chapter 28: Oh, Brother!	225
Chapter 29: Gone, but not Forgotten	243
Chapter 30: Running in Heels	253
Chapter 31: My Grit, His Grace	259
Chapter 32: Into the Shark Tank	267

Chapter 33: Boy, Oh Boy!... 281
Chapter 34: On Borrowed Time.. 291
Chapter 35: Mrs. C... 299
Chapter 36: From the Inside Out 303
Chapter 37: Transition.. 309
Chapter 38: Mama Mía... 319
Chapter 39: Happy Birthday!... 329
Chapter 40: Storms Strike – 1990 333
Chapter 41: This Too Shall Pass 343
Chapter 42: The Catch 353
Chapter 43: Full Circle.. 367
Chapter 44: A Leaf in the Wind 375
Chapter 45: The Best for Last... 381
Epilogue... 383
About the Author... 392
Questions and Topics for Discussion 395

Running in Heels: A Memoir of Grit and Grace

Part 1

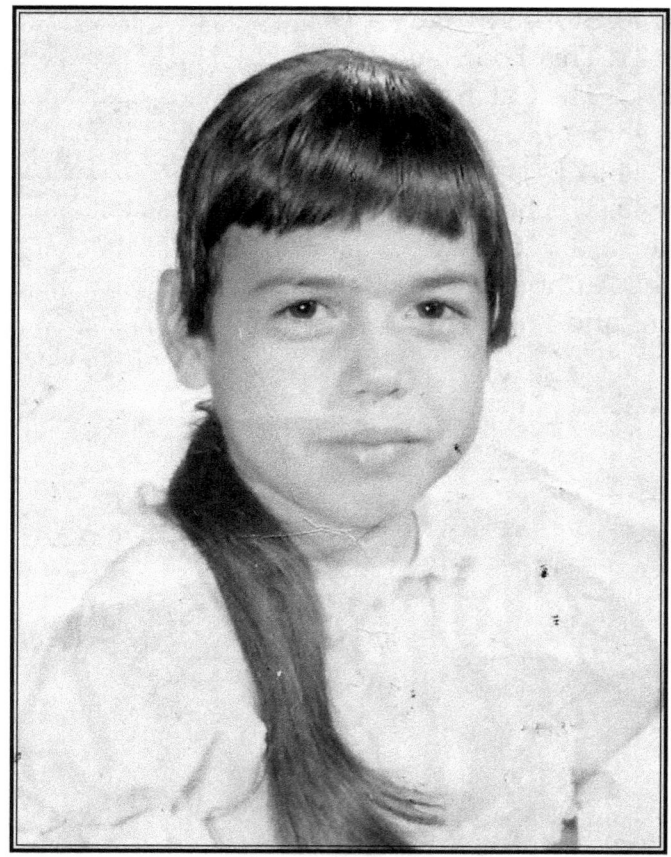

School Picture - 8 years old

Read on to learn the mystery of those crooked bangs.

Mary A. Pérez

PROLOGUE

THROUGH HALF-DRAWN CURTAINS, I watched the other children at play, chasing one another in a circle, chanting, "Duck. Duck. Goose!"

Humpty Dumpty, the daycare where Daddy dropped us off that morning, operated on a strict schedule. I knew I didn't fit in there. At lunchtime, they sat me in a dimly lit kitchen to finish the tough, chewy meat on my plate while the others went out for recess. By the time I cleaned my plate, they announced, "Lights out." I hated naptimes too.

By the time I was three, my parents were separated. My brother Ruben lived with Daddy while I stayed with Mama. Daddy had started coming for me, but on one visit he said I could stay and didn't need to go back. I was perfectly happy. I didn't know that Mama never agreed to him keeping me. Early one morning, determined to know where he took Ruben and me before he headed for work, Mama called for a taxi. She hunkered down inside and followed us to the daycare.

Later, parents came to collect their children. While my brother and I waited for Daddy, we played on the swings. That's when the clunking sound of an engine caught our attention. We were not expecting them, but Mama and her boyfriend Jimmy — my new stepdad — drove up in a gray jalopy.

Mama stuck her head out the window and waved us on.

"*Tout de suite!*" my mama shouted in the single French phrase that she knew, her arm pumping for us to hurry.

Trained to move *fast* whenever we heard the phrase, we bolted in their direction.

Jimmy yelled at Mama, "Stay in the car, Ruthie. I'll get 'em." He hoisted Ruben over the massive stonewall, and dropped him down the other side. Then he grabbed me by the arm and lifted me before sprinting toward that old heap. We clambered in and sped off. I glanced back to see the daycare worker running after us, screaming.

Mama and Jimmy, cackling with glee, celebrated their successful kidnapping scheme. A strong odor of beer permeated the air inside the car. I peered over at my brother who pretended to be brave with his gaped mouth and eyes gawking. I glanced down and noticed my scraped knees. A lump lodged in my throat; a tear escaped my eyes as I thought: *What will Daddy think when he comes for us?*

Even so, that wouldn't be the last time I'd be taken.

CHAPTER 1: HUMBLE BEGINNINGS

IN NEW YORK, Ruth "Ruthie" Méndez still lived at home in her twenties with her parents and brother. Benjamín "Benny" Pérez, a native from Puerto Rico, became her first boyfriend while attending church at *Roca de Salvación* and eyeing her there. Their courtship lasted a year. On the week of Ruthie's twenty-second birthday, they married. Benny was twenty-three. They moved to 594 Union Ave. in the Bronx. A year later, Ruben was born; I came along two years after him.

In 1962, we migrated south to join my maternal grandparents who had settled in Miami. Daddy began working at Grand Way, a large grocery chain store on Northwest Fifty-Fourth Street and Twelfth Ave. He paid the bills; Mama stayed home. We should have been a happy family. But I don't recall our living under the same roof together, let alone being "happy." I remembered Daddy being gone. I couldn't understand why he didn't take me too, and wondered if he loved my brother more than he did me. How could I have known the judge had ordered it that way?

After my parents' marriage dissolved, a neighbor seized the moment. James "Jimmy" Molloy had sleek combed-back hair, deep blue eyes, and a lanky build. In the guise of friendship, he showered my twenty-eight-year-old, naive Mama with attention and wormed his way into her heart. Far from being reliable or a provider, he was more of a schmoozer who loved to "shoot the breeze" and "drink it up," Mama had said.

Jimmy had orchestrated that entire kidnapping plot. Mama, fearing the cops, called my daddy soon afterward to let him know what they had done. Although Daddy was upset with Mama, neither one wanted the law involved. With that said, they returned Ruben.

Looking back, I had been glad when Mama and Jimmy came to take us away from that strict daycare where I felt deserted, although surrounded by kids. Those kids didn't speak to me and the women who worked there paraded with stark faces, snappy voices and rough hands. But I would learn about loneliness even when surrounded by others.

After Jimmy moved in with us, Mama took on his last name, yet they never married. Like a cunning spider building a web for its prey, my "stepdad" lured my mama into a world she never knew existed. She never stepped foot inside a bar before, but soon after, The Rainbow and The Bamboo were the notorious honky-tonks where she sat with Jimmy until dawn.

Mama said her first sip of wine she found so sweet that she drank it much too fast. Before long, I watched as Mama guzzled large amounts of beer and wine, puffing away on Jimmy's Pall Malls. She liked go-go dancing to *Pretty Woman* playing on the jukebox. She did this with a drink in hand while rolling and swaying her hips to the music.

They shot down drinks and scoffed, calling each other "loopy-looped." Twelve years her senior, my stepdad toyed with my mama as a lazy cat would with a helpless mouse. By the time Mama realized Jimmy's dependence on alcohol, it was too late. I watched her develop an insatiable thirst for the same poison. Once her appetite was whetted, its flame burned out of control.

Mama started to leave me home alone, saying I was mature for my age. Before she left for the night, she'd repeat specific instructions to me.

"Mary, don't open the door to anyone," Mama warned. "Don't let anyone know you're home alone."

She needn't have worried. If someone were to knock on the door, I wouldn't have uttered a sound. Alone in my own world, I sometimes pretended to be Shirley Temple. Her dimpled smile and blonde curly-locks got her noticed. I imagined if I pouted like her and smiled like her that I'd be pretty like her. But in the bathroom mirror, a brown-eyed, freckle-faced girl peered back. She had straight, dark hair and dingy clothes that hung loosely over scrawny legs. She looked plain, clumsy and insignificant. She was me.

I didn't know we lived below the poverty line. I knew the hunger pangs that clawed at my belly. I remember sneaking outdoors once, taking cold cuts away from stray cats so I could eat. I remember surviving on government surplus with tins of soft butter, brick cheese, powdered milk and creamy peanut butter. When we had it, nothing tasted better than smearing slabs of mayo over a slice of bread.

Food was scarce. Even after Daddy started sending money to Mama, I saw little food on the table. Liquor bottles and empty beer cans reeked and saturated the air. Constant bickering between Mama and Jimmy punctuated the tensions in our rodent-infested, cockroach matchbox. I'd see those creepy-crawlers on the walls, tables and dirty dishes on the counter. I'd hear them scratching behind the walls or running across the linoleum floor. I could even smell them. Those pests were our relentless, unwelcomed guests.

Early one morning, I stood on my bed too frightened to move, crying, "Mama! Mama!" A hideous, brown creature on the bare floor stared at me with a curled-up, pointed tail and claws ready to pinch.

Mama ran in with a look of horror with Jimmy close behind. "What is that thing?" she shrieked.

"See that tail?" Jimmy pointed. "You don't want it touching you."

"Get it away from me!" I squealed, stomping my feet. My bed—a cot pushed up against the wall—made me feel trapped. I imagined nearly stepping on the monster and the tail stabbing my foot. I wanted to turn away but couldn't. "Doooo something," I pleaded.

Jimmy disappeared for a second and returned with a small bottle in his hand. "This oughta do the trick," he said, pouring bleach over it, splattering the linoleum.

The fumes burned my eyes and made me cough.

Satisfied with the results, Jimmy lifted me out of bed. "That there is a scorpion, but he's kaput. He can't hurt you now."

Relieved, I hugged my stepdad's neck. At that moment, I thought him brave and smart. But because he pulled many disappearing acts whenever he latched onto some money, Mama didn't trust him and she later would call him a "louse," and "the biggest con artist ever."

"You see? If I don't watch him, he'll go off with some *puta*," she often complained.

"What's *puta*?" I asked her once.

"Don't say that," Mama had warned and added, "Means she's bad, a hussy."

I may not have known the meaning, but I knew it wasn't good.

I noticed after a drink or two, Jimmy would say he needed to go to the store but then wouldn't return. One evening, Mama wanted me to join her on a hunt for "the bum." After much walking, we found him in a hole-in-the-wall beer joint sitting beside a female friend. I'd seen this friend before, except Mama called her a *puta*. She wore too much perfume and too much makeup, her bleached blonde hair swept away from her face, tied high in a ponytail. She sat with her arms wrapped around Jimmy, wrists dangling with clusters of glittery bracelets and shiny rings.

I knew Mama had plenty of drink in her and was in one of her fearless Puerto Rican moods as we trudged up to the bar. She coached me on what to say.

"What are you doing with my stepdaddy?" I demanded from the evil *puta*.

She turned to me, but before words came out of her mouth, Mama shoved her off the stool. When she got up, she and Mama pushed, pulled and shoved, shouting horrible words—words I was never allowed to say. Jimmy stepped in between them. Soon, he and that *puta* left. Those close by who witnessed the catfight told Mama not to worry about the ditsy Blondie. But I thought they had said "dizzy." I gleamed with pride knowing my mama did that to her.

A day after my fourth birthday, a man named Martin Luther King, Jr. led a quarter million people in a march. As I watched him on TV, I asked Mama about him and she said he was someone famous. I liked his voice. The tone of his words

echoed like distant thunder when he delivered his "I Have a Dream" speech. I wasn't sure why some loved Mr. King's dream and others didn't.

Mama said some people were two-faced, yet she herself acted like two different people.

She loved to eat. She hated to cook. She loved acting *muy grosero* yet shrieked from the sight of palmetto bugs. She loved her drinks. She hated drunks. She loved Jimmy. She hated him. According to Mama, "Jimmy's full of it and craves attention." She never knew what to expect from him. She hated that too.

On a rare but cherished winter night, Jimmy unexpectedly came home with a surprise and tossed a brown sack onto my lap. Puzzled about what could be inside, I hesitated to open it. The bag moved. I jumped. I glanced at Mama and she nodded her head to continue. The bag moved again. I inched forward and peered in. Then the eyes of a black puppy looked back at me. Holding my breath, I lifted her out. Her long, wet tongue washed my face and made me giggle. I loved her and named her Blackie.

She followed me around. She kept me company. At night, she slept on my neck and kept me warm. Once, when my parents yelled at me, she growled. I laughed inside and hugged her. I knew she loved me, too.

My joy turned to heartbreak the day she disappeared.

"Mama, have you seen my puppy?"

"We can't keep her."

"Mama, why? Why can't we?"

"Because Blackie's full of fleas."

"I'll give her a bath."

"We can't feed her."

"She can eat my food," I sobbed.

"That's enough, Mary."

Again, I asked, "But why, Mama?"

"Nothing lasts forever," she said, still reading her magazine.

I'd have kept Blackie forever.

Mama wouldn't look at me. I hated her then and cried for weeks.

But there were some better days. A neighbor, a hefty woman with floppy arms, lived alone and liked children. Whenever I stopped in for a visit, she'd have a treat to offer me. She handed me a large chocolate Easter bunny once and then asked what I wanted for breakfast.

"French toast!" I sang, bouncing up and down. The neighbor put on an apron and shooed me out of her kitchen with her jiggling arms.

In the dining room, I sat on a chair with my legs swinging. I got up to stretch. I walked around and traced my hand over a flower arrangement, almost knocking the vase over. My eye caught a candy dish that sat in the center . . .

"Don't you touch anything," the neighbor called from the kitchen.

"I'm not," I replied and returned the purple jellybean that I had licked.

A black cat-shaped clock hung on the wall. I followed the big, moving eyes and long, swinging tail—back and forth, back and forth, tick-tock, tick-tock. I gazed across dusty photo frames that filled the shelves and windowsills and wondered if any pictures were of her as a child. I wanted to thumb through her assortment of worn-out picture books and *Life* magazines stacked on bookshelves and floor. But I didn't dare.

The aroma coming from the kitchen made my stomach rumble. I heard footsteps and raced to sit back down. The neighbor put a plate in front of me stacked with golden-brown French toast. She poured warm maple syrup over the fluffy slices of sweet bread. I knew I never smelled or tasted anything so delicious. My one regret: eating too fast and becoming full too quickly. Then I watched, horrified, as she collected my plate and tossed the rest into the trash, because I had eaten half a slice and tried to hide it in the bottom of the stack. I would have brought the rest home to share with Mama and eat later.

At four, I already had a keen mother-hen instinct kicking in, especially over my brother, a shy six-year-old. On one of his occasional visits, we played barefoot in the dirt road nearby. A neighborhood bully with a thick neck, arms and legs lived in the same area. He began poking fun at Ruben, calling him names like "chicken" and "sissy-pants." Then he flung a crushed soda can at my brother and nicked the top of his forehead. Blood oozed down Ruben's face and he started crying.

I became furious; I threw rocks at the meanie. "Go'n! Scram, you doongyhead!" I yelled at Ruben's tormentor. "Leave my brother alone or I'm gonna shove your head down your throat!" I imitated one of Mama's threats in my loudest voice until he ran off.

From the window, Mama saw the entire scene but didn't try to stop the bully. She belittled Ruben for being a scaredy-cat even though she herself grew fearful, especially whenever Jimmy was gone all night.

From my cot early one morning, I gawked over at Mama's bed and rubbed my eyes, unsure of the scene before me.

My heart pounded in my chest. Someone was in bed with my mama and it wasn't Jimmy, because I knew Jimmy was in jail. The stranger's unshaved face turned to one side, lips parted. One arm lay across his chest, the other extended toward Mama. Hairy legs stuck out from under the sheet.

Mama was sitting like a stone. When her gaze met mine, flecks of fear swam in her eyes. She placed a trembling finger to her lips, motioning for me to keep quiet. I didn't dare twitch. Finally, the stranger stirred and opened his eyes. He turned his head and looked about the room in a drunken daze.

Wide-eyed, I couldn't stop staring.

"Tell your little girl to turn around." He spoke in a deep voice that made me leap.

"Mary . . . ," Mama's voice sounded terrified.

"Yes ma'am." I turned to face the wall. I heard him pull his pants on, his belt jangling. When the screen door slammed shut, I rushed toward Mama who was peeking out the window.

"Mama! Who's that man? What did he want? Why was he here? Did he hurt you?"

"Hush, Mary." She stared at the door. "It's over. He's gone."

Mama sat on the edge of the bed, biting her nails. I wished she'd talk to me. I started to ask her questions, but she shushed me and went to take a shower.

That's when I saw the broken screen. The intruder had climbed in through a side window. He forced himself on Mama, and he took advantage of her while I slept close by.

Mama, fearing for her life, never cried out. She never reported the incident to the police.

Jimmy's release from jail, where he'd been held several

days for public intoxication, didn't make our lives any better. Mama's attempts to explain the rape led to never-ending arguments. I wasn't sure what "rape" meant but Jimmy called her a "damn liar" whenever she said it.

Many things were beyond my comprehension.

The week before Thanksgiving at my grandparents' house, I enjoyed the peaceful ambiance where I felt loved and cared for. My grandparents showered me with attention. I looked forward to the upcoming holiday, especially Grandma's stuffed *pavo* with tons of mashed potatoes, gravy, and cranberry sauce.

On that particular day, I lay on their living room floor, watching the crowds on TV who stood in respectful silence observing a funeral procession. The clopping sounds of horses' hooves echoed as they pulled a carriage carrying a coffin draped with the Stars and Stripes. I knew the world lost an important man. As I studied the sorrowful faces of my grandparents and peered into their misty eyes, my heart broke, too.

One morning, a serious Grandpa gazed out the window, deep in thought. With a sad but loud voice, he bellowed, "He was a greaaaat man! He was a greaaaat man!" I later realized that Grandpa referred to President John F. Kennedy.

A month later, back home with Mama, my first memory of a grand Christmas with her was marked by the image of beautifully wrapped gift boxes circling a "Charlie Brown" Christmas tree. My eyes grew bigger and bigger, taking in so much at one time. It looked like a fairy-tale picture book. Tons of yummy desserts, candies and food—more than my wildest dream—lined the table. Glazed ham, yams, cranberry sauce, apple pie, cherry pie, cookies, candy canes. There was even a gingerbread house. Mama said not to be greedy. Even so, I couldn't keep my mouth from watering. Then I couldn't decide whether to eat or play first.

I loved my new stuffed orange, huggable tiger. His face calmed me. His soft whiskers tickled me. It felt comforting to carry him around. When I asked Mama where everything came from, she said with a frown that Grandma had called a local church asking for help.

Why did Mama have to ruin everything? Didn't she want me happy? Couldn't she say I was good and that Santa Claus came by?

Mama wasn't cheerful. She was sad and going to have a baby. I heard her say how mixed-up she was, uncertain who the father might be. After the welfare folks pressured her, she agreed to give her baby up for adoption. I wasn't sure what that meant either.

In May of 1964 at Miami Jackson Memorial, a baby boy came into the world. For a moment, Mama cradled him in her arms. She then handed him to the caseworker who carried him away. They had called him Steve.

Mama returned home from the hospital empty-handed and heartbroken.

Hurricane Cleo struck Miami with 100-mile-per-hour winds in late August of 1964. Fallen branches and debris flew across the yard. The pelting rain rattled against our old wooden door and the thin, sheet glass-paned windows.

Jimmy placed a dresser against the front door to our efficiency apartment to keep it from flying open. Mama and I hunkered down in the dark bathroom like cornered animals. I sat on the floor with my knees pulled up. I covered my ears with my hands, trying to drown out the deafening gusts of wind and my mama's panicking cries.

Yet in the same instant that I closed my eyes, the thoughts tumbled through my mind: *Gosh, today is my birthday; I am five years old. Mama said I'm a 'big girl' now.*

I wondered if my big brother Ruben remained safe from the storm. Was he ever afraid like me? Felt lonely? Invisible?

Then I heard that Ruben and Daddy were safe, vacationing in Puerto Rico during Cleo.

Lucky him.

Three months later, Mama and I waited in line at the clinic for a checkup. On the opposite side, the same woman who had handled the adoption waited. She held a baby in her arms. We noticed Steve—with piercing blue eyes—the same color as Jimmy's eyes.

"Look, Mary," Mama whispered. "There's your baby brother. He's so big now."

I heard sadness and pain in Mama's voice.

The caseworker noticed us and scurried away.

"Go get him," I said, looking up at Mama. "Take him from her."

"No, Mary," she said before pausing to sign her name at the check-in, "we can't." The longing in her voice spoke volumes. I wanted to look for that lady with my baby brother, but Mama grabbed my wrist to go into the waiting lobby instead.

Sometime later, the loudspeaker blared, "Ruth Ann Méndez-Pérez-Molloy! Please come to the front desk!"

I often thought about Steve. *Where did he live? Will we ever see him again? Did he have enough to eat? Can he feel us missing him? Is he lonely?*

Mary A. Pérez

CHAPTER 2: HEAVEN, HELL OR HOBOKEN

Jersey, 1965

WE MOVED TO New Jersey when I was six. The term "upper class" didn't mean us. Neither did the term "middle class." We didn't move *up* in the world, but we did move way *down*. Down into a hellhole. At least that's what Mama often said. Our residence: a drafty basement at the bottom of a five-story building. Pipes covered the walls and ceiling; we even had a boiler room.

Hoboken beckoned my stepdad for its bars—one on every corner. A stand-up bar nearby served steamed clams, the shells tossed onto sawdust-covered floors. Those delicacies accompanied a tall glass of beer. No one appeared to mind my presence, as I remained by my stepdad's side. Jimmy gave me my first sample of clams—a bit salty but tasty.

In those bars, women and children sat in the back, the front reserved for the men at the counter on stools. While Mama and I waited for Jimmy to satisfy his thirst, he ignored us and threw down drink after drink, joking with the fellows around him.

"That louse," Mama mumbled, drumming her fingers on the table, glaring at him from across the room.

The jukebox played my parents' favorite songs one after

another: Frank Sinatra's *Strangers in the Night,* Eddy Arnold's *I Can't Stop Loving You,* and Nat King Cole's *Ramblin' Rose.* Jimmy waved his hands as he sang along but never in tune.

Peanuts were plentiful, the shells scattered about on the floor. I didn't care for the peanuts. I preferred pickled eggs in the large jar. The bartender brought over a sandwich and chips for Mama and me to share. He placed a bottle of cola in front of me and winked.

"Mama, why does the bread have seeds in it?" I asked, sniffing it after the man left.

"It's rye bread, Mary. Just eat it."

I took a bite but couldn't swallow. I grabbed my soda and knocked it over.

"Oh, for heaven sakes, wipe that up," Mama huffed and reached for my plate, still eyeballing Jimmy. "I'll eat this if you're just going to play with it."

My stepdad's singing and laughter echoed across Hudson River to Manhattan. Mama's eyes narrowed, her face turning red. "I oughta go over there, smack him in the face and take his money away."

She was mad enough to do it too. But Mama, being co-dependent, tolerated Jimmy's out- of-control behavior. Despite my young age, she griped and complained to *me* but seldom knew what to do. I listened while my mama rambled, until I'd fall asleep at the table with my head on my forearms.

Mama never cooked. Jimmy knew how to throw anything together and make it edible. I even saw him once gather fistfuls of snow to make a pot of rice because we lacked running water. One time he gave me a quick cooking lesson so he could leave me to prepare a meal.

"Break the spaghetti in half," Jimmy began his instructions. "Put it in the pot after the water boils," he continued. "Then drain it like so . . . ," He deftly held the empty pot with lid over the sink.

I wondered how I might lift that heavy pot to drain the water and keep a lid over it.

". . . toss in some tomato sauce, a dab of sugar . . ."

What if the spaghetti spills out all over the floor?

". . . season it with a pinch of salt, pepper . . ."

My head swirled with visions of one big mess.

"And," Jimmy added with a wink, "don't forget to stir."

The instruction over, my parents headed out for a nightcap. I stayed home as Chef Mary, kneeling on a chair, trying to remember the difference between a "dab" and a "pinch."

Sometime later, I awoke to voices and the clanking of dishes. It wasn't unusual for my parents to come home squabbling in the wee hours of the night. Through my sleepiness, with my chin resting on my hands, I watched as they devoured my cold pasta creation, unmindful that the noodles were chewy or the sauce soupy.

"You're a quick learner," Jimmy said.

I beamed with pride before dozing off.

In general, my stepdad was good to me, but Mama often called him two-faced. I don't recall when he started hitting her. But I'd hear her crying and I saw marks on her jaw.

Jimmy thought himself wise and became philosophical whenever he drank. He routinely came home in the middle of night, long-winded. After he flipped on every light-switch and opened all the windows, he cranked up the radio, blubbering to songs like *Winchester Cathedral*.

Once I was awake, Jimmy often called on me to listen to him rant and rave about everything and nothing. He'd sit on the windowsill, peer up toward the sky and ramble about the heavens, the moon, and the stars. He repeated adages like:

"Nothing tells the truth like the mirror."

"Never let your right hand know what your left hand is doing."

"No two leaves on a tree are alike."

I never wanted to miss a word but couldn't keep from yawning. I tried staying alert, but my eyelids grew heavy, my mind foggy as Jimmy's voice faded in and out:

". . . or get off the pot . . ."

"Die . . . pay taxes . . . go to jail!"

Mama didn't work outside the home on account of emotional problems, so she depended on Jimmy. Jimmy depended on intoxicated wit. Holding on to long-term jobs wasn't in his vocabulary, so he sought temporary handy-man work. He'd wear clothes with paint stains splattered on them on purpose, "just to play the part," Mama had said.

Often unable to pay rent, we'd find ourselves locked out, with our stuff even tossed out on the curb. We suffered our losses and trudged on, wandering like "some damn gypsies," according to Mama.

Jimmy, nowhere in sight, sometimes left Mama and me roaming the streets hungry and tired throughout the night. Those hellacious events happened in our lives as a recurring nightmare . . . filled with hideous monsters prowling in my dreams.

Two evenings in a row, Mama and I took turns peeking inside Jimmy's favorite hangouts. Since we couldn't find him, we'd trudge on over to the police station hoping for assistance. Each time, they put us up in a motel and gave us enough money for a meal or two.

We stayed in a small dingy room with a bed. We drank tap water from the bathroom faucet located down the narrow hallway. The food left in our room consisted of a can of pork and beans to eat cold between slices of bread. Sometimes we ate sandwiches that were just mayonnaise spread over a single slice of bread, rolled up. It tasted good to me, plus I had Mama to myself.

When we sat in a crowded charity hospital's waiting room to warm ourselves from the chill in our bones, an observant security officer walked us to the exit.

Out in Jersey's bitter cold, the moon full, the trees rustled. Mama and I spent half the night shivering, huddled together on a bus bench, my head on her lap.

"M-Mama," my teeth chattered. "I'm cold."

"I am too. Now stay still."

"But I'm hungry."

"I know, Mary. Close your eyes. That *bum*. Where is he?"

We would have frozen if a kind woman hadn't invited us up to her place to sleep on her sofa overnight.

Whenever Mama cornered Jimmy in a bar, drinking his pay away, after bickering over *dinero*, she'd remain with him. If I happened to be around, they sent me away, or Mama left me at home by myself. It saddened me how she preferred being with him than with me. Often they'd stagger home and pass out in a stupor. Only then did the arguments cease and the fights end.

More often than not, I'd gone to bed with the sound of my stomach rumbling. Mama and Jimmy routinely barged in from a night of carousing.

"Mama, I'm hungry," I mumbled, rubbing the sleep from my eyes.

"Why are you awake?"

"Can you fix me something to eat?"

"Oh, for goodness sake. It's late." She turned on the hotplate to fry a hotdog. A few minutes later, she'd have one for me rolled inside a slice of bread. "Here. Sit up."

"Fix me one, too," Jimmy demanded.

"Hold your horses," Mama snapped.

As soon as I finished, I laid back down, my eyelids heavy. Eventually, the bright lights in the room faded. My parents' fussing drifted away as sleep overtook me, but not before I heard familiar sounds. A can popping open. A curse word. A slap. Sobs.

Although I was unsure why, one evening Jimmy overturned the bed that Mama and I slept in. We tumbled onto the hard floor. As Mama struggled to rise, Jimmy pulled her by the arm and shoved her into a windowpane. Jimmy became aware of my presence and after he flipped the bed upright, he ordered me back into it. I faced the wall sniffling until I fell asleep.

The next morning, I awoke to the sight of a blood-spattered Mama hobbling on crutches. I ran to help her.

"Mama, what happened?"

"It's nothing, Mary. Stop crying! I tripped, that's all."

I couldn't help but wonder, *Why did she think I didn't know anything?*

I knew some things. I hid loose change and planned to save enough money to take care of Mama one day. In my childish mind, I knew that one day we were going to live in a big house, have plenty to eat, and Mama wouldn't ever have to worry again.

That afternoon I heard cursing and knew it wasn't good. A rattling sound carried around the wall like something whirling in a container. Then, to see Jimmy shaking my pink, plastic kitty-bank upside down in mid-air — my pennies, dimes and nickels clattering onto the floor — made me weak and sick inside.

I followed the coins that rolled under a chair and dove for them. I looked up, my eyes darting between Mama and Jimmy, hoping she'd do something. Mama called him a "jackass," but that didn't stop him. He couldn't care less that I knelt there sobbing. He expressed zero shame as he scooped the scattered change into his pocket. *My* coins.

Later, Mama told me that Jimmy was just thirsty and to stop sniffling. "He'll return the money soon enough," she said. I knew that wasn't true.

On my knees, I gathered up the broken pieces of my kitty-bank. With no more tears left, I seethed, thinking, *maybe Mama can take care of herself. And maybe I'll never talk to her again. Or to Jimmy. And maybe I'll run away . . . to my real daddy.*

In my dreams, I escaped hideous monsters by floating away to safety. But those nightmares continually turned into never-ending terror as my real world infiltrated them.

Once, in the middle of night, I tossed and turned in my underwear, hot with fever and drenched in sweat. My mind fuzzy, I climbed out of bed. I wanted a drink of water but froze when a strange distorted image blocked my path. Confusion, panic and terror blinded me. I couldn't make out *who* or *what* I was seeing. In slow motion, *it* slithered closer and closer.

I raised my hands in sheer fright and pleaded, "Noooo,

stop! Go away!"

When I came to and the vision cleared, Mama stood in front of me, her expression twisted with amusement. Instead of treating me with a kid-glove approach, she chided me.

"What s'matter with you? Sleepwalking again? Get back in bed."

"Mama! You scared me . . . you looked funny."

"Oh, for heaven's sake." She groaned. "Go to sleep."

Confused, I lay down on my cot and eventually dozed off.

In yet another harrowing episode, lying in my bed with fever, the ceiling appeared rubbery like I'd seen in a cartoon. It rose and fell, back and forth, back and forth—closing in and expanding. Faster and faster. Nearer and nearer. Almost touching my face. Even with eyes shut, I imagined the same odd sensation. I didn't try to explain it to anyone.

Years later, as I worried over my own daughter's fever, I understood the danger my mama's lack of knowledge could have caused me. Untreated high fevers may accompany hallucinations in children. My hallucinations as a child could have become life threatening.

September 1966

A month after my seventh birthday, Mama went into labor with baby number four. When we arrived at Margaret Hague Maternity Hospital, Mama's face twisted in pain and an attendant sped her away on a wheelchair. Before disappearing behind the huge metal doors, she shouted for me to stay put and to wait for Jimmy.

Unable to keep my eyes open, I pushed two chairs together, curled up, and went to sleep. No one bothered me; maybe they thought I actually belonged to someone.

The next morning, Jimmy appeared and took me to a woman's apartment. Bent over, she walked with a limp. She wore a wrinkled face that frowned. When she talked, teeth were missing. She smelled funny too. Mama said don't talk with strangers, but wasn't this lady one?

"Why I gotta stay with *her?*"

"Gonna get your mama and your new baby sister," Jimmy answered, his breath smelling of beer. He promised the lady some money for my care in a couple of days. The old lady mumbled something. I didn't want to stay with her. Jimmy patted my head and then left.

He failed to return.

The first night, she told me that she had drowned kittens one by one in the tub filled with water. I refused to take baths there. I had a difficult enough time trying to erase the horrible image of her single breast whenever she undressed.

A week later, the old woman called the authorities to come for me. "Are you gonna arrest me?" I asked the cop as soon as he walked in. "I'm a good girl."

He spoke in a soft voice and assured me that I wasn't in any trouble. We walked together to his car. I hesitated to climb inside; he was a stranger. He lifted me and let me sit in the front seat. He reassured me that he wanted to find my parents. My tears still fell.

Sometime later at the police station, I sat cross-legged on top of the counter with an ice cream cone one officer bought to cheer me up.

A tall officer with kind eyes peered down at me and said, "Why, aren't you something?"

"I'm Ruthie's little girl," I corrected him.

He chuckled. "They tell me your name's Mary Ann.

What's your mother's name?"

I slurped on my vanilla cone. "Ruth Ann."

"Last name Pérez?" asked another with a warm smile.

"Nope. It's Méndez-Pérez-Molloy," I said between licks.

"Three last names?"

I nodded.

"Right. And your father's name?"

"I have two." I grinned. "My real daddy is Benjamín Pérez."

The tall cop handed me a napkin.

"And what's your other daddy's name?"

"My stepdaddy is James Francis Aloysius Molloy," I answered, proud for knowing his full name.

The ice cream dribbled down my chin and on my shirt. The officer with the warm smile chuckled, pulled a napkin out and dabbed my chin.

Soon my parents walked in, carrying a bundle in a pink blanket. Jimmy handed it to me, saying, "Her name is Anna."

"Keep your hand holding the back of her head, now," Mama instructed.

While they talked with the officers, I held my new baby sister close and cradled her head.

Soft, velvety cheeks. A round rosy nose. Dark hair like mine, but curly. Eyes, blue that sparkled like the ocean I'd seen in storybooks. I kissed her sweet-smelling face. Her soft, pudgy hand with tiny fingers, curled inside mine. Anna melted my heart. *I won't be alone anymore.* I caressed her cheeks and whispered, "I'll stay by your side for always."

Soon left with the responsibility of caring for Anna, I became her substitute mother. I loved her and took care of her as best as a seven-year-old could.

The day we ran out of baby formula and diapers, I didn't know what to do. I waited until Anna stopped fussing and fell asleep in her carriage (we didn't have a crib for her). Then I ran to the corner to a hole-in-the-wall where I knew my mama and stepdad were.

A blinking neon beer sign over the door clattered when I pushed it open. Dimmed lights hung from the ceiling. The haze of cigarette smoke made my eyes water and nose run. Loud music played on the jukebox. Boisterous men and women engaged in a game of shuffleboard, others threw darts. Still others, sloshing their drinks, perched themselves on barstools, carrying on like screaming peacocks.

"Whataya have?" yelled the bartender. I jumped at his voice, thinking he meant me.

"Hey Charlie, whose girl is this?" a man grinning with a silver tooth asked.

"She's Ruthie's little girl," Charlie answered, pointing in the direction where Mama sat.

The all-too-familiar, rowdy voices of my parents' cursing at each other reached my ears. I ran toward them. When I told Mama about Anna, she and Jimmy started arguing over money.

I waited, feeling forgotten, wishing Mama would hurry and come home with me. Then someone handed me a nickel to play the jukebox. I remembered my manners, thanked him, put my coin in the slot, and punched in the numbers to *Spanish Eyes*.

At last, Jimmy gave Mama what she wanted, but he continued to roost on his stool.

When we got home, we never imagined that someone had called the cops. They met us at our front door holding my naked sister, wrapped in a soiled blanket.

"Is this your baby?" an officer demanded of Mama.

"Yes . . . yes . . . ," her voice cracked.

"Ma'am, have you been drinking?" the other cop asked in a gruff voice. But before Mama answered, he stepped forward and said, "Turn around and put your hands behind your back. You're under arrest for child abandonment."

"Ma—?" I choked back the burn in my throat.

To my horror, the police officer put handcuffs on Mama and started telling her something about "remaining silent."

Why can't she talk? "Tell him, Mama," I insisted and started to cry. I turned to the officer to explain, "We *were* going to buy milk and diapers for my sister . . ."

He didn't hear me and shoved Mama in his police car. She looked at me; her face glistened with tears running down as they drove away.

"Where . . . is he taking my mama?" I choked, sobbing. I hovered close to Anna, ready to grab my sister, to run fast and hide before he took us to jail, too. In my confusion, I don't recall what he said except that they were there to help and to take us to protective custody. *I protect my sister*, I thought. I begged him not to separate us.

The cop drove us to a children's hospital for routine examination and to remain there for safekeeping until a suitable family member claimed us.

No one showed up.

Ragamuffin

Before suppertime, Anna and I needed a much overdue bath. A nurse's aide took my sister to get one and another helped me with mine. I sat on the ledge of the tub waiting for it to fill. The warm water running over my feet felt good, washing the dirt and grime away. When the aide added bubbles, I plopped right into the inviting suds with glee.

"You're splashing water everywhere," the aide said and smiled, dabbing a washcloth on her high cheekbone. She was pretty and talked in a soft voice. Her hair was up in a bun. She pushed back a ringlet behind her ear. "Let's get that long hair shampooed," she said.

After we were done, I giggled to see the tips of my fingers and toes wrinkled. Given jammies to wear, I marveled at how clean they smelled and how soft they felt.

With my hair still dripping, the aide tried to comb out my tangles. Then she said my hair needed cutting. "When I'm finished, you'll be a pretty little ragamuffin," she promised.

Ragamuffin? I thought to myself. *I don't wanna be that. I just wanna be Shirley Temple.* Minutes later, my sense of well-being came to a halt. When I glanced in the mirror, a boy stared back. I remember thinking: *I won't ever look like Shirley Temple.*

The lady had chopped my hair clear off to my ears. The drastic cut, owing to huge, tangled knots—some the size of my fist—from not having my hair combed for long periods. I then felt another blow to the gut when she said, "Honey, we need to get you some medicine. You have ringworms on your back, feet and ankles."

Days later, I celebrated my eighth birthday at that hospital. The staff surprised me with a birthday cake, ice cream, and a blonde Twist-N-Turn Barbie.

At bedtime, I thought about Mama. My eyes welled with tears. I missed her nonstop chatter. I missed the way her soft, fair skin smelled of Jergens lotion, and the scent of Alberto VO5 in her brown hair. Before I went to sleep, I sensed her near, saying to me, "Happy birthday, Mary, wherever you are."

On a Sunday morning, I colored on my bed, still in the hospital. Anna napped in hers.

Suddenly, Jimmy bolted in.

"Jimmy!" I cried.

"*Ferme la bouche.*" The tone of his voice made me flinch. He wanted me to hush and I braced for the worst. His breath smelled of booze. His eyes were fierce like that of a wild man's; his forehead dripped with sweat. He glanced behind him before pulling my half-asleep sister out of her bed in her blanket and headed for the door.

"*Tout de suite!*" Jimmy barked over his shoulder.

No time to think.

Dead on his heels, I ran to the stairwell, down four flights of concrete steps and out the exit, nearly running into security guards pointing guns to our heads.

"Freeze!" a guard shouted. Jimmy did a tailspin, bouncing Anna in his arms.

"*Run*, Mary!" Jimmy bellowed without looking back.

Among the parked cars, Jimmy zigged one way, I zagged the other. The security guards scrambled in hot pursuit. In all the commotion and half out of my mind, I froze.

Petrified that they'd shoot Jimmy while he held Anna, I became frantic. "Don't shoot!" I pleaded. "Please don't shoot my stepdaddy! Jimmy stop! Please stop!" I bawled.

Jimmy quit running and surrendered. They took Anna from him and then restrained him in handcuffs. Anna never uttered a sound. They hauled Jimmy to jail. I felt at a loss knowing I had two parents locked away. Exhausted from the chaos, a security officer hoisted me in his arms and carried me back to our room.

To my amazement, hospital staff and patients witnessed the kidnapping attempt, their faces glued to the windows, cheering. I felt like an instant celebrity—the topic of everyone's conversation—the most attention I ever received.

I lost all track of time while we stayed in the hospital, but the happy day came when a familiar face claimed my sister and me.

Running in Heels: A Memoir of Grit and Grace

Mary A. Pérez

CHAPTER 3: TO *ABUELA'S* HOUSE WE GO

MY NOSE WAS pressed to the window. "Are we still in New Jersey?" I stared at the billowy clouds below and bounced on my seat when I saw a bunny shape, pointing it out to Anna.

"Dun worry, dear," Grandma said in her Spanish accent, patting my arm. "We will be in Miami soon enough."

At 5'2", Grandma was a pleasantly plump woman with a round face and full lips. She had a light olive complexion and wore reading glasses that sat on a nose "too fat," she would often complain. Her soft, wrinkled skin smelled like Jean Naté.

I couldn't wait to arrive in Miami. "Will Grandpa be there?" I asked.

"*Si, niña*, Papa will be waitin' for us at the airport," Grandma explained patiently.

The tall flight attendant looked pretty, dressed in blue. She served feasts of wrapped sandwiches, chips, fruit salad and sodas. She even gave Anna and me extra chocolate chip cookies. "Grandma, can I be a stewardess one day?" I asked, turning to her.

"You can be anythin' you want, but dun talk with your mouth full, dear."

When we got off the plane, I glimpsed up and noticed rows of people standing at a glass-wall balcony. Grandma said they waited for their family members or friends. My eyes traveled across them and stopped on a man wearing a hat. He waved.

Grandpa!

As we approached him, I squealed with excitement when he greeted us with hugs and kisses. Clean-shaven, he smelled like Mennen Skin Bracer and Vitalis. He affectionately pinched our ear lobes, making Anna and me laugh with delight. His laughter was so jolly it made his belly jiggle.

At my grandparents' home, all was peaceful. Plenty of food. No arguments. No smelly booze. No crawling bugs. My room wasn't stuffy; I had my own soft and comfortable bed. Naptimes were easy here, unlike in that old, gloomy Humpty-Dumpty preschool daycare.

Within a couple of days, Mama showed up. As fast as she came, she left again, this time taking Anna with her. I stood by the door, my heart heavy as I waved to my sister when they drove away. I wished Anna stayed with us. But Mama said that Grandma and Grandpa were too old to care for a toddler, and they might spoil her as they were doing with me. I couldn't grasp that concept. With them, I felt loved, happy and safe. In their home, we were *familia*.

Boricuas

My grandpa Florentino was born in 1897 in Arecibo, Puerto Rico, and the youngest of six siblings. Average in stature, he had fair skin, gray hair, and quick eyes with a broad smile. Fastidious about his appearance, he was a sharp dresser and carried a gold pocket-watch tucked away in his vest. Whether he needed to or not, he visited the barbershop once a month. Although English was his second language, he practiced enough to speak without a Spanish accent. He read his Bible and the *Daily Bread* and often recited Bible passages. From across the room, his powerful voice resounded whenever he quoted his favorite verse, I Corinthians 13:11, "When I was a child, I spoke as a child; I understood as a child. I thought as a child: but when I became a man, I put away childish things." After devotions, I'd see Grandpa read *The Miami Herald* from front to back.

He was a reserved man who measured his words with razor-sharp wit. With a no-nonsense approach to life, he rose before dawn and believed in the saying, "The early bird catches the worm." He prided himself on discipline, stemming from his years in the military. On a weekly basis, he cleaned our shoes, the way he said he had learned in the Army.

"Do you know what I'm getting ready to do, young lady?" Grandpa asked.

I sat Indian-style and watched him scatter newspapers on the floor, laying out the shoes in a neat row and placing an old wooden box beside them. Inside the box, he kept brushes, old socks, rags, and cans of black polish. "You gonna spit and shine shoes," I shouted.

With one hand in a shoe and the other in an old sock, Grandpa rubbed the wax back and forth, polishing the leather. I never tired from following his hands, moving like flashes of lightning.

My grandma's name was Ana, born in 1898, the second of six siblings. She lived at home and cared for her elderly mother until her mid-twenties. Living at home, she worked as a secretary for a steamship company, typing and transcribing in Gregg Shorthand. She was soft-spoken, a temperate woman. Seeing her on her knees by the bedside in prayer was the norm. I witnessed her faith in action. She expressed love and devotion by being a "doer of the Word and not a hearer only," forever willing to help others. Even during the times when I'd see her wincing from the pain in her knees and feet, she'd still make treats to hand out or write cards and letters to encourage someone.

Grandma suffered from arthritis. If ever she mentioned that her feet hurt, my grandpa, whom she affectionately called her *"flor de té,"* would prepare a tub of warm water and Epsom salt for her to soak them in. My grandma blamed the tight pointy shoes she wore in her earlier years for causing her aching feet and overlapping toes. All her current shoes in black were odd-looking and clunky like the ones worn a long, long time ago. I enjoyed playing in them.

Clip-clop. Clip-clop. Grandma's shoes echoed as I walked in them across the tile floor.

"Mary," Grandma called to me, sitting at her sewing machine, rubbing her eyes. "You have good eyes, dear. *Por favor*, thread this needle for me."

With one eye shut, I squinted, concentrating on the task of getting the string into that tiny hole. "Grandma, does Mama know how to sew?" I mumbled, pursing my lips with the tip of the thread in my mouth to moisten it—the way I'd seen Grandma do—making it easier to go in the eye of the needle.

"I taught her, *pero* she dun like to."

I wouldn't either, it takes too long. "All done," I said, giving the threaded needle back.

Grandma wanted me to learn how to sew, but I preferred sitting on the floor, playing with her sewing stuff instead. I either sifted through the Mason jars she kept filled with buttons of all sizes or rummaged through her large, round tin can packed with spools of colorful threads. Inside also were porcelain thimbles, a pincushion, and even a wood darning egg for sewing Grandpa's socks.

We had chores to do. The weekly wash we did at the laundromat, a short walking distance away. Once home, Grandma ironed all bed sheets, linens, pillowcases, cloth napkins, and even Grandpa's white hankies on her chrome-edged dining room table. I helped her to fold but knew I didn't like ironing.

"Mary, it's good that you give me a hand," Grandma said as she sprinkled water over a napkin before ironing it. "You must learn to do these things yourself one day," she added.

Gonna get me a maid for that, I thought.

Overall, I liked helping Grandma with chores. She saved S & H Green Stamps that I enjoyed pasting in a book. She did many things differently from the way I saw Mama do with her time. Even when she was busy, Grandma always talked to me. I studied her. I thought it funny the way her mouth moved, her lips still closed, whenever she read. I marveled how her fingers typed fast and hard on the keys to her black manual typewriter.

In retrospect, Grandma liked my curious mind and eagerness to learn. When she gave me a small, white leather Bible for my own, I felt special.

"*Mija*, have you been studyin' your Bible verses?"

"Yes, ma'am. I learned it all."

"*Bueño*, let's hear it."

"The Lord is my Shepherd . . . ," I began. As promised, when I finished, she gave me a crisp, two-dollar bill.

"Can I take my nap now?" I asked, yawning.

"Go ahead, dear. You may. I'll wake you before dinner."

Sometimes I watched Grandma in the kitchen cooking and helped by peeling carrots or potatoes using her peeler. I didn't like it much, but Grandma enjoyed making Chicken á la King. I watched the way she washed and chopped white onions, celery stalks, bell peppers, and cut up a boiled chicken once it cooled.

"It's good that you pay attention, dear," Grandma said, wiping the chicken grease from her hands on her apron. "*Señoritas* must know how to cook."

"Why?" I asked, rubbing my eyes burning from the onions. "Mama doesn't."

"Even so, you had better learn, young lady," she replied, throwing everything into a pot, adding milk. "You dun want to become *vaga*."

"What's *vaga*?" I asked.

"It means lazy. You dun want to be that; you'll have a family to care for one day."

My husband gonna have to help cook if he wants to eat, I mused.

Even though my grandpa didn't know how to cook, he fixed breakfast. In the mornings, I'd linger in bed until he called for me. I liked the feeling of the cool softness of the bed sheets between my toes. I liked listening to the cooing sounds of doves close by my window. The tinkling of dishes, the opening and closing of kitchen cabinets were all music to my ears. And I especially liked the aroma of coffee coming from the kitchen.

The first thing my grandpa ever fixed for me was soft-boiled eggs. I stared at them. Grandma was sitting across the table eating a grapefruit with a serrated-edged spoon. *Paul Harvey's* mellow voice came over the radio, but when I complained to Grandma that the eggs were too runny, Grandpa overheard.

"Well that's all you're going to get," he bellowed, slamming down my glass of milk, some of it spilling over. "So, you had better be satisfied."

I wanted to crawl into a hole and hide.

My grandma, the buffer in the family, felt that if Grandpa ever needed straightening out, she'd let him know it. That morning she charged to my defense. Grandpa listened to her chewing him out, and after she finished, he exclaimed, "Well! I consider myself bawled out!"

That's when I knew he was no longer angry. I laughed nervously, gobbled my eggs with toast and asked to be excused.

We knew Grandpa's bark was bigger than his bite. Did I fear his bark? Oh, yeah. We *all* respected him, knowing about his quick temper. But whenever Grandpa agreed about something, he'd have a funny way of saying, "That's about the size of it!" Overall, he had a soft spot and never stayed upset for long.

School Days

Because Mama liked to sleep in, she never bothered sending me off in the mornings to kindergarten or pre-school. We moved so much that when I should have attended first grade, I was only in school for brief periods at a time. Before my sixth birthday, we had traveled across three states and changed addresses more than a dozen times. Mama jokingly called us gypsies, saying she lost count after the eighteenth time we moved. I laughed with her then.

But since I had missed so many days of school, I would

always be a year behind, one more thing that gnawed at me as I got older.

After my grandparents took me into their home, they enrolled me in Shadowlawn Elementary. I walked to school and back, logging in a mile and a half each way. Without fail, Grandpa accompanied me. Rain or shine, I counted on his presence waiting for me after class.

"What did you learn today, young lady?" Grandpa asked.

"We're reading a book about Dick and Jane and their dog Spot. And today in art," I piped up, "my friend Vicki ate paper paste."

"You don't say!" Grandpa's eyes twinkled, peering over his bifocals.

"Yep. I dared her. Watched her do it, too," I volunteered.

"Well, I'll be doggone!" Grandpa exclaimed.

One sunny day at the schoolyard, I found a black, woolly caterpillar crawling in the shrubs and unafraid, gently placed it in my palm. A classmate asked to see what I held. When I opened my hand to show him, he whacked it so hard that the caterpillar flew out and disappeared onto a bush. Without hesitation, I slapped him on the face, hard. The boy stood stunned, mouth opened.

I never liked getting into trouble, but if needed, I defended myself. Mama warned me not to be a show-off or bring attention to myself.

Mama's words registered in my head the day my teacher wouldn't let me go to the bathroom during recess. When she told me to hold it longer, I didn't think it possible. When I asked permission a second time, she reluctantly called the others to gather in line. Everyone needed to hush before leaving the playground. How I wished she would hurry it along.

But getting twenty or more kids to settle down after playtime wasn't easy.

And then it happened. Before the line started moving, I wet my pants. Horrified, I tried forcing myself to stop, but once the dam broke, there was no stopping the warm waters from streaming down my legs. Mortified, I glanced around. How I wanted to wipe the smug smirk off each face that snickered and never go back to school. It wasn't easy being good.

Days later, I overheard Grandma talking with Mama on the phone. I knew Mama wanted me back home with her. When the call ended, Grandma noticed me sulking and said, "You mind your mother and be a good girl now. She needs you to help her."

Help her do what? I wondered, as I stomped away to my room.

My first year in school was a triumph, especially in receiving my report card. My teacher's observation:

```
"Mary Ann is a very creative
child and likes to draw. She
has made satisfactory progress
this year." IR 1968
```

The beginning of the school year, back home with Mama, I'd begun to notice how much of a nervous wreck she was. She bumped into things or dropped them and then complained and said bad words. She always bit her nails so low they bled.

One morning I twirled around while looking at myself in the mirror.

"Mary, stop that and come here."

"Watch me, Mama." The faster I spun, the more my dress flared out.

"Okay. Now c'mon and sit down," Mama said holding a large pair of scissors. "Your bangs are too long. They need trimming."

I didn't want her to, but as soon as I sat, she started to cut away. I listened to the *snip, snip* of those scissors with my eyes closed. Then Mama asked me to turn my head. I complied, inching around, when—

"Ouch!" I yanked my head back, covering my ear with my hand.

"Mary! You okay?"

"No more, Mama. You almost poked another hole in my ear." I checked my dress for droplets of blood.

"Wait. I have to finish," she insisted.

Snip. Snip.

"There, now I'm done."

"Lemme see." I reached for the hand mirror. I gasped. Mama trimmed my bangs all right—too short. And oh, so crooked. That's the way they took my school picture: short, crooked bangs, the rest tied in a ponytail, draped over my right shoulder so I wouldn't look like a boy.

That photo of me sat in a frame on my grandma's dresser. Also on her dresser was a dome-shaped musical box that I enjoyed playing.

Years later, I heard the words to that tune. *Always* by Irving Berlin:

Days may not be fair. Always.

That's when I'll be there, always.

Not for just an hour,

Not for just a day,

Mary A. Pérez

Not for just a year,
But always.
In the days ahead, I would come to wish that my sister and I had stayed with my grandparents.

Running in Heels: A Memoir of Grit and Grace

Mary A. Pérez

CHAPTER 4: THE LITTLE GREEN DRESS

Miami 1968

I ADORED MY little sister growing so fast. To see her beaming face at the window highlighted my day after school. She always reached up to carry my books, no matter how heavy. After we shared a snack, then time for homework. Anna took naps or played alone while I finished my studies. Then we'd go out for a walk.

She loved the outdoors. Our outings became adventures — it made me feel good to see her hopping and skipping alongside me. If something piqued her curiosity, we stopped, whether it was to find a fallen bird's nest or to watch a worm squirm under a rock to hide. We'd listen to the mockingbirds while we gathered sprigs of white wildflowers, and the red hibiscus and puffy yellow marigolds in bloom, smelling their fragrance before taking some home for Mama.

Anna cheerfully greeted everyone we passed. "What a beautiful angel she is," they'd say. Her enchanting smile and deep blue, watchful eyes mesmerized. The warmth of her merry laughter penetrated hearts, including mine. "She's *my* sister," I'd proudly boast. Anna's countenance radiated joy. I cherished her carefree spirit and relished her innocence.

Since Mama stayed in bed until the afternoons, Anna and I usually ate a bowl of corn flakes for breakfast. We'd watch *Sesame Street* on the black-and-white tube. Whenever Big Bird appeared, my sister squealed and clapped. Then when *Mr. Rogers' Neighborhood* came on, we sang along with him.

We ate our meals sitting on cushions on the floor. We didn't have a scheduled time to eat. Chow time consisted of simple bologna sandwiches, a heated can of SpaghettiOs, or sometimes a can of tomato soup. On special occasions, we ate Swanson chicken TV dinners.

Mama expected me to care for my sister. In the evenings, when she and Jimmy went out, Anna and I stayed home by ourselves. We'd lay on the floor to color or played inside our blanket tent, having tea parties with our plastic cups. I sometimes read aloud, making up the words I didn't know. We stayed up until we grew sleepy.

Whatever we did, doing it together was more fun than being alone.

One particular evening, as I gazed into my sister's baby-blues, a sudden feeling of sorrow swept over me. Tears clouded my eyes. Something burned within my chest. I cried out, "Please God, don't let nothing bad happen to her!"

Anna gazed at me with her gentle, trusting eyes.

"I'll protect you," I whispered to her. "For always."

Before bedtime, we repeated a child's prayer Grandma taught me, one that hung on the wall:

"... I pray thee, Lord, my soul to keep ..."

That night I clung to my sister and kept the strange premonition to myself.

❖ ❖ ❖

After a number of arguments and fights, Mama and Jimmy would split up but then get back together. It was during one of those "split up" periods that she and I were living with a couple that befriended my mama in one of her hangouts. We could stay if we cleaned and cooked.

Mama didn't like to clean. Or cook.

Every other Saturday, Daddy would come by and drop my brother Ruben off for an overnight visit, then take me to stay overnight or for the weekend at his place. I loved going to Daddy's yellow house in Hialeah and visiting with him and his new wife, Gloria. I liked her. She chatted away in Spanish to me. She always made certain I had plenty to eat.

On one of those weekends while I visited Daddy, Jimmy showed up at Mama's, uninvited and drunk. He wanted to take Anna for a stroll.

Later, Ruben recounted, "Mama was upset over the stove trying to cook a pot of rice. She knew Jimmy was drinking, but he wouldn't leave her alone. They started to argue, scream and cuss." My brother heard Jimmy demanding to take Anna. Mama shouted, "Hell no!" When he saw them starting to pull on Anna's thin arms as if it were a rope in a game of tug-of-war, he yelled for them to stop.

"Let me take Anna out to play," Ruben pleaded.

But they wouldn't listen.

Jimmy snatched Anna and demanded, "I'm gonna spend time with *my* daughter. We're going for a walk and coming right back."

We never knew the full story of all that happened after that.

Jimmy must have decided to buy beer at the local 7-Eleven store. He sat Anna on the curb to wait for him. She was still barefoot and wearing her favorite green dress. When he crossed the busy intersection, Anna darted after him. A hit-and-run driver struck her down.

Around that same time, Daddy brought me back home. As we kissed and said our goodbyes, we heard the wail of a siren in the distance but didn't think anything of it. Then Daddy drove off with Ruben. He waved to me. I waved back.

Still the siren blared.

I turned to Mama and asked, "Where's Anna?" She was always here to greet me.

"That louse came by to bother me again," she huffed.

"Mama, you said you were finished with him."

She swatted the air with her hand as if shooing a mosquito. "He only wanted to see Anna."

A neighbor came running and whispered breathlessly with Mama. Right then, a police car pulled up, its radio static coming from within. An officer climbed out of his cruiser and walked toward them. Within seconds, someone let out a cry that sounded familiar, and then I watched my hysterical Mama sprinting down the street. I stifled a scream. My heart pounded in my chest. I didn't know what happened, where she was going or why.

I don't remember who drove us to the hospital. But once we arrived, a nurse pointed down the hall to where they cared for Anna. Except I couldn't go to see her because they said I was too young.

I *had* to see her.

My legs trembled as I crept to her room and peered through the glass-paned door on my tiptoes. I saw a blinking monitor. Then I saw her — my baby sister — with soiled feet, still in her little, green denim dress, tattered and torn. Anna lay motionless on her back, her curly, brown hair matted with blood. Her face bruised and swollen, her baby blues closed tight.

I felt light-headed as I slumped on the floor, pulling my knees to my chest, crying.

That night, we returned to the scene of the accident. I will never forget the puddles of congealed blood that saturated the street. I wanted to scream. Blood-soaked rags from my sister littered the pavement.

Others offered shallow words of comfort. "Don't cry," they said. "Think positive thoughts," they chimed. "The doctors are doing everything they can for your little sister." But all I heard was my sister's blood calling out to me, along with my broken promises pounding in my head: "I'll protect you."

Two days later, I awakened to the sound of rain and a car door slamming. I peeped out my window and saw a taxi pulling away from the curb. My grandparents, their faces grim and eyes downcast, walked to our doorstep. A shiver ran down my spine and a horrible dread washed over me. I threw myself on the bed, a knot lodged in my throat. Then I heard my mother's wails. I curled up in a ball and covered my ears. *God, it hurts!* I cried. *Make the pain go away.*

My sister was gone. Forever. A month earlier, we had celebrated her birthday. She had just turned two. I was nine, but felt ancient. Empty. Heavy. The weight of the world on my thin shoulders.

Like a fuzzy video tape, fragments of blurred images and sounds played across my mind: Anna's dancing blue eyes, laughter like the morning sun, vibrant flowers . . . Mama's primal screams, hushed voices, muffled sobs.

At the funeral, I held my breath and willed my feet toward the small white casket. Grandma squeezed my hand. I took my finger and stroked my sister's face, which reminded me of a plastic doll's, stiff and cold to the touch. Heavy make-up could not conceal her bruises. Her grotesque head cradled by a bonnet, much too small. She wore a new green dress, cleaned and pressed, with no stains. Nor traces of blood.

I glanced up at Grandma. "Your sister's in a better place now," she choked. Then I placed a small cross under Anna's tiny, rigid hands. My tears blinded me.

". . . If I should die before I wake, I pray thee, Lord, my soul to take."

Why, God? Why? Why did you have to take her?

Anna, I'll love you for always.

Mama sat by the farthest wall away from people, away from the coffin. Her eyes were swollen and red. I went to sit by her.

My mama did her best, but this setback became one too many. Her six-year relationship with Jimmy-the-louse ended. And for that, I was glad.

Later I understood it had been a monumental year for our country: A hidden gunman assassinated Rev. Martin Luther King, Jr., and another shot down United States Senator Robert F. Kennedy.

A year of deaths shocked and changed the world.

But the girl in her little, green dress was the one who mattered to me. She was my sister. My best friend. She lay in an unmarked grave.

Mary A. Pérez

CHAPTER 5: BUMP IN THE NIGHT

AFTER MY SISTER passed away, both Mama and I moved in with my grandparents. Mama, thirty-five years old then, took on a small house-cleaning job—the first job I had ever seen her go to. In the beginning I had thought, *Now I have Mama to myself and we'll do stuff together*. But it wasn't long before she grew restless and visited the bars again. There, she met a new boyfriend who would be my next "stepdad."

"I want you to meet a friend of mine," Mama chimed. "His name is Warren."

Her voice sounded phony; she never talked that way to me.

"Why do you always have to have a *friend?*" I asked.

"Because it gets lonesome," she said cheerfully. "Now, I want you to be nice to him."

I didn't want to be nice to him . . . she was *my* mama.

Before long, we left the comfort of my grandparents' home to move into a dump with Warren. Then Mama took on his last name too.

My new stepdad, funny-looking, low-key and ultra-passive, was more subdued than Mama's usual taste in men. Although he appeared mild-mannered and kind enough, there wasn't anything eye-catching about him. He may have been tall but he walked slumped over. His features included an unusually high forehead with thinning hair, bulging eyes and a bumpy nose. He wore false teeth.

Unlike Jimmy, Warren couldn't hurt a *cucaracha* if our lives depended on it. But like my last stepdad, Warren loved to drink plenty bottles of *cerveza* in between his smokes. After a few of them, he nodded off, even with a lit cigarette in his mouth.

I still had to take care of Mama.

We heard a racket once. When Mama ran to investigate, she found Warren out cold, in the tub, his feet sticking out. We laughed then. We often found him sound asleep out on the cold, hard ground with cigarette burns on his chest. He also developed a disgusting new habit: wetting the bed when sloppy drunk. Even worse, he did it while Mama slept next to him.

Another incident imbedded in my memory bank: In the middle of night, awakened from a sound sleep, I shook cobwebs from my head to the sound of guffawing and rowdy chatter. Throwing caution to the wind, my parents brought home a stranger whom Warren had met earlier—at a bar, of course. After a night of carousing, they continued drinking, and talking gibberish in our small, single room.

Surrounded by enough drunken behavior for my young years, I already developed a guarded distrust of those who drank, particularly the loud ones.

Warren's friend laughed too much and joked too much. I thought he toyed with my dumb stepdad, pretending they were old bosom buddies when I knew they had just met.

A gnawing feeling ate at me. I sat cross-legged on the bed, my nightgown over my knees. I colored as I observed the creep's performance and his furtive glances toward my mama. I was nine years old and knew enough not to trust anyone like *Señor Creepo*. No one paid attention to me.

I colored. Listened. And watched.

The merriment ended after *El Creepo* said his goodbyes.

"Don't forget to go to the bathroom, you jerk." Mama snapped at Warren as he stumbled around. Soon, they conked out.

In our tiny efficiency, as I lay in pitch darkness, my eyes remained opened, growing accustomed to the dark. The yellow moon peeked through the window shade. Eerie shadows traveled across the walls and bounced off a tattered chair whenever headlights from cars passed by.

Mama and I shared a narrow bed then. Because Warren had "accidents" in bed at nights, he slept on the opposite one from us. Like the sound of a freight train, his incessant snoring rattled my eardrums. Asleep in her underwear, Mama's gentle snoring came in spurts. Those sounds became my lullaby in the evenings, lulling me to sleep.

But not tonight.

I was never afraid during the night, but with a sense of foreboding I couldn't shake off, I got up and propped a chair under the doorknob. Time passed. *Thump!* The chair toppled over and my heart hammered against my chest. Then I heard the knob turn and the door creaked. The hair on my scalp pricked me.

In the dark, I turned ever so slowly, peering through half-closed lids.

The silhouette of Warren's weird friend crawled, cat-like, on all fours. He inched his way closer. And closer. Warren snorted and rolled over. *El Creepo* froze. Then he continued his way toward Mama. His hand reached her leg and started feeling upward . . . With sheer determination, I hopped up, screaming at the top of my lungs. Like a wild animal caught in blinding light, *El Creepo* jumped and made a bee line toward the door. He crashed into a chair, tripped over the box fan, and then collided with the dresser before hightailing out. Crying and shaken out of my wits, I turned the light switch and called out to my parents in zombie-land, to no avail. It took a long time before I shut my eyes. The next morning, I gave a full report. With stupefied faces and mouths agape, they attempted to process my words.

"What?" Mama shrieked. "I didn't hear anything!"

"Mama, he *touched* you!"

"How did he . . . ?" Warren stammered.

Mama gave him a dirty look. "The door doesn't have a lock, you dope, remember?"

"Well, you just wait 'till I see that jerk again," Warren hinted, getting up to check the knob. One may think that this frightening episode caused a rude awakening in my party-animal parents. It changed nothing. Sometimes, I think Mama didn't know what to do with me. Some days she wanted me close. Other days she didn't. So, she sometimes sent me to my grandparents. Then she changed her mind and demanded me back.

Through my grandma, I learned that some relatives wanted me to live in Manhattan with them. I got excited thinking about living in New York. But Mama refused to let me go. "It doesn't matter that she can't give Mary 'proper care,'" I heard Grandpa say.

I wasn't certain if it was over jealousy or stubbornness from pride or the possibility of being guilt-ridden from the aftermath of Mama having lost three of her kids: one by divorce, one by adoption, and one in death. Whatever the reason, unyielding, my mama reminded me that *she* was the mother.

Two important events happened later than year. On July 21, 1969, Neil Armstrong, the first man to walk on the moon, uttered the legendary words: "That's one small step for man, one giant leap for mankind."

And then on August 17, 1969, ten days before my tenth birthday, the second most intense hurricane on record hit the United States. Hurricane Camille, a Category 5, had all south Florida feeling her wrath. Warren, Mama and I took shelter in the gymnasium of Miami Edison High School. Many people talked in loud voices. Confused and frightened children fussed and cried as they clung to their mama's skirts and their daddy's necks to ride out the storm.

On a floor mat I sat, glancing around, clutching my raggedy doll and our meager chow in a sack: a single loaf of Wonder Bread and a jar of Welch's Grape Jelly. When Warren suggested that I offer some to another girl close by, I recoiled. Even in normal times, sharing food wasn't so easy for me.

Comfort and tranquility were as far away from me as the moon and blew past like shingles from the roofs of so many of the homes that felt Camille's fury.

Running in Heels: A Memoir of Grit and Grace

CHAPTER 6: THE CRUX OF THE MATTER

MAMA HAD DIFFICULTY sharing pleasant thoughts about her own childhood. Her memories seemed hazy or hidden, too deep or too painful for her to discuss at will. Nevertheless, she once mentioned to me that in her teens she wanted to "get away" from home.

"Why Mama?" I asked. "Were you abused?" I had learned about child abuse when the teacher talked about it in school.

"No, no," Mama scoffed. "Where do you get such crazy ideas? My parents loved me."

"Then, why?" I persisted.

"Oh, in those days they were too strict."

What Mama wanted and needed to escape from remained uncertain, but that feeling led to an even more drastic decision. At seventeen, she agreed to go to Rockland State Hospital in Orangeburg, New Jersey, and become a patient there for several months. She went through electroshock treatments and insulin shots afterward.

I never understood why she subjected herself to such an aggressive treatment. Was it because of anxiety? Or deep depression? Or an attempt to erase a memory?

My grandparents were overprotective with Mama. They doted on her out of pity that may have unwittingly stifled her from becoming independent. At least that's what Mama always said. I overheard her once yelling at Grandma for keeping her in the house like a prisoner as a child. "You people never taught me right from wrong or let me do anything. No wonder I was so *stupid!*"

"You see, Ana?" Grandpa had said. "See the thanks we get? She forgets all we did for her and how I even threw my own brother out the house in order to protect her."

I realized that secrets were in every generation. But I never found out what Grandpa meant by that statement, and gathered by the glances between them that I shouldn't ask either.

On more than one occasion, Grandma confided in me that Mama had trouble retaining the subjects her teachers taught. Children ostracized her. Bashful and timid, she kept her mouth shut. Her shyness prevented her from asking necessary questions regarding class assignments.

Long-limbed and with large feet for a girl, Mama was often teased and ridiculed. Kids even stuck chewing gum in her long, thick hair or made fun of her big front teeth. Their words cut deep whenever they taunted, "Hey, rabbit, wanna carrot?"

Around kinfolk, Mama was quite talkative. But when surrounded by outsiders, her timid disposition took over and inhibited her from voicing opinions or in making healthy decisions. She depended on others to make choices for her, whether good or bad.

"*Pues*, your mother was so withdrawn," Grandma said with sadness in her voice, "that she lived in a shell, always hidin' from people, and seldom smiled."

I asked Mama about herself as a child.

"The word 'love' wasn't spoken in those days," Mama

emphasized. "Any displays of affection were withheld. You know, children were seen and not heard."

I often thought about Mama's comment during those times when she expected me to wait for her to finish eating before I could. When we had it, she would sit with a steaming cup of coffee with extra milk and heaps of sugar. She loved her toast dripping with butter stacked on a plate eight, ten, or even twelve slices piled high, leaning like a tower ready to topple.

"Mama, I'm *hungry*," I protested, watching as she dunked her toast in coffee before it went in her mouth. My stomach rumbled. "Can I eat now?"

She turned and snapped. "You hold your horses; I just sat down!"

I tried to look away, but from the corner of my eye, I noticed how she devoured every crumb on her plate before she fixed me something.

When Mama let me stay with my grandparents again, I was glad. Grandma and Grandpa were flawless in my eyes. I didn't feel anything but love in their home, with family who actually had my best interest at heart. Their kindness and selflessness offset my mama's negligence and indifference. In their trusted care, I felt loved, protected and carefree. I had clean clothes *and* my own room. I slept in the spare bedroom big enough for two narrow beds, a nightstand, an oversized dresser, and Grandma's Singer by the double window. The *click-clacking* of her sewing machine in the afternoons were soothing to my ears. Listening to her humming to *His Eyes Are on the Sparrow*, whether she sewed, crocheted, worked in her flowerbed or bathed me, always gave me a warm sense of belonging and well-being.

At my grandparents' house, I'd run about or play hide-and-seek as much as I wanted. Except maybe when I tried playing an April Fool's joke on Grandma.

I waited, crouched down low behind a chair and listened for her. I thought myself witty and barely could keep from snickering. As her footsteps came closer, timing it just right, I sprang up with arms raised and yelled, "BOO!"

But it so happened to be my grandpa instead.

He popped my bubble of enthusiasm, letting me know it was too early in the morning for such nonsense. He might have popped me on my bottom too, if he hadn't missed when I shot past him like a dart and hopped back into bed.

I would even enjoy guilty pleasures like standing in Grandma's linen closet sniffing the scent of mothballs. Of course, the aroma of her apple turnovers calling me to the kitchen was the best.

Mealtimes meant family time at the table. "You be a good girl now and clean your plate," Grandma suggested. "Lots of children are starving all over the world."

Although Grandma wasn't a fantastic cook, with her I had plenty of food to eat. With mama, never enough. While Grandma hated to throw anything away, particularly food, I always tried to "clean my plate."

"Young lady, are you satisfied?" Grandpa asked.

"Yes, I am."

"Well, praise the Lord!" he boomed without fail. He never liked it if Grandma put too much food on his plate. He believed that one must leave room for *postre* after meals. Often Grandpa brought his favorite home: a New York cheesecake.

I knew if I didn't finish my food, there'd be no dessert for me.

Grandma, conscientious about her health, watched what she ate as much as possible. She avoided fried foods and loved baked fish. She enjoyed her salads with a little olive oil. I ate salads that way, too, but didn't care for some vegetables Grandma liked, such as watercress, radishes, and onions. I never understood how she stomached drinking buttermilk and why it was supposed to be "so good for you" when it tasted so terrible.

After *Walter Cronkite* and the *CBS Evening News*, it was bath time. I continued playing in the bubbles until Grandma said I looked like a prune. She helped me climb out the tub and stood me on the commode while drying me with a big towel. She gently combed my hair and put baby powder all over me. It wasn't this way at home with Mama.

At my grandparents', we watched TV together. I lay on the carpeted floor with a pillow. Grandma would perch herself in her rocker, her hands busy either sewing or crocheting and Grandpa would sit in his recliner, his legs raised. TV shows like *Ed Sullivan, Red Skelton,* and *Jackie Gleason* were favorites.

Although my grandparents weren't dancers, they never missed *Lawrence Welk* on Saturday nights. I liked the sisters that sang together, wishing I could sing like them. When I grew bored with the rest, I'd color or draw pictures nearby.

We all had our share of chores. One never used the word "bored" around my grandparents. They did not believe in idle time. My weekend chores: dust-mopping the tile floor and polishing the furniture, including Grandma's various collectibles.

"Dun break anythin' now," my grandma cautioned. "Be sure to put everythin' back."

Curiosity got the best of me. I couldn't resist examining her knick-knacks while I dusted them. "Grandma, where'd ya get these?" I asked, trying on an old wooden Dutch shoe, the same size as my foot.

"On one of our many trips we took by Greyhound, Mary," Grandma explained, holding her hand out for me to give her the shoe. "Papa bought it at a shop in Holland, Michigan."

"Oh," I said, already losing interest, going on to look at some cute ceramic ducks. When I dropped one and its neck broke, I felt awful and ready to cry.

"Dun worry, *mija*," Grandma coaxed, helping to pick up the two pieces. "I'll get your grandpa to glue it for me."

Back home, Mama would have been furious over my breaking something of hers. She wouldn't be so forgiving, forever shouting, "Look, but don't touch!"

The tedious task of wiping the baseboards in all the rooms became another duty singled out for me. Grandma called it cleaning the woodwork.

"There's a lot of work to be done, but I think we'll catch up with it." Grandpa would sing out during chore time. That common phrase put a bounce in my step whenever I heard it.

Once a month, the refrigerator needed defrosting. I remember watching with fascination the way Grandpa placed old newspapers on the floor, and then carefully jabbed an ice pick at the block of ice in the freezer.

On Saturdays, I watched my favorite cartoons, *Bugs Bunny* and the *Tom and Jerry Show*, while I ate an egg sandwich and drank a big glass of chocolate milk made with Bosco. And I loved it whenever a Jerry Lewis movie came on and my grandma and grandpa would laugh with me.

Weekends were also shopping days at Pantry Pride.

Grandma pulled her two-wheel cart behind her, and Grandpa and I carried the rest of the groceries, chitchatting along the way.

"You know, young lady," Grandpa said, "you're going to have long legs when you grow up."

"Are they going to be long as yours, Grandpa?" I asked, trying to keep in stride.

"No, I don't think so."

"Will they be long as Grandma's?"

"Well, I'll say there's a good chance."

"What about Mama's?"

"Yep. I think they're going to be longer than your mother's are."

"Then I'll be taller than her." I skipped along, thinking about it.

"Yes, yes, I think you're right." Grandpa chuckled.

We couldn't walk at a fast pace on account of Grandma's bad feet.

But one morning we left for church later than usual. Grandma insisted that Grandpa and I run on ahead to stop the bus when we saw one. We took a shortcut along the sides of the railroad tracks. Trotting over the loose gravel became tricky, but we hurried on, determined to catch that bus.

"*Papa,*" cried a small voice. We couldn't quite make out that first call. The cry came again, followed by a moan. When we turned, we saw Grandma laying facedown over pebbles and rocks. Grandpa moved with surprising agility and helped her sit up.

Grandma's forehead bled from the fall. I cowered at the sight of so much blood. I felt sorry for her, and helpless. Why couldn't I have stayed close and given her my arm to hold onto?

Together, we walked back to the house. When we got there, Grandma limped into the bathroom and Grandpa helped her clean her face with a washcloth. To our surprise, she then insisted that we go back out.

"We are goin' to church even if we are late," she said.

"Aren't you going to change your blouse?" Grandpa asked.

"¡No señor!" Grandma said with finality. "I'm goin' just as I am."

Grandma maintained a deep faith in God and rarely missed church, and this would be no exception.

I'd never forget the time we went to a tent revival. Straw and hay covered the ground. The service—held under a humongous tent—filled with people with lifted hands in the air. I attended services with this type of worshipping before with my grandparents, but this one was more intense. Loud music played on an organ. The evangelist held my complete attention as he preached and then, with the "laying on of hands," prayed over certain ones. Captivated by an unseen power that filled the atmosphere, my skin tingled and I knew that others did too.

Grandma felt "touched" and couldn't stop crying; tears streamed down my own face as well. I hurried to join her when she went forward for special prayer.

The evangelist turned and then stood before me. He said that the Lord loved me and held me in the palm of His hands. He prayed over me saying, in my teens, I would drift away from God, but would return to serve Him again in my later years. The thought comforted me. From that point on, I believed my life was in God's hands.

❖ ❖ ❖

Mama said Grandma babied me whenever I stayed at her place. At least my grandma cared when I didn't feel well. I remember the unpleasant chalky taste of Phillips' Milk of Magnesia and the fishy-tasting cod liver oil by the spoonfuls, administered for any complaints or discomforts, given to me as cures by Grandma. Those cures also included green rubbing alcohol, Vicks VapoRub, and Mercurochrome for fever, colds or scrapes. They were Grandma's tried-and-true remedies, coupled with a prayer or two.

I never considered myself "babied" while I played alone since no other kids were around. Deprived from owning four-legged friends, I grew an interest in the behaviors of tiny critters, such as insects. Fascinated with ant piles, I liked to dig apart their colonies to watch the different activities of the workers, the soldiers, and the queen ant that I read about in books. I never developed a fear of grasshoppers, even if they spat "tobacco" on my fingers, or of handling caterpillars that pricked when they crawled on my hand, or of sneaking up on lizards that left their wiggling tails behind—I was too caught up wondering what the funny red thing on their throats going in and out was all about.

But sometimes I couldn't go outside.

"Can I watch TV?"

"*No señorita*, you may not," Grandma chided. "You go wash your hands and set the table, and then get your grandpa." I tried to obey right away, never wanting Grandpa to hear that I was naughty.

As a treat before bedtime, Grandpa always gave me a cup of eggnog made with warm milk, an egg yolk, and sugar. He said it would help me to sleep after a hot bath. Sleep came like a welcomed friend.

After I'd say my prayers, Grandma or Grandpa would

take turns tucking me in.

"God bless you, Mary. Sleep tight, dun let the bedbugs bite."

"Good night," I said, pulling the covers up to my chin so no bedbugs could get to me.

Special Visitor

In the summertime, Uncle Richie flew in from New York and drove straight from the airport to Grandma and Grandpa's house in a rented car.

With jet-black hair and long legs, Uncle Richie towered over us all with his 6'2" frame. Like Grandpa, he too worked at the post office. He spoke slowly, with a gentle voice, and told funny jokes. Along with his sense of humor was a natural talent for sketching. Every year he'd send Grandma homemade cards he drew himself. Watching him draw made me want to learn, so I started doodling.

Uncle Richie loved the outdoors. He made everything into a fun adventure. If we visited the Crandon Park Zoo, Uncle Richie made me laugh for mimicking the silly monkeys. Another time, at Parrot Jungle, I marveled at how the pink flamingos rested on one leg. I tried to stand like them, but not without hopping to keep from falling. Biscayne Boulevard led us to Miami's sandy-white beaches. On our drive there, I always anticipated passing by the Sears Tower with the giant Coppertone billboard that pictured a sunburned girl's puppy halfway pulling down on her bathing suit bottom. It reminded me of my own black puppy I couldn't keep years earlier.

We parked near a pavilion to unload and sort out beach chairs, blankets, baskets, and an ice chest from the trunk. I was anxious to dig my toes in the warm sand, run into the sparkling blue ocean, and to feel the cool water on my face.

"Mary, stop wigglin'," Grandma said from under her big, funny straw hat. "First, I must put dis sun screen on you, and den you may go and play."

I grew impatient.

She laughed and said, "*Ten calma*, Mary."

"Grandma, why do you put so much on me?"

"You have lovely color, white skin, Mary. You want dark, wrinkled skin like mine?"

Uncle Richie waved me on and soon we were playing in the waves. We hunted for hermit crabs and made sand castles. He even let me bury him in the sand. Grandma and Grandpa watched from their chairs under the shade. Sometimes Grandma joined us to help collect seashells while Grandpa stayed behind reading.

When time to eat, I liked that Grandpa treated us to Royal Castle for their miniature burgers or to a Carvel's creamy vanilla ice cream cone with rainbow sprinkles. Sometimes we'd stopped at Woolworth's Five-and-Dime Store before heading home. My grandpa never left without buying me a box of Cracker Jacks or animal crackers.

On Sundays, we took two buses and then walked the rest of the way to attend our church, First Faith Cathedral. Once service was over, we hopped on yet another bus that took us to the Painted Horse, a favorite all-you-can-eat restaurant downtown on Biscayne Boulevard. Adults ate for 99 cents and kids for 49 cents. I preferred the hamburger steak with macaroni and cheese, and even though they displayed Jell-O in every color, my favorite was red.

After lunch, we would head for the Miami Public Library,

near Bayfront Park. Grandpa walked ahead, while I strolled along with Grandma under her umbrella. We'd stop by a large pond filled with giant goldfish and feed them crackers. The park was adjacent to a waterfront where fancy boats and exquisite yachts sailed by. As I waved to them, I imagined how the rich folk lived.

Once in the library, I'd take the elevator to the children's section on the second floor while my grandparents read in the downstairs lobby.

My imagination ran wild as I read fairy tales about faraway places. In my mind, I turned beautiful and clever all in one.

I pretended to be *Cinderella*, overjoyed that the glass slipper fit my foot perfectly and that my uncle, the tall *Prince Charming*, singled me out to dance. I imagined that Ruben was *Hansel* and I *Gretel*, hunting for food, and then eating chunks of candy broken off the cottage with no evil witch in sight. I pictured myself as *Little Red Riding Hood*, saving my grandma from the *Big Bad Wolf*. While reading, I became all those characters and more—until Grandpa called for me, saying, "Mary, time to go home."

My real so-called adventures didn't take me to faraway lands like those in the books I read. My adventures included riding around town on the city buses. If the bus was crowded, we stood while swaying back and forth. Back and forth. Grandpa held onto straps. Unable to reach them, I held onto the bars instead.

"Mary, hold on tight now," Grandma cautioned. Grandpa stood nearby, ready to steady Grandma or me if needed. But I don't think he enjoyed riding on the bus much.

When it was time, I liked to pull the cord to signal the driver to let us off.

"Now, Grandpa?" I asked, not wanting to miss our stop.
"Not yet. Be patient, young lady."
"How about now?"
"I'll let you know when it's time."

Eventually, the sunny, brightly colored Sable Palms apartment complex came into view.

"Okay, *now*, young lady," Grandpa nodded.

I would kneel on the seat and reached for the cord, or sometimes Grandpa hoisted me up. I pulled on the cord fast, once, twice, and sometimes even three times for the bus driver to stop. Then, *swoosh*, the rear doors opened; we exited, and then the door swished closed.

Palm trees lined winding roads and shaded the path to my grandparents' home. Often coconuts fell from those towering trees and I'd run to pick one up for us.

Once, when we arrived home, I overheard Grandpa complaining to Grandma about being too close to so many people.

"*¿Tu ves*, Ana?" he said, showing her something. "See? They stole my wallet."

From the hall, I listened.

"Oh, no!" Grandma gasped, staring at his inside-out pocket in disbelief.

"We have to stand so close we are like sardines. Too easy for someone to put his hands in my back pocket, taking my wallet out without me knowing."

It made me sad to think someone would do something bad to my grandpa, stealing from him as if we were rich.

I looked forward to when the holidays rolled around in school. Grandma helped me wrap a Christmas present to exchange. I didn't have anything new to give, except a couple of small bendable doll figures of mine. That week in class, everyone took turns picking untagged gift boxes. I chose one with candy canes taped over wrapping paper decorated with gingerbread men. Wanting to savor the moment, I caressed my package and tugged at its wrapping. At last, I reached in to remove the tissue paper and found—*ankle socks?* With pink lace. I glanced across the room and glared at the girl who had picked *my* gift. Her face beamed with such a grin that I saw she was missing two front teeth.

"It's not fair!" I shouted when I got home, choking back bitter tears. I threw away those socks.

"*¡Eso no se hace!*" Grandma chided, reprimanding me for complaining. "You be a good girl and be grateful for whatever you have."

"I am," I whined, kicking the puny box.

I tried to be good. A boy I knew in school had the worst, most offensive body odor, and a pungent, sour smell. Every day his white shirt was dingy, the back of his neck gray, and his frizzy hair unkempt. The other kids talked about him behind his back saying he carried "cooties." I kept quiet, thinking how he possibly came from a poor, simple family and didn't have much, like me.

I was pretty much a loner. I knew no one my age to play with at my grandparents' neighborhood. My minimal toys occupied my time. They included a curly-haired doll with a little plastic baby bottle and chair, a few Archie comic books, ball-and-jacks, Etch A Sketch, sticker books, and cut-out paper dolls. Other pastimes included reading my books checked out from the library and coloring on the floor with my 64-count box of Crayola crayons.

The Barbie doll was ten years old at this time—the same age as me. Everyone had one. Everyone but me. A classmate let me borrow hers, along with an assortment of Barbie out-

Mary A. Pérez

fits and matching shoes that she kept in an overstuffed suitcase. I played with a blonde doll and a brunette one whose legs bent. I liked changing their stylish clothes. I pretended to be the dark-haired Barbie; all those cute outfits were mine and I practiced saying, "I don't have a thing to wear."

Like a sponge, I absorbed the elementary school years in Miami. My favorite subjects were penmanship, reading, and sometimes language arts. I tried my best with all subjects but didn't care for math quizzes and science projects.

Like my uncle, I developed a knack for expressing myself through art. I danced with glee the day I won a $50 U.S. Savings Bond from the fire department for my artwork after entering a "Smokey Bear Fire Prevention" contest. But I couldn't have been more excited than I was after winning a free two-week course at a nearby art institute.

Our assignment was to copy a couple of still-life pictures. One was a fruit bowl, the other a colored pencil drawing of a woman. I enjoyed the challenge and turned in my best work. On the last day of class, my art teacher handwrote a two-page letter for me to take home, saying I showed "natural artistic abilities." She recommended that I take private lessons.

We couldn't afford such luxuries.

No one knew how much that sadden and disappointed me.

My third grade teacher's observation:

```
"Mary shows outstanding abili-
ties in art. She is also an ex-
cellent student." M.J.W. '69
```

Running in Heels: A Memoir of Grit and Grace

CHAPTER 7: BIG BROTHER

"I CAN DRAW just as good as our uncle can, or you," Ruben said matter-of-factly.

"No, you can't," I corrected.

"Can too."

"Cannot."

"Can—"

"¡Niños! Cállense ya!" Grandma cut in. "Dis is why you two can't be together."

Ruben and I looked at each other, puzzled by what she meant. But that statement became the reason Ruben and I usually traded places during Daddy's visitations. Because we siblings horsed around and played too "wildly" together, our daddy would come for me to go to his house over the weekends, while dropping Ruben off. That was the normal arrangement. On rare occasions, we visited together. And my big brother loved to tease me.

"Com'on, will ya?" Ruben impatiently waved his arm as if it would fall off, standing with the bathroom door open.

Curiosity got the best of me. "Hold your horses," I said, trying to sound like Mama.

Big brother looked like the cat that swallowed a pigeon, a canary, or something.

"You better not be foolin' me," I warned.

"Don't be so sentimental," he said, practicing the use of big words.

"Am not."

"Are too. And you're never gonna guess what's in here."

"Can too."

"Cannot."

"Gimme a hint."

Ruben shook his head. "Negative."

"Cuz, it's gonna be nuthin'." I stomped my foot and crossed my arms, dying to know what was inside. "You tryin' to trick me again."

He stood in front of the closed shower curtain and held onto it. "Ready?" Ruben asked, with eyes wide.

"Go on . . . it ain't nuthin'."

"It's too . . . it's—" With one swoop, Ruben yanked the curtain and cried, "¡El Chupacabra!"

I let out a long scream at the huge form floating in the tub.

Daddy came running, out of breath. "¿Qué fue?" he demanded. "What's wrong? What happen in here? I hear you all da way outside."

"Daddy, Ruben told me it's 'El Abra Ca Dabra, the goat sucker,'" I whined, mispronouncing the word.

"¿Qué? ¡Oye! What s'matter wit you?" Daddy demanded. "Why can't you play nice? You dun do dat to your sister." He popped Ruben on the head with his hand.

My brother flinched but kept grinning at me, mouthing the word, "boba" before he disappeared.

"Mija, you know what dis is?" Daddy asked, holding me by my shoulder.

"It's a pink, dead pig!" I screeched. "Why is he in the tub of water?"

"Gloria is goin' to make *pernil*. We gonna eat him."

"Roasted pig? No, Daddy, that's yucky."

"Whachu talkin' 'bout? I betchu never had it before," he said, closing the shower curtain. "You'll see," he winked, taking my hand. "It's gonna be so good."

It was yummy.

Even though Daddy had full custody of Ruben instead of me, Daddy was my hero. Brown in complexion and with a bounce in his steps, I admired him as much as I loved him and wanted to remain in his company. I was jealous that Ruben lived with Daddy in a small but immaculate house with a big backyard, in a great neighborhood with charming neighbors.

I imagined my brother knowing nothing about skipping meals, or going to bed on an empty stomach. Daily he ate to his heart's content. He had the love of *both* parents who didn't curse and yell at each other. He attended great schools. Ever since he was seven, he slept in his own bedroom where Gloria kept his closet and drawers filled with clean, tidy clothes. I envied his stability and security—things I lacked back home with our mama.

I liked playing with my brother's toys, which he never cared for me to do. When I accidentally flushed one of his small cars down the toilet, he wasn't too happy about it.

"Did that on purpose, didn't ya?" Ruben yelled.

I snapped back. "That's for me to know and you to find out!"

Another time, Ruben told Daddy that I had done something. It must have been something awful because Daddy scowled as he stomped toward me in one of his Puerto Rican hot-temper flares.

"C'mere. You did dat?" Daddy shouted, holding a branch

he snapped off from a nearby bush. He pointed with his chin to a neighbor's broken window. I wasn't sure what he meant, but I was ready to deny anything, especially if it meant avoiding a whipping.

"No, Daddy. I didn't do it."

"Whachu mean you din't?"

"*Ruben* did it!" I wailed, not knowing who else to pin the apparent crime on.

"How could he?" he exploded. "¿*Oite*?" his voice rose in a high pitch as he grabbed my arm. "He's been right here wit me all da time."

Before I escaped, in quick motions Daddy switched my legs with the branch, all the while saying he now must pay for that window.

I ran into the house, crying. The stinging in my heart from my daddy's harshness toward me hurt more than the stinging in my legs.

When I glanced back, Ruben stuck his tongue out.

CHAPTER 8: MY DADDY'S HOUSE

"WHY DID YOU and Daddy divorce?" I asked Mama. At twelve years old, I never understood why they had separated when I was only three. *Didn't they meet at church? Fall in love? Supposed to be married until death do you part? Why didn't their love last forever?*

After a long pause, Mama answered, "Your father, he was too impatient with me." Then she added, "Well you know, I guess I didn't know how to prepare his meals."

Once I stayed with my grandparents, Daddy started coming for me more often, taking me to his house on weekends.

I loved going to my daddy's house. Feathered friends scurried about in his backyard, a number in cages nestled on eggs. I liked feeding the ducks and watching them swim in the pond. Not so much with the chickens though; I knew they were for consumption. But I couldn't keep from watching in agony whenever Gloria ran after one, caught it, and then wrung the poor creature's neck. It gave me the creeps. Then I'd stay clear from the messy job of plucking feathers.

I felt the same way about gutting stinky fish. But none of it fazed my stepmother. She was always willing to clean and cook anything that my daddy brought home.

Daddy first spotted Gloria shopping in the produce department where he worked. She had an eye for him as well. After several invites over for dinner, they soon fell in love. I was five when they married. By the time I turned ten, they owned a cheerful yellow house in Hialeah and started their family: a girl first, a boy two years later.

I knew then I had the best Daddy in the world. He didn't forget about me. Throughout the years, he'd come for me in various cars. The prettiest I remember was a shiny, red and white '57 Chevy Impala. But the most fun was when he drove up in a bronze station wagon with enough room in the back for me to stretch out and color.

I loved it when he drove me to Morningside Park before going to his house. My daddy may have been short, but he was a big kid at heart and loads of fun. He had a knack for mimicking different sounds. Children laughed whenever he cried out like *Tarzan* on the jungle gym. He wouldn't hesitate to push me high on the swing. I squealed with delight when he ran in front and scrambled away right in time before I would kick him. He'd spin me on the merry-go-round as fast as he could until we couldn't go anymore; then we would tumble, exhausted, onto the ground—he from running in circles and I from laughing so hard.

Daddy worked as the produce manager at Grand Way, a huge grocery chain store that later became Grand Union. He was a model employee. A friendly, robust, people-person, he never grew tired of greeting his customers and telling them jokes. His dark eyes twinkled with glee. The mirth in his thick Puerto Rican accent, combined with his animated personality, charmed all.

Sometimes Daddy caused havoc, but always in fun. He

often mimicked the sound of a kitten near the produce stand at work to see the children's reactions. Once an elderly woman hunted everywhere for the *pobrecito*. Then another time, while whistling like a bird, he had customers looking up for one. He even imitated a newborn's cry.

"Excuse me, sir, but don't you hear a baby crying somewhere?" a worried customer asked.

"A baby? No, no," he answered. "No baby over here." Daddy chuckled as he related to me how he watched the mystified customer walk away, shaking her head.

Daddy told me a story about a little boy who stared at him from the shopping cart while his mother across the aisle weighed her vegetables.

"I smiled at da boy and asked his name, but he dun say noteen," Daddy explained. "He just keep lookin' and lookin' at me, like I'm so ugly or somethin'."

"Then what did you do?" I asked and chuckled, knowing of his pranks.

"I dun do noteen . . . just smiled big and stuck out my bottom dentures at da boy."

"No, Daddy, you didn't!" I laughed, remembering him doing that very thing before; it was enough to startle anyone.

"Yeah, but then da boy started cryin', so I got outta there fast," Daddy said guiltily. "I dunno where I get these jokes. You got a funny *papi*, eh?"

"Yeah." I giggled. "*Muy loco*, all right."

Daddy had a habit of freely passing gas. Whenever he tooted at home, my stepmother frowned and cried, "¡*Fo!*"

"¿*Qué fue, Mami?*" Daddy asked, feigning innocence.

"*Ay* Benny, *qué mal huele*," Gloria complained, holding her nose.

Daddy pretended to look hurt. "*Fue un peoito, no se huele.*"

"*'Peoito' nada.*" I giggled. "That was a big, stinky one!"

My daddy's habitual antics, however, backfired on him while at work one day. Thinking no one near, he let one of his SBDMs (silent but deadly missiles) out while working at the vegetable stand. Suddenly, a customer with a disgusted expression approached him.

"Hey mister, do you know you have some rotten potatoes here?"

"*What?* Oh, yeah! Yeah! You're right," my red-faced, quick-thinking Daddy responded. "I better get dis thin' outta here," he said, quickly hauling off the bag of supposedly "rotten" potatoes.

I laughed so hard I couldn't breathe. "Daddy, tell me the story about the goat sucker in Puerto Rico," I said, wiping my eyes.

"*¡Oh, sí!*" Daddy exclaimed, slapping his thigh. "*¡El Chupacabra!* Dis thin' dat went round to all the *animales* suckin' their blood dry."

"Yep, that's the one," I said, remembering the time Ruben frightened me like crazy when he made me think one was in the bathtub.

"Man, da people get so scared and say it's some kind of *diablo*. They say, '*sierra la puerta*', close your door, *El Chupacabra* is goin' to suck your blood!"

"You ever see one, Daddy?"

"No, no, I never see dat thin' in my life." He chuckled and added, "I dunno if I believe it."

"Well, it's sure an awful scary story." I shuddered at the possibilities.

My daddy was a natural born storyteller. I could sit and

listen to him for hours. "Daddy, tell me again about the first time you left Puerto Rico on the plane."

"When I left my home town in *Utuado*?" His eyes flickered and his gaze suggested he was miles away as he mused. "Flyin' on dat twin-engine *avión* made me so scared. I needed to go to *el baño* so bad. The stewardess want to tell me somteen. *Pues*, I dunno what she say; I dunno any English then. She talk louder but I dun understand; I just wanna go. I try to make her understand me, so I jell to her, '*I no spic inglish! I no spic inglish!*'"

"No wonder we're called, 'Spics,'" I teased.

"Is dat right?" Daddy winked.

His broken English made me giggle until my sides ached and my eyes watered.

"Daddy, you didn't know how to speak English when you were nineteen?"

"No *hija*, I didn'. Later, my cousin in New York explained to me dat stewardess just wanted me to put my seatbelt on. *Ay bendito nene*," Daddy laughed. "I didn' understand noteen."

"Hey *Papi*," I said, wiping my eyes. "You know what?"

"*¿Que mi vida?*"

"You still have an accent."

"You tellin' me, man." He laughed.

My daddy loved to watch *Lucha Libre*. His favorite wrestler then was Rocky Johnson. Also a die-hard Yankees fan, he loved his baseball team. "*¿Vite?* You see dat?" Daddy shouted and pointed to the TV, asking no one in particular. "Man, dat Mickey Mantle can hit dat ball sooo hard...."

But I especially loved watching him play dominoes. "*¡Oye! I win again!*" he'd yell, making the losers groan.

Daddy enjoyed many hobbies. He knew his fruits and

vegetables. He loved gardening and showing off his avocado and *gandules* (pigeon pea) plants, which he himself planted, as much as he loved chewing and sucking the juice from raw sugarcanes. The one thing he liked to make for breakfast was banana pancakes. So good!

Gloria was such a great cook; we all loved her *comida*. It was common to see her working in the kitchen preparing mouth-watering delicacies. Meals were her priority. She often cooked wearing rollers under a hair net, sometimes in a floral housedress and with *chanclas* on her feet.

She chose whatever Daddy planted in the yard to complement any one of her flavorful, traditional entrées, like *arroz con pollo* (rice and chicken), *arroz con gandules* (rice and pigeon peas), or *pernil* (roasted pork).

Each dish was first sautéed in *sofrito* (a mixture of bell peppers, garlic, onions and capers blended into a paste) in a deep *caldero*. The aroma alone made your mouth water. Gloria served side dishes of fried sweet plantains, large Florida avocadoes, red beans simmering with new potatoes, and always with a big pot of yellow rice.

One Sunday after a tasty meal of chicken stew, we drank *café con leche*, a strong espresso made with hot milk and sugar.

"Mary, did you like *Mami's pollo guisado*?" Daddy asked, sipping from his cup.

"¡Sí!" I answered, practicing my Spanish. "*Muy bueno.*"

"Oh, yeah? You wanna know somteen'?" Daddy's eyes twinkled.

"¿Que?" I asked, blowing on my *cafesito*, too hot to drink.

"Dat's no chicken you ate . . . dat was *un pato*."

A *duck*? I stared at Daddy, and then at Gloria, then at the leftover duck in the pot. I didn't feel so good. My stomach felt queasy. I raced to the bathroom without a moment to spare when my entire lunch came up.

Gloria helped wipe my face in the bathroom and pleaded, "*Ay, Marí. Perdóname.*" I knew she felt terrible about what had happened. When I looked out the window, I couldn't quit thinking about how I fed those cute, adorable ducks. And then had eaten one.

With no hard feelings over anyone about the duck incident, I enjoyed being at Daddy's house and forgetting my troubles back home with Mama. I noticed the way Gloria fussed and cleaned house, the same way she enjoyed cooking: fast, thoroughly, and *con mucho gusto*. She didn't like dirt. She had every chair in the house and even the couch covered with plastic. When time to clean the bathroom, she'd use a bucket and throw soapy water on the floor, walls and tub, scrubbing, mopping and drying until everything was squeaky-clean. She never relaxed until evening when one of her *novellas* came on TV.

Daddy and Gloria were affectionate and called each other pet names. Because Daddy's skin was brown, Gloria called him, "*Negro.*" While many knew my stepmother as "*Pita,*" Daddy called her his "*Mamita.*" Seeing their love in action made me smile.

Although Daddy spoke both languages to me, I never became as fluent as my brother had become in Spanish. I understood the language more than I could speak it. But I learned that love was felt and expressed in any language.

During those weekend and summertime visits, my stepmother treated me like her own child, showering me with loud smooches and tight squeezes. She always asked what I wanted for breakfast. I was satisfied to have cereal. She'd gladly bring me a box of *"Con Fley"* and then asked if I wanted a *huevo frito* too. Since Gloria hardly spoke English, we communicated well enough. I enjoyed being around her. She liked talking to me. When she spoke to me in Spanish, I answered her in English and in my broken Spanish.

Although Gloria didn't speak English, her hugs and warmth said more than the words from my own mother.

And she could cook.

Mary A. Pérez

CHAPTER 9: GROWING PAINS

NOT ALL SCHOOL projects were memorable, but one stuck with me for years. When the teacher assigned a report on any subject, I picked caterpillars. On a large poster board, I drew the four stages of the butterfly: (1) egg, (2) larva, (3) pupa, and (4) adult. I described *metamorphosis*. Though not a Picasso, my work earned a ranking on my school's hallway wall, posted for all to see, with the highest mark in class: A+.

My grandparents sang my praises for weeks.

Such proud moments were rare, but I lucked out with another opportunity when chosen to work as a patrol guard before and after school. I wore a bright orange sash signifying my status. I instructed students to "Get off the grass," "Walk," and "Don't run," and helped younger kids cross the street. No one got hurt under my watch.

Those happy occasions aside, as I matured into my preteen years—although I tried to hide my true feelings—I became self-conscious and ultimately developed a guarded inferiority complex. While not shy as my mother had been, I felt like an outcast: I came from a broken home, my family was poor, and I was still on the school's free lunch program. My clothes were hand-me-downs. We didn't own a car. I didn't even own a bike, although I always wanted one. We didn't go on vacations like other kids bragged about; nor could we afford the latest trends or luxuries.

As I wrestled with these feelings of mediocrity, I became ashamed of my Puerto Rican heritage. I didn't play the blame-game, but felt second-rate, forever on the outside looking in. I aimed to not allow anyone see through my brittle exterior and find a weakling. In school, because I didn't feel part of the "in" crowd, I enviously watched as the popular kids were voted for class president, vice-president, or secretary. In my mind, I believed the ritzy kids went to summer camps, swimming lessons, and Girl Scout gatherings. After all, they and not the state paid for their school lunches. They wore the latest fashions, not hand-me-downs. Their straight, pearly-whites glistened when they smiled. They even pronounced their words perfectly. They lived in big houses and their parents had "nest eggs."

"Some are more privileged than others," Grandma explained to me. "But we are all the same in God's eyes."

I wasn't about to argue with Grandma's statement. All I knew was that there never seemed to be enough funds to do anything extra. My grandparents were extremely frugal. They didn't believe in splurging or in keeping up with the Joneses.

In the early seventies, several public schools were still racially unbalanced, so the federal courts stepped in. Miami's school districts bused students from one neighborhood to another to achieve integration.

Busing made my life plummet from bad to worse. I attended Miami Shores Middle School, a predominantly white community where kids commonly called brown skins *"spics."*

Because I was of Puerto Rican descent, I was the target of

their taunting. "You *spic* English?" they scoffed, using their favorite line. They even gave me grief about my naturally full-sized lips (something others now pay good money to have done).

To make matters worse for me, my grandma—unpretentious and a bit old-fashioned—insisted I wear to school dresses with hems below my knees, even though other girls wore the trendy mini-skirts and mini-dresses. Almost all my clothes were second-hand, and at eleven years old—going on twelve—that bothered me.

"Grandma, this isn't what the girls wear nowadays!" I groaned.

"Dis is what *you're* wearin', and you shouldn't be ashamed. Your clothes are clean and pressed," she said with finality.

I threw up my hands. "Grandma, you're gonna make me get into fights!"

"You are a Christian girl," she retorted, her eyes wide and fierce. "Dun you forget that."

But I wanted to forget. I was beginning to feel restless, as if I, like my mother, needed to make up for lost time.

During physical education, we girls changed into hideous, white gym uniforms, snapped down the front, cuffed at the thighs. The other girls complained bitterly about their uniforms, but I didn't. At least in this class, except for my skinny legs, I didn't stand out in a bad way. Besides, I found my niche and proved myself the best at something: I was a fast runner.

At the track and field events, I earned many awards and ribbons. I raced along, my eyes on the mark. Momentum built as my arms pumped with energy and my long legs pounded the grassy field. The warmth from the sun's rays kissed my face, and the breeze caressed my long, flowing hair. My mind, clear and free from childhood worries, centered on one thought, one goal: crossing the finish line.

The school's P.E. coach never encouraged me. His disregard led me to believe he was biased. Although I was considered the fastest girl in my class, Coach never praised me but favored a blonde girl, instead.

Coach gave Goldilocks pointers and techniques for becoming a stronger runner and routinely paired us to race against each other. I beat Goldilocks to the finish line but gained a hollow victory. Coach normally brushed past me, refusing any congratulatory remarks, and scolded Goldilocks about letting "that girl" beat her. I knew I was "that girl," and "that girl" wasn't good enough to mention by name.

"How many times do I have to tell you to run with your head up?" Coach yelled at Goldilocks. "Your slumping-over allowed her to beat you again."

As I turned and walked away, I still heard his voice. "You're so much better. You're better than *she* is!"

I continued to the gym with my head high, thinking, *She may be better but she ain't faster.*

Another day at practice, I experienced difficulty breathing and gasped for oxygen. I stopped sprinting, hunched over in a fit of coughing and wheezing. I'd never suffered from an asthma attack before, but I'd heard about them. On my knees, crouched over, I motioned for someone to slap my back, until a student came to my aid. Minutes passed before I regained my composure.

The next day was Field Day; we were to race in a 400-meter run—three times around the track. My stomach twisted in balls. I thought about the unusual asthma-like symptoms the day before. Overwhelmed with the what-ifs, I wondered, *What if a similar coughing spell hits me? What if I can't breathe and start to wheeze again? What if I collapse on my face, in front of everybody?* I tried to swallow but couldn't for having dry cotton-mouth. I needed to shake off the nerves and do my best. *Hadn't my grandparents said nothing worthwhile comes easy?*

We took our places and lined up in a row, waiting for Coach's command.

"ON YOUR MARK . . ."

Nerves hit the pit of my stomach.

"GET SET . . ."

I willed my mind to focus, my eyes fixed straight ahead.

"GO!"

We were off. My foot slipped; two of us bumped. I regained momentum, pumping my arms, elbows high. I needed to pace myself or I'd run out of wind. I decided to hold steady at a comfortable third place. I knew that if I stretched myself, I'd pick up speed and pass them one by one. Needed to time everything just right.

Breathe. Keep your eyes on the back of their heads.
Don't get in too much of a hurry.
Steady . . . Steady . . .
Not yet. Not yet.
Almost . . .
Now!

I passed one girl. Then another. A burst of energy flooded me as I gained a second wind. I closed in on the leader.

Goldilocks! I heard her breathing. Our feet pounded the ground in unison, inches apart. It was now or never.

We came onto the turn. I moved to the right. Willing my legs to move faster, I passed her up, taking the lead. In record time, I beat her to the finish line.

With my blue ribbon in hand, victory tasted sweet that day. I couldn't keep from smiling.

Thank goodness, I never suffered another asthma attack. Furthermore, during that period of my life, I knew I was better at something.

My fourth grade teacher's observation:

```
"Mary is a very good student.
She is a fine all-around pupil.
She has shown very good prog-
ress in reading and spelling."
D.S. 1970
```

CHAPTER 10: A ROCK AND A HARD PLACE

MY LIFE IMPROVED while living with my grandparents, yet one shadow lingered: Four years after the birth of my sister and two years since her premature death, I still counted years by the accident.

Grandma and I flew to New York one summer for an entire month. Her brother was my great-uncle Aniceto. I went with Grandma to the hospital to see him. My first impression was of his bony features with two sunken eye sockets staring back. Paper-thin skin clung to his bones. Grandma sat at his bedside talking in Spanish, trying to feed him Jell-O. He didn't have an appetite, but she still tried to get him to eat. He lasted two more weeks before he died.

Uncle Aniceto's daughter, Irma, wanted me to address her as my aunt. She was a stocky, dark-haired, Puerto Rican woman, short in stature, with a strong, loud voice. She spoke more with a New York accent than with a Spanish one. I was both shy and fascinated by her: "a city woman with class who used to be a tomboy," Mama had said.

Aunt Irma loved her father and, when he died, she mourned for him a long time.

"Grandma, what's mourning?" I whispered.

"It means when someone is very sad, dear." Grandma explained. "They are grievin' because their loved one is gone."

The way I felt when I lost my sister.

Aunt Irma cried a great deal. She wept even when we went with her to Macy's to buy an armful of dresses. I thought, *How wonderful to be able to wear a different black dress every day.* I owned four dresses and not one in black. Grandma reminded me that it didn't matter how many one owned if they were clean and pressed.

Aunt Irma's husband, my uncle Jimmy, was originally from China. A cheerful, friendly sort, he was easy to talk with. Because of his thick Asian accent, I needed to pay special attention whenever he addressed me; otherwise, I feared I might miss something.

In mid-Manhattan on East Fourteenth Street, lush green parks surrounded the complex where my aunt and uncle lived. Bluebirds nested, and bushy-tailed gray squirrels scurried in the maple trees above. Park benches alongside playgrounds and courtyards invited parents to watch their children at play. Grandma waited close by while I stooped to feed a squirrel my pretzel.

"¡*Ten cuidado*, Mary! These are not tame *animales*."

"Why, Grandma?"

"They are wild. Your mother didn't pay attention when she was young, and a squirrel bounced on her and bit her on the face."

The thought bothered me but not enough to make me afraid.

At eleven years old, I thought my aunt and uncle were rich. I remembered the cramped places I used to live in, and nothing compared to their grand apartment. Grandma and I stayed in the lovely guestroom in their two-bedroom, fourth-floor apartment. A white, laced canopy bed sat against the wall in the middle of the room. A matching hutch spilled over with Walt Disney storybooks on its shelves. I found the room and all the goodies enchanting, fit for a princess. How I wished that room was mine. But all had been prepared with my aunt's twelve-year-old stepdaughter in mind to welcome her upon her impending arrival from China.

We also visited my favorite uncle Richie in his home for a couple of weeks. My two younger cousins and I watched *Romper Room* and *Captain Kangaroo* with a plateful of pancakes, scrambled eggs and a glass of fresh orange juice. I noticed my auntie didn't remain in bed sleeping the mornings away. She never waited for us to say if anyone was hungry before preparing something to eat. In the mornings she cleaned, swept, and mopped The whole time there, I thought about how much my own mother slacked in these areas.

I awoke with a start.

"Disgraceful!" Grandpa's voice boomed.

"Leave me alone!" a shrill cry answered from the living room.

Another late night visit from Mama.

Grandpa chided her like a child. "Why don't you wash your face and go to bed?"

I studied my mama's features: Mouth twisted. Lipstick smeared. Hair faded of Sun-In spray. Bobby pins missing. She couldn't keep her balance and she talked with a ridiculous slur.

"You should be ashamed of yourself!" Grandpa bellowed.

"You don't know what you're talking about!" Mama spat.

"¡Ay Dios mío! Flor," Grandma pleaded. "Let her be."

Grandpa waved his hand as if swatting a fly and stormed out of the room.

Alcohol deceived my mama, giving her a false sense of power. After drinking, like the caterpillar in my book report, Mama metamorphosed into a social butterfly fresh out of its cocoon. She felt glamorous and intelligent, able to walk with her head up, look others in the eyes and go-go dance the night away. Gone were the restraints that crippled her emotionally. She laughed wildly, conversed freely, and flirted openly.

The more attention and compliments Mama received from men, the less she knew the difference between genuine praise and mere flattery.

Grandma sighed, facing my mother. "Ruthie, Mary is watchin' you."

Mama peered around as if in a daze and stumbled backward. Grandma helped her into bed and then took her shoes off and pulled up the covers. Mama mumbled something. How I wished she'd hush and hurry to sleep.

I'd seen her like that many times, but I felt terrible for my grandma. I didn't think she'd ever seen Mama "loopy-looped" before.

But Mama's behavior wasn't all doom and gloom. With drink in her, my mama—never at a loss for words then—rehashed some wild and hilarious stories. They always held my interest, even the ones about those "riffraff folk and their hanky-panky," as Grandpa had labeled them.

"We were driving down a dark road, but they didn't know the way to go," Mama recounted of the time she, Warren, and his brother drove around in the middle of night. "Then I saw where we were supposed to go, so I yelled, 'Turn here!' That's when Warren crashed the car right into a bus bench." Her face turned so red from laughing hard that I laughed too.

She also shared about the time she was mad at Warren. He always slept with his dentures under his pillow. "I took them, opened the door and threw them as far as I could," she roared.

"Mama, you didn't! Is that why he doesn't have 'em now?"

"They landed in the bushes. Those false teeth are lost and gone forever!" she hooted. "Did I tell you about the time I shaved his sideburns when he passed out . . . ?"

As late-night cocktails turned to daytime binges, Mama—becoming the aggressor—left Warren behind when she went for nightcaps. She often repeated his embarrassing episodes, like the times he would pass out in a bar; his head slumped over the counter. She then started going out alone.

"Once he tried to follow me on the bus," Mama began, "but I turned and stopped him short, striking him over the head with my umbrella." She laughed. "He never boarded that bus."

On another occasion, Mama told me about Warren finding seventy-five dollars she hid in a tin box. "He had the gall to lock me in the bathroom by jamming something against the door," she began. "I not only busted out, but I chased him outside, running down the middle of the street."

When Mama noticed a police car, she shouted, "Stop that man! He has my money!"

The cops pulled over with guns drawn. After discovering the ruckus was a domestic quarrel and not a mugging, the officers threatened to throw one or both in jail overnight. Thank goodness, they returned home safely. I pictured them hammering at each other verbally throughout the evening until they both zonked out from exhaustion.

That same summer, three days before my twelfth birthday, Mama gave birth to baby number five and named him Willie. After him, she decided to have her tubes tied. A history of blood clots prevented her from being a good candidate for birth control pills.

While being prepped to have the procedure done, Mama explained that when hooked to an IV she began to suffer such excruciating pain she felt her arm would fall off. Alarmed and panicking, she screamed, "Take it out! Take it out!" until a nurse removed the IV. She never did have her tubes tied.

Fear often prevented Mama from doing whatever was necessary.

She also never attended any of my extracurricular activities. She came up with one excuse after another:

"I have no way getting there."

"I have to take care of Willie."

"I haven't anything to wear."

At least my grandparents cheered for me the day I proudly won a Christmas carol-singing contest. When I took on a leading role in a school play, singing "Let There Be Peace on Earth," again their smile beamed in the audience as they clapped for me. They couldn't attend my track and field events, though, and Mama remained either too busy or too preoccupied to show up.

In spite of her involvement, my fifth grade teacher's observation was:

```
"Mary Ann is often talkative,
but does do all her work; ma-
ture for her years." 1971
```

For three blissful years, I lived with my grandparents. Then Mama insisted that I move back in with her. At first, I was excited, thinking it might be fun. Until I realized she didn't have much to offer me: a door-less closet for a bedroom, with a lumpy old cot to sleep on.

"This is it?" I asked, thinking she'd gone off her rocker. "You expect me to sleep on *that*, in *there*?"

"Pipe down. It's the best I can do," Mama reasoned. "Things have been worse."

"Well, I was perfectly fine living with Grandma and Grandpa."

"Well, too bad. *I'm* the mother, and besides, they're too old to care for you."

"That's bunk and you know it!" I kicked the puny cot. "You just want me here to babysit Willie while you go out at nights."

"You think you know everything—"

"I know *enough*, Mama. I'm not a baby anymore."

At twelve and a half, returning to live with Mama wasn't the best situation for me. With no structure, stability or sanity, I took an emotional nosedive. No one cared to do housework or take out the piles of trash. I'd do my own laundry, yet soiled clothes still littered the dirty floor.

I'm sure keeping kittens indoors didn't help. I loved cats. Having had no furry kitties when I was smaller, I consoled myself about my living situation by taking in strays. I named them all: Skippy, Bootsy, Fluffy, Sugar, and Wanda (because I found her wandering about). The rarely-changed litter box contributed to the odor and debris in our tiny place.

Life with Mama, history repeated. I spiraled downhill fast.

I loved my grandparents and continued to visit them on occasion. Although everything about them remained the same—nothing about me did. They continued firm in their faith; I became weak in mine. They drew closer to the Lord; I pulled farther away. I started wearing short dresses and hot-pants borrowed from friends. Even my speech patterns changed—I began using slang to sound more street-wise.

Because my mother never took me to church, I placed God on a shelf, like the many dusty knick-knacks Grandma displayed on hers. Eventually, doing things my own way left me blindly headed for more pain and disaster.

Once upon a time, I was content being "Ruthie's little girl," the dutiful daughter who adored and respected her mother. As a child, I competed for Mama's time and attention over the drunken bozos she met at bars. I wanted to please her and never intentionally disobeyed her. I tried to protect *her* and keep *her* out of harm's way, even more so when she drank too much. But because Mama didn't seem to care, my regard for our well-being felt unwarranted and unappreciated. I grew bitter. Ice cold. A sense of defiance festered. Then once I became a teenager, I resumed the role of caretaker, but with a rebellious streak. Mama no longer held me in an iron-grip. With our quirky, mother-daughter roles reversed, our relationship felt awkward. I grew weary of the role of Mama's mother. Listening to her tell her rehashed, zany stories wasn't funny anymore.

Mama didn't want me to hang out with any of my friends,

although *she* never stopped going out. Even ending the three hell-raising years with Warren hadn't interrupted her social lifestyle. She then went out and frolicked with younger men, men who seemed to have nothing at all in common with one another. One boyfriend putted along in a blue Volkswagen Bug, another sped around town in a noisy, red Pontiac GTO.

My mama was having the time of her life while I cared for Willie at home.

O Brother, Where Art Thou?

Curiosity forever led my squirrelly, oddball kid brother into mischief. He preferred to be alone. He saw the world through different lenses, playing by his own rules. His communication skills were lacking as he scarcely spoke in complete sentences. Because he didn't speak plainly, we didn't always know what he wanted. We worried about the foolhardy behavior caused by his strange way of thinking.

"Mary, he did it again!" Mama's voice sounded like nails over a chalkboard, waking me.

"What?" I rubbed my eyes, trying to make sense of what she had said. "Who?"

"*Willie!*" she shrieked. "Go find him before someone calls the cops."

Crazy with worry, Mama paced the floor, chewing on her nails.

Half awake, I tripped over a couple of kittens, kicking their bowl of soured milk. I stumbled down the stairs, barefoot in my gown, and frantically began my quest for the missing two-year-old.

I searched near the overgrown mango trees where I had found him countless times before. Not there. I peeked under the old, vacant house next door, where he sometimes hid. *Nada*. Minutes passed. Then I spotted him. Oblivious to my call and still in his underwear, Willie played in the mud with a stick. How long he'd been roaming the neighborhood was anyone's guess. I half-dragged him upstairs and washed him in the kitchen sink, amidst the scattered dirty dishes and a few floating roaches.

Mama shouted the whole time. She worried about Willie's running off and getting her into trouble with "those damn welfare people."

My immediate concerns: drown out her voice and crawl back into bed under the covers.

That same month, when the landlord called the law on us for causing a ruckus, Mama and I were screaming at each other, throwing stuff around. By the time the police arrived, I was livid. With nothing to lose, I reported to them that my brother and I hadn't eaten for two days. I even dared them to look in the refrigerator and search the cabinets if they didn't believe me.

Unable to find adequate food, the cops whisked Willie away to Children's Protective Services and left me behind. I hadn't planned *that*. Guess they figured I could take care of myself, bare cupboards or not.

Months of dealing with social workers and attending court-ordered appointments went by before Mama got Willie back. Mama led me to believe that her headaches were entirely *my* fault.

"Those jerks will want to know my business and never leave me alone!" she complained for the umpteenth time that day.

Weeks later, Willie returned home more despondent than

before. He wouldn't laugh, wouldn't even crack a smile.

So, I aimed to fix him.

I tickled him and tossed him up high to make him giggle, nearly knocking his head against the ceiling. Then Mama yelled at me to stop before I made him "more cuckoo."

Making matters worse, Willie came back infested with lice that then spread into my long hair. Interruptions didn't make Mama happy—interruptions from watching her daily soap operas, or reading *Ann Landers* columns, or any of her endless collections of *True Story* and *True Love* magazines, or last but not least, the *Enquirer*. Running a fine-toothed comb painstakingly through our hair several times a day was her breaking point.

"If you wouldn't have opened your big mouth," Mama said scornfully, jerking my hair between each word, "none-of-this-would-have-ever-happened."

"Ouch, Mama! Stop it! I only told the truth. We didn't have food in the house."

"Willie isn't a big eater, and it's not like you're starving."

What was the use? She always blamed me.

I argued over a boy with a girl who lived downstairs. We grappled with each other and started throwing punches. Fists flew. Handfuls of hair were yanked and pulled. The squabble that started with us on our feet ended with us on the ground. The next thing I knew, the girl's mother joined the scrap—biting—with a painful death-grip on my thigh. I held unto the girl's neck with my forearm and wasn't about to let go.

The police arrived and broke us apart.

And where was *my* dear Mama? Upstairs. In the safety of

her doorway, gawking at the entire brawl. I became angry, thinking that she might as well have been munching on *chicharrónes* while enjoying the show. I blurted a few choice words and she blurted some back.

"Who's the mother here? Who's the daughter?" the police officer asked.

"Now that's a good question," I sassed, as Mama and I glared at each other.

Undeniably, Mama had been lax in protecting me and, now that I was older, was clearly incapable of managing me. Not quite thirteen, I had become *more* than a handful.

When the landlady came swinging at me with a broom for mouthing off at her granddaughter—without thinking—I swung back with my fist. She promptly called the police.

Bam!

The judge's gavel pounded down on her desk. She sentenced me to thirty days in Miami Juvenile Detention Center.

Slam!

The gate shut behind me.

Juvy Hall was a rough place. Everyone there claimed his or her own turf. The dudes in one area, we *chicas* in another, all kept under lock and key. At least they allowed us to wear our own clothing.

I wasn't in for drugs, so I didn't have to attend the substance abuse classes. I figured nothing was wrong with my brain, so I skipped the mental health sessions. Still, having to sit in on group counseling, I never classified myself as "a threat to society." Almost all the other kids there had issues I hadn't even thought of yet.

Whatever the counselors said went in one ear and out the other. While I bitterly nursed my emotional wounds, I trusted no one, and maintained a false bravado.

"You *Cuban*?" challenged a tall black girl, with an attitude the size of her Afro. She and her sidekick glared at me and blocked my path.

"Naw. I ain't Cuban." I mustered up the toughest stance I knew and added, "*¡Soy Puertorriqueña!*"

"Far-out! We can dig it."

"Right on. Gimme some skin," I said, sticking out the palm of my hand.

Afro-chick slapped my hand so hard it stung.

"So, whatcha in here fer?" Afro's sidekick asked.

"Kickin' butt and smokin' pot!" I lied.

"Groovy, man. You can hang with us."

I wondered, *What if this conversation turned out differently? I don't have any beef with Cubans. Some are friends and even part of my own family. Besides, I love their food.*

Afro-chick, the ringleader of the pack, knew her role. Whenever she wanted something, others forked it over. No questions asked. When she "borrowed" my bottle of musk perfume or my sandals for one too many days, I snuck in her room and took them back. Thankfully, she never confronted me on it. But she was one girl I never wanted to have to tussle with.

One weekend Ruben paid me a visit. I appreciated him reaching out to me as my big brother, and he tried to encourage me the best way he knew. As we reminisced, he reminded me that Jesus loved me. Even though he meant well, I felt his efforts were in vain.

Earlier, Ruben confessed how he always envied *me*. He

felt I had loads of "freedom" while growing up because I hadn't rules to obey, while he had strict ones.

I noticed a pack of Kools hidden in his sock. He shrugged his shoulders and reached down for them. After tapping the pack of cigarettes on his palm, he pulled one out with his teeth like a real pro. I watched as he lit it, inhaled deeply, and then exhale smoke from his nose.

"Well, now, sis," he said, blowing smoke rings and lighting a cig for me, "ain't never said I was perfect."

"Right on," I agreed, taking my smoke.

Once I was back home, the tensions between Mama and me heightened. We argued relentlessly, exchanging harsh and bitter words. I threatened her once, saying that *I* was going out whether she liked it or not. In a wild rage, Mama reached for a curtain rod and lunged for me, whacking down on me hard across my arm.

Pain shot through me, bringing me to my knees. The blow left a long, red welt. Then I leaped and threw a fierce punch that struck Mama in her eye. An ugly bruise quickly appeared. Inwardly, I cringed. Outwardly, I put on a tough façade. I stormed out of the apartment and, with nowhere to go, I sat under an overpass, sulking. After dark, I sauntered on back home.

Mama never hit me again.

Stuck in a rut, with nothing going for me, I felt suffocated and restricted. I knew right from wrong but chose wrong. Peer pressure clouded my judgment, and I hung out with the rough crowd. I skipped school and sneaked behind Mama's back whenever possible.

School had become boring, no more than a means of escape from home. Fighting became a way of life. I had a few

Mary A. Pérez

run-ins with a teacher who didn't like my attitude in *her* classroom. She even escorted me out once, walking behind me with a big ruler in her hand. So, I didn't think she'd mind if I skipped *her* class.

Regarding my numerous absences, my sixth-grade teacher wrote:

```
"Mary is talkative and wastes
time; has had several weeks of
'illness' the last 9 weeks."
'72
```

Running in Heels: A Memoir of Grit and Grace

Mary A. Pérez

CHAPTER 11: TO LIVE AGAIN

MY DAYS AND nights were for my friends. I rarely went home to Mama. My wild conduct got the best of me. My motto: "If it feels good, do it." I skipped classes, hung out with the gang to drink cheap wine and smoke menthol cigarettes, far more fun than schoolwork. Sometimes we'd get hold of grass and, after smoking a couple of joints, hop on the city bus and ride around town going nowhere, giggling like idiots.

After getting a buzz once, we went to the movies to see *The Pink Panther*. We cut up and laughed until our sides hurt and tears fell when the slow-motion fight scene flickered across the big screen. Those seated around tried shushing us to no avail. We didn't care. We'd stopped long enough to breathe and when we glimpse at one another, we'd cracked up laughing again. Then we had the munchies. We ate so much popcorn and candy, anyone else may have gotten sick.

One hot, sticky summer afternoon we thrill-seeker teenagers strolled along *Haulover Pier*. The boys horsed around and dared one another to hop into the ocean, some ten to fifteen feet below. Not only was I skittish about heights, I never learned to swim.

The boys jumped in one by one, hooting and hollering, and the girls followed. The one rule: Whoever dawdled was shoved over the side. For the benefit of all who considered me fair game, I gave all nearby a fair warning at the top of my lungs, "Don't even think about it! I can't swim!"

No sooner than the words were out of my mouth, a prankster shoved me over the edge. I careened into thin air and plummeted into the waters below. My face and chest slammed against the deep, turquoise ocean and the air was sucked right out of me. A solitary thought came to mind as I sank into the murky depths:

Not this again!

I was seven years old when my new friend, Gina, and her mom invited me to a public pool. Gina's mom wore headbands and tie-dyed psychedelic tee shirts. Mama had labeled her a "free-spirited hippie." I thought she knew how to have fun.

Not used to being in the water, I lay contentedly on my stomach along the edge of the pool, watching the others dive and swim.

Behind me, the hushed voice of Gina's mom urged her to do something. How I envied Gina. She had a mother to encourage her, who enjoyed the pool instead of going out all night and sleeping during the day.

"Go on," I heard Gina's mom say, closer now.

Suddenly, *thud!* Someone shoved me over the edge.

Splash! The cold water slapped me.

The water smacked my face and swallowed me. My mouth, my eyes popped open. I saw underwater for the first time. My nose burned from the chlorine. I pushed and pulled to *get air, get air!*

I surfaced and tried to gasp out the word *help,* but water filled my mouth.

A man jumped in and pushed me toward the shallow end. I barely had the strength to hold onto the rail and reach the steps. Weak and trembling from the cold, I grabbed my towel and wrapped it around me.

Gina's face turned pale, her eyes wide with terror. I plopped down on a chair, too stunned to move, too ashamed to speak. Then I heard Gina's mom say, "I can't believe she couldn't swim."

Six years later, *I still couldn't.*

As I floundered toward the surface, my eyes were burning, my throat raw. When my mouth opened, I gulped more seawater.

Choking!

I couldn't catch my breath.

God, I'm drowning!

My lungs screamed for air. My muscles burned. I felt like lead.

So weak . . .

The current swept me farther from shore.

Too far . . .

Suddenly, a pair of hands reached for me. I saw arms. I clawed at them desperately — wildly climbing over the shoulders and heads of anyone brave enough to come near. I nearly drowned my rescuers. After what felt like an eternity, someone pulled me until I reached shallow water.

With what strength I had left, I paddled to shore and collapsed on the beach. The others followed and dropped next to me. Their expressions showed concern.

"That . . . that was close," Earl croaked, coughing up mucus.

"Yeah," his brother, John, chimed in. "We thought you

were a goner for sure."

"Man. You nearly took us down with you!" Sandra choked.

"I told you!" I grumbled. "I told you all I *couldn't* swim."

"Man, we didn't believe you really couldn't."

I hated being afraid, feeling out of control.

Determined to overcome my fear of drowning, several months later, I learned to float and to dive off the diving board in a neighborhood pool. Although never considered a strong swimmer, I enjoyed swimming races underwater.

I conquered that fear.

I rode the bus to Miami Beach to my first paying job.

"Hold the pickles, Hold the lettuce, Special orders don't upset us, All we ask is that you let us, Serve it your way."

Our uniforms reminded me of ketchup and mustard, and the hats were large and goofy-looking. I pasted on a smile, greeted customers, took their burger-and-drink orders, and handled the cash register. Considering myself slick, for several months I worked full shifts at two different locations, pulling in long hours until a store manager caught on and stopped me. Even though he mentioned what a hard worker I was, he worried about child labor laws.

When not working, I spent my leisure time, "chillin' with the gang." We jive-talked in Pig Latin, played FISH, and spin-the-bottle, and drank *Mad Dog*, MD 20/20.

I had since learned to stay afloat on water and joined in on the fun of pool-hopping with my friends. We roamed the streets of Miami, up and down Biscayne Boulevard, believing there was safety in numbers. When kicked out of one pool, we strolled on to the next motel and hopped into theirs.

Long, straight hair parted in the middle, heavy green eye shadow, ruby red lipstick, Musk, *ToujoursMoi* perfumes and black polish over long natural nails were my trademarks. I proudly displayed Virgo zodiac signs and the symbols that represented love and peace. My choice of clothes: bell-bottomed hip-huggers, and hot-pants. I preferred walking barefoot to wearing my clogs. I enjoyed listening to MoTown music like the Stylistics, but when I was by myself, I'd crank up Karen Carpenter and sing along with her.

I became infatuated with a twenty-something Puerto Rican boy. One look at him spelled t-r-o-u-b-l-e. I liked that. Although he was shorter than me, I didn't care. He became my *Sonny Bono*, and I his *Cher*. Johnny, with perfect teeth, long hair, and lean features, loved to party-hardy. He knew how to dance and was some kisser.

One night, I went home late with hickeys circling my neck.

"Oh, so you're showing off now, are you?" Mama spat.

"Mosquito bites," I retorted, brushing past her.

Mama knew all about Johnny. We were at the gathering where he and I had met. As a kid living under her roof, I had to grow up fast. Yet it never occurred to me that I was still so young. Except for my grandparents and my daddy, I didn't care what others thought.

Our favorite Spanish album was by a Puerto Rican group called El Super Trio. Our song was *"Tu Fuiste Mi Primer Amor."* While Johnny could be loving and tender, he was also selfish and arrogant. Still, I succumbed to his hot-cold treatment. At thirteen, I figured our union was my wretched lot in life and assumed that I couldn't do better anyway. During our tumultuous, two-year, on-again-off-again relationship, we lived together; we lived apart. Johnny became a regular jailbird for drugs, intoxication, and violence. He repeatedly broke my heart, put me down, cursed me and shoved me around. I shoved back. He smacked me in front of Ruben once. That my own brother hadn't come to my defense hurt more than Johnny's slap. As a teen, I had learned to fend for myself, depending on no one.

My early adolescence involved scores of unstable living arrangements. They included a single-women's facility like the YWCA, where I was the youngest resident there. I also shared an apartment with my brother and his girlfriend, lived with a few friends, even rented a motel room and shacked up with my boyfriend (and of course, there was the thirty days in Juvy).

When I was fourteen, Johnny and I lived at The Haven, which was nothing more than a bungalow in a dilapidated rental property. A month later, I found myself alone when he landed in jail again.

One hot July morning, Daddy and Gloria paid an unexpected visit. My daddy's voice called as he knocked on my door. "Mary, it's me, *mija*."

I held my breath.

He knocked again. "Mary."

I didn't answer.

"Please, Mary, open da door."

But I couldn't.

"*Te quiero mucho, mija.*"

Hot tears traveled down my cheeks.

Daddy kept knocking and calling for me. Hoping he'd

leave, I didn't make a sound except for my stomach growling. My eyes skimmed across my meager furnishings, which included a mattress to sleep on, a tattered armchair, and a cable-spool table. What would he think, seeing his daughter living in such pitiful, dark and dreary conditions?

I peered out the window to see Daddy, Gloria, and Mama having a conversation. *I knew it!* Mama lived four doors from me. *She* must have let them know that I was home.

After an hour, I peeked to see my parents drive away. My throat burned as I tried to swallow the shame and disgrace I felt. I had let God down, my father down, my grandparents down. I even let myself down. I walked away from the window and flipped on the light switch, forgetting the electricity was off since the bill hadn't been paid. I was tired of being alone, living in the dark.

That night, I resolved not to stick around for Johnny's release. No more tears, no more false pride. I played "La Cadena se Rompió" and went to a payphone to call Daddy.

Next morning, they welcomed me into their home. I walked in carrying my belongings in a small bag, my clothes wadded in a pillowcase over my shoulder. At Daddy's house, I occupied Ruben's old room and slept comfortably in his bed, amazed that he was in such a hurry to leave home.

Ruben, sixteen then, was already gone. He told me many times that he couldn't wait to live out on his own and taste sweet freedom. For me, freedom tasted more like a bitter pill.

I relished the idea of putting a kink on my younger siblings' pampered world. By then, they were five and seven, and a great deal more boisterous than I ever was at their age. I poked fun at my whiny brother whenever he'd bellyache to Gloria at mealtimes, "*Mami, picame la carne.*" She would then cater to him and skin the meat off the bone for him.

Good grief! Wasn't he old enough to eat chicken without eating the bone?

If the kids didn't want what my stepmother cooked for dinner, she prepared something else for them. I never knew such privileges as a kid.

I taunted my slightly overweight sister—not because of her weight, but because I imagined it was from eating so good. I found it hilarious to see her try to run fast. I roared with laughter as she shrieked whenever I chased after her with a green *lagartija* (lizard) and tried to hook its jaw onto her earlobe for fun.

Fortunately, my stepmother tolerated my silly pranks. "*Ay, Marí.*" She pronounced "Mary" by rolling the *r* with her tongue, and making the sound more like the letter *d* than the letter *r*. "*Yo va decil la verdad,*" Gloria said. "*¿Tú eres loca?*"

I shrugged my shoulders and chuckled. "*Quizás.*" Perhaps I was *un poquito loca*. For once, I could act *loca* and be a kid again.

I might have gone too far once (or twice) like when I went shopping with Gloria and my sister at the department store. My stepmother hated escalators. She liked elevators even less. More tired than nervous on this particular day, we took the elevator to the third floor. Gloria hung onto my sister for dear life. Their eyes were about to pop out of their heads. I couldn't resist the urge . . .

I pulled the red STOP button.

The elevator jolted to a halt.

Cries, yelling and stomping of feet as if putting out a fire, echoed and shook the elevator.

My sister tugged on Gloria's arm, screaming, "*¡Mami!*

¡*Mami!*"

My stepmother's wide eyes filled with panic as she pleaded, "*¡Ay Marí, no! ¡Ay Marí, no!*"

Their fits got me all in a tizzy. "Okay, okay," I said, trying to think fast and punching the OPEN button. The doors opened between floors.

Oops.

Screams grew louder. Arms-a-flailing. The bouncing and stomping intensified.

My nerves worked overtime. *What if the door jams? Lord, if you get us out of this mess, I promise to act right.*

I pounded the CLOSE button. The doors shut. *That's better.* I pushed the STOP button back in. The elevator trembled before starting, and finally carried us to our destination. We walked down the stairs when it was time to leave.

Gloria liked shopping at the *bodegas* over department stores; I figured I knew, then, one of her reasons.

"You did *what?*" Daddy asked me when we were alone. He'd been given an earful from my sister and Gloria about our hair-raising day.

"I was just goofing around," I said guiltily.

"Heehee." Daddy chuckled. "You're better than your old *papi*, eh?"

This turned out better than I thought. "*¡Ya tu sabes!*" I hooted. "I learned from the best."

My daddy and his wife tried to live right and set a good example. They attended a Pentecostal church called *Biblia Abierta* (Opened Bible). Although I understood only part of what the preacher said, his messages were upbeat and positive. I liked the music and joined in by clapping my hands. During the praise and worship, women played tambourines. I marveled over the loud, charismatic congregation. Latinos didn't do anything quietly.

Daddy came home late from work one night. "*¡Ave María purísima!*" he exclaimed as he plopped himself in his chair. "Dis never happened to me before." By now, he had our full attention.

"*¿Que pasó, Benny?*" my stepmother asked, hand over her heart.

We crowded around, fearing he'd been in an accident or something. "Daddy, what happened?" I asked impatiently.

"Dis da first time I see long, long lines for gas." His arm circled the air. "They go all da way 'round the block!"

"*¡Qué barbaridad!*" Gloria lamented.

"*Sí, Mamita. Parece mentira.*" Daddy turned to me and continued, "And then, after all dat, I could get noteen. When it was my turn, *¡Dios mio, no hay gasolina!*"

Hearing that, I felt relieved that Daddy had experienced a shortage of gas and not something worse. Everyone talked about the oil crisis then. If the economy didn't get better, we'd all have to depend on the bus, as I had to as a child and still did on occasion. I didn't want that for my daddy. He had broken the mold in our family. He taught himself how to drive. I was proud of him and enjoyed riding in his Gran Torino.

Months went by and I began to think some of Daddy's rules strict. What bothered me most was that I couldn't go anywhere alone or with my friends. I even got in trouble when Daddy found a male cousin and me watching TV on his and Gloria's bed with the bedroom door half-closed.

Daddy barged in looking as if he wanted to strike me on

the spot but he ordered me to my room instead.

I stomped passed him and spouted, "You never let me do nothin'!" His footsteps closed in behind me. I dove for my bed. Before he reached me, Gloria came to my rescue and stopped him. They shut the door to let me sulk. Just as well. I'm certain I might have said something I'd come to regret.

After eight months in their home, I decided to leave and be on my own again. Used to having *no* restrictions, I felt as though they treated me like a baby. While I respected my father and Gloria, especially for their efforts to help me — it was too little, too late.

Eventually, having nowhere else to go, I landed back at my mom's crib.

Home again with Mama, I noticed that three-year-old Willie was a slow learner. He exhibited odd behaviors that prevented him from focusing on details. After undergoing a battery of tests, he transferred to a special education program. Surprisingly, one of his special-ed teachers told Mama that she was wasting everyone's time by sending him to school. Since neither Mama nor regular school could help Willie, social workers soon placed him in a Catholic home, even though neither of us were Catholics.

I had my own cross to bear.

The year 1974 slammed the brakes on my standard education. The court system had labeled me a juvenile delinquent, due to fighting in school and truancy. After my bout in Juvy, a case worker decided to place me in an alternative school until deemed ready to return to my regular home school.

For me, the atmosphere felt more laid back than standard school was. A number of pregnant girls attended Douglas MacArthur, North, but most of the students were boys. I soon discovered that the females got lots of attention from the males. I also learned that if they paid more attention to you than they did the other girls, then those girls called you a "tramp."

I liked the smaller classes and attentive teachers. But I hated the long, bumpy rides to school and back in the long, yellow tanks on wheels. Usually another girl and I were the last ones on the bus heading home. She didn't speak to me. I didn't speak to her.

From the corner of my eye, I noticed her swollen belly attached to her small frame. She gazed out the window, her face hard. I imagined how I'd feel being in her shoes. Pregnant. Scared. Alone.

Eventually both of us ended up napping on those hard, squeaky, bouncing seats until we reached our destination.

Back home, I cranked up the radio whenever Eric Carmen's song came on. I drowned in my bowl of sorrows, singing:

All by myself
Don't wanna be, all by myself anymore.
All by myself
Don't wanna live all by myself anymore . . .

Like an itch that couldn't be scratched, I yearned for fulfillment, searching for love and acceptance in all the wrong places. I dated the cute boys who showed me attention and ignored the unattractive ones. I became my own worst enemy, thinking myself invincible, doing my own "thang," as if I had a noble reputation to maintain.

But I was running on empty. Hungry. Unsure of when I'd eat again. Tired from being on my own. Sick of the dreariness that consumed me. Feeling ashamed. Useless and *sucia*.

Circumstances beyond my control as a youngster and my responses to those circumstances during adolescence served to make my loneliness worse.

I had a dream. It went something like this:

I returned to the refuge of my loving grandparents who believed in a loving God. Because they were strong in their faith, I could be strong as well in mine. As they mentored and encouraged me, I completed high school with honors, learned a trade, saved money, and purchased my own car. I was proud of me.

That's not what happened.

Part 2

At 17 years old with my 5-month-old firstborn, Anna Marie. I am hiding a black eye under makeup.

CHAPTER 12: MY DARK AND SHINING KNIGHT

HE PRANCED ROUND the corner.

His arresting, mystifying air captivated me: suave, debonair, and oh, quite a looker. I thought, *I'll stroll on by and check him out.* Quickly making mental notes: *tall, dark, high cheekbones, broad shoulders—*

He turned with a mischievous grin, showing *dimples!* I averted my eyes and sauntered on by. He whistled. A warm sense of elation swept over me as I thought: *He seems older; more mature than the other boys I've dated. Surely, this one has already sown his wild oats.* I didn't grasp how *much* older until later. But at the time I didn't care.

He was a native of West Indies, thirty-two years old and born on June 6, 1943. If he had claimed that a year after he was born they had named a memorable day on his behalf, calling it D-Day—the "D" standing for Don—I would have believed him. Starry-eyed, I hung on to his every word. He could have said he hung the moon, and I wouldn't have doubted him.

I was staying with Mama again when I met Donny. When we invited him over for a bite to eat, I cooked boxed macaroni and cheese. He brought over a bottle of wine, set it down and peeked at the pot on the stove. He chuckled graciously accepted a plate from me and added, "Well, I guess I'm going to have to show you gals that I can cook."

Before long our days turned into nights, nights turned into weeks, weeks into months. He told me things I wanted to hear. He promised his undying devotion. I was a smitten sophomore thinking, *he embodies the escape from my pathetic home life.*

"Tell me about you growing up," I asked, curled up in his arms on his couch. The smell of his aftershave was intoxicating. The TV flickered in the background, but I had lost interest.

"My mother was Caribbean, her skin the color of charcoal. Just fifteen when she had me."

That's a year younger than me, I thought.

"Relatives and neighbors helped raise me and gave me whatever I wanted," Donny continued. "My father, an American of Scottish origin, died serving in the United States Navy. I never knew him. After my mother remarried, she stayed gone traveling a lot."

Even though Donny's parents weren't around for him, his description of his childhood painted the picture of a privileged life; his every wish fulfilled. Unlike me, he never went without. An only child, money never became an issue—unlike me. And unlike me, he attended a private school and then even college for a couple of years. He said he had enlisted in the army in his early twenties. In Vietnam, he went through the terrors of war, dodging bullets and losing close friends. A handful of his buddies went in; one came out. Renowned for shrewd acts of bravado, Donny boasted about being a leader—even as a boy—proud of the fact he'd sooner run *to* a fight than *from* one. "You get respect that way," he said with a wink. "Two go into a barn but only one comes out."

Wounds of battle were visible on Donny. While running through rice fields in combat, dozens of poisonous booby traps called Pungi sticks had pierced his legs. Deep embedded scars traced his legs and remained as mementos. Months later, when a bullet traveled straight through him, it clipped a kidney, resulting in the loss of that kidney. Besides the ugly surgical scar on the right side of his body, I could see where the slug had entered and exited.

I would later come to know that his internal scars were deeper than his external ones.

By his late twenties, Donny's mother had passed away. As trustee of her estate, he made her funeral arrangements. Already married by then, he and his pregnant wife bought a house with his inheritance. One year later, he left for work and never returned home to her or their young daughter. He simply vanished! Walked away from his responsibilities. Donny admitted to me that, in a moment of weakness, he impregnated another at the *same* time his wife was expecting their child. After their baby, when things got too hot for him to manage, he left. Eventually, his wife sued him for desertion. Upon their divorce, they agreed that she keep the house. Once their daughter became of age, they'd sell the house and split the profit.

I knew something like that would *never* happen to us. Why would it? Hadn't he promised to take care of me and give me his undivided attention? What girl wouldn't want that?

Donny owned a large assortment of records, 45s, mostly collections of oldies-but-goodies from the 50s and 60s stored neatly in a carton. He replayed his favorite record of Otis

Redding's, *Sittin' on the Dock of the Bay* — old fashioned for me, which I didn't mind.

He often talked of "moseying" along to see the world, never cared about staying in one place too long. I admired that he was an early bird who enjoyed staying busy. He took pride in working with his hands, those hands strong, meaty and calloused. His back solid, his shoulders square, he believed in working by the sweat of your brow. I was amazed to see that he even sewed, washed and cooked better than most women I knew (including myself).

Donny was a true fisherman. He loved to fish. Sometimes I'd tag along and fish off bridges and piers alongside him. But when he and a friend went — for fun and sometimes for profit — they'd go in a small boat, casting out huge nets. What they caught, they mostly sold at fish markets.

Around his friends I felt left out, which he made up for when we went to the drive-in theater and watched movies under the stars. Be it a Clint Eastwood or a Charles Bronson flick, I enjoyed our time, especially since I didn't have to compete with any of his buddies or hobbies then.

When I came across a number of old love letters (a majority left unopened in sealed envelopes) in Donny's briefcase, with hundreds of photos of women, I felt a twinge of jealousy. I discovered that he had been involved in various romantic flings, and fathered children by several women. Shrugging his shoulders, Donny assured me he had nothing to hide, even suggested that I toss everything away. Undoubtedly, he had lived a full life, while I had hardly begun mine.

Donny maintained a bristly sense of humor. If I joined him in a drink, he'd call *me* a "lush" even though he'd talk up a storm and his speech slurred. Even so, that man enjoyed his liquor. In abundance. And while he'd begun to display dominance, control and extreme possessiveness, his drinking amplified those behaviors.

Did I run? Nope. Even when I noticed how easily his friends forever pulled and yanked him away from me. Sometimes I felt like the losing side of a tug-of-war, but I felt like I didn't have a choice. I was hopelessly in love.

Soon, Donny persuaded me to quit school; I had lost interest anyway. He prohibited me from associating with *any* of my peers, more so the male population. If I dared glance at, talk to, or even stand near another boy, I'd face consequences. He'd browbeat me with accusations. He wasn't bothered that *he* was a big flirt.

No wonder hometown friends in Antigua nicknamed him "Saga Boy."

Several weeks passed before he and I went to Publix Supermarket to visit Daddy at work. (Daddy and Donny were only ten years apart in age.) Anxious about introducing my man to Daddy, I hoped my worries would disappear once they met. I spotted Daddy in the produce department and grabbed Donny's arm, leading the way.

As we approached Daddy near the fruit stand, he looked up and smiled warmly at me. But as fast as it came, his smile evaporated. He wiped the grime off his knuckles on his green apron, hesitantly accepting Donny's extended hand. Although Daddy appeared polite and pleasant enough, the twinkle in his eye was missing, the mirth in his voice vanished. Whether due to our age difference, or because he had heard how callous he could be, or because he'd seen something I was in denial about, my daddy did not like Donny. It troubled me that their first meeting turned out so somber.

A couple of weeks later at his house, Daddy and I were alone. We sat at the kitchen table, and I asked him about Donny. "What is it, Daddy? Why don't you like him?"

His forehead wrinkled as he poured coffee. His dark eyes, deep in thought, pierced my soul. "I know he's *moreno*, but do he treat you good, Mary?"

I gazed down at my cup, stirring the sugar to collect my thoughts. I needed to sound convincing and believe my own answer. "Daddy, he's mixed. His father was white, his mother black." I glanced up and added, "And he treats me just fine."

Daddy leaned toward me and in a quiet but serious tone, urged, "*Mary, por favor tenga cuidado, hija.* I worry 'bout you."

"Please stop worrying," I said with a smile, placing my hand over his.

We finished our *café con leche*. I went into the kitchen to place the cups and saucers into the sink. My insides fluttered with my dilemma: *How I love these two men, yet so different. If I continue in this relationship, Daddy is hurt. If I walk away from Donny . . .* I couldn't bear the thought.

Before I left, my daddy hugged me and said, "*Él parece muy duro*, Mary. He looks too mean."

I felt I'd been walking a tight rope as I looked into my father's misty eyes. "He will protect me, Daddy."

Undaunted, I clung to Donny wholeheartedly, followed his every footstep, subservient to his every whim. I adored the ground he treaded, wondering if I'd become as needy as my mama, so desperate for love that I let him walk over me. "I don't need him," I told myself, "I *want* him."

I didn't know that my man was more than a social drinker, or that his doctor had advised him to lay off the booze for having one kidney. In the beginning, I believed alcohol alleviated his pain from the memories and injuries of Vietnam. However, I'd begun to realize that Donny's social drinking *and* wandering eyes became his Achilles' heel. Liquor, combined with war recollections, fueled his combative behavior. Even in his sleep, he would shout out profanities, and I regularly got the brunt of his explosive outbursts.

We were at a gathering when a drunkard spurted beer from his mouth into our path.

"Hey, you! Wipe that up," Donny demanded.

"Why don't you take a flying—"

The intoxicated fellow never knew what hit him. With nerves of steel, Donny cold-cocked him, knocking him off his feet. When that dude staggered to rise, blood covered his entire mouth. He wore dentures and the impact of Donny's smack slit his mouth wide open.

I knew what that felt like. I already suffered from the force of those cuffs.

The first instance I ever mouthed off at Donny, a slap landed across my face. Overcome more by rage than fear, I grabbed a vase and targeted his head. Next thing I knew, the ground gave way. I gawked up; dazed from the effects of a blow that felt like it came from a two-by-four.

Bruised. Swollen. That one strike jolted me and left my entire face throbbing.

I had once hoped that loving another might give me the resilience of Teflon, to guard off and shield against the blemishes and corrosion from a torn and broken heart. Instead, disappointment and betrayal chipped off layers of raw emotion, wounding the soul.

The shine in my knight's armor dulled, turning rusty. The weight of his steed trampled upon my spirit.

Running in Heels: A Memoir of Grit and Grace

CHAPTER 13: PIPE DREAMS

May 1976

Dear Mary,

   The first couple of nights we slept in a cheap motel. Finally, we got a place that George found for us. We pay only $80 a month. It's not what we really want. George wants a nice 2-bedroom house, farther out, to raise chickens and have a garden with tomatoes. There's a lot of land around that I saw growing corn and large watermelons. The things at the store are cheap. Willie likes it here, at night we sit out on the porch. We are only here until we save some money and then get what we want. I would like to have a mother cow with her baby calf, a horse with her pony, a white goat that I'd

```
name, "Billy the Goat," and
raise chickens, too . . . Love,
Mom
```

WHEN I FINISHED Mama's letter, I couldn't help thinking: *Fairy tales, fantasies, and pipe dreams. Mama has them too.* After much talk, her current boyfriend George from Tennessee had finally moved them from Miami to a rural area in Ocala.

In the beginning, Mama shared her excitement about their expected move to the country. She smiled wistfully while recounting her childhood days of many summer vacations in the country surrounded by chickens, ducks and cows.

Her enthusiasm would soon fizzle.

Within a week, George fought with Mama, went on a drunken binge and left her and Willie stranded with minimal groceries; no phone, neighbors, or transportation; and the nearest town too far of a walk.

Earlier, Donny and George became buddies, sharing drinks, working on cars, and going fishing. We didn't hear about the abandonment until George dropped by for a visit a week later, and alone.

"Where's Mama?" I asked.

"Left her in Ocala," George answered flatly. "Wouldn't listen. Started to argue. Complained about everything and—"

"And so you just *left* her there?"

What a pompous ass.

"No woman is going to tell *me* what to do!" George retorted, as if he had bragging rights.

Yeah, and you're another conceited, male chauvinist pig! Something I'd always wanted to tell Donny but never dared.

Soon after, Donny and I drove the 300 miles to Ocala to rescue Mama and Willie. They were happy and relieved to see us. Thinner, both were weak from lack of food for more than a week. We loaded their stuff into our van and stopped for burgers before heading back to Miami.

Riding over miles of country road, Mama perked up, relishing the idea of having a captive audience. She rehashed long, drawn-out stories of her hair-raising ordeal living with George, and made no bones about how he had stranded her and Willie.

When Mama laid her head back and closed her eyes, Donny and I stared at each other, hoping she'd exhausted herself enough to take a nap. Then, she opened her eyes, jerked forward, and added for good measure, "No one would do this to a dog or a cat!"

But that didn't stop her from taking George back.

The Square State

On a whim, Donny decided to leave Miami, get away from Florida altogether. With mixed emotions on my part, and high expectations on his, we headed for Colorado.

God's paintbrush, I thought, as we neared the Rocky Mountains. The beauty of those peaks gave me goose bumps and brought tears to my eyes. The clouds were breathtaking and enveloped the crest as they shifted across the horizon.

But apprehensions about the future felt as insurmountable as those Rockies. Nerves consumed me. Fear roiled in my gut. Away from the familiar: home, family and friends.

Once we arrived in Denver, we stopped and settled into a one-bedroom, furnished apartment, minutes from downtown. Because Mr. Popular had lived in Colorado before, in no time he re-connected with longtime friends, acquaintances *and* old female flings.

A natural at landing on his feet, Donny found employment as a machinist at Band-It, a large engineering company. He insisted that I be a stay-at-home girl. His favorite lines: "No gal of mine has to work." And the never ending, "I'm the man; you're the woman."

Donny picked arguments over trivial matters. He was right. I was wrong. If I didn't hear it once, I heard him say those hurtful words to me a zillion times: "When we met, you carried nothing but a small georgie-bundle around."

Even so, they were my things. And I was my own person then.

"Remember," Donny added, "I own you. I bought and paid for you, gal."

Damaged Goods

Hollow. Pure loneliness. Dark like a bottomless pit. Ripping in my chest. Again, he stayed out all night. Overcome by torment, abandonment accompanied me. Consumed with depression, isolation wrapped itself around me. My mind raced with wild imaginations of where he had gone, what he was doing, and with whom.

Instead of going to bed to sleep, I was wearing a hole in the couch. At the sound of every car approaching, like a jack-in-the-box I sprang to peek out the window hoping Donny had returned. With every disappointment, my stomach turned into knots. My own sobs mocked me until I cried myself to semi-unconsciousness. Hideous lies followed after he returned and added to my anguish and emotional decline.

I had begun to feel lightheaded and tried hiding it from him. He wouldn't tolerate me being sickly or feeble, so I said nothing.

Time took its course and eventually he noticed.

"What's the matter with you now?" Donny demanded, glaring at me with a raised eyebrow.

My body felt like lead. I looked at the clock and realized I had overslept on the couch again. "Nothing," I whispered, feeling dizzy. Even though I rehearsed the answer a hundred times, my voice cracked and wasn't really assuring. I stumbled for the bathroom to throw up. Truth told: I figured *something* wrong.

The following week I made an appointment for a checkup. In my mind, I figured I was anemic and most likely needed to take an iron pill, at best. Or maybe I had caught the flu, at worst. Once at the clinic, after routine questioning and a urine sample, I learned the truth:

I'm going to have a baby! Although relieved that I wasn't going to die, I was also scared to death. *Sixteen and pregnant, must be the record in my family.* I didn't know if Donny wanted the responsibilities of a kid. He fathered children before and went AWOL. One thing I knew: this would either make or break us.

The day that Donny galloped into my world, my young heart had been over-confident, thinking my love for him was enough to change him into being content as my soul mate, protector and confidant. Now with the pregnancy, I wondered if maybe the knight I'd dreamt about would emerge after all. That he might be pleased since I carried his child, and show me a smidgen of tenderness or affection.

When I made my announcement to him, I expected at least that an inkling of pride might register across his face. No feather in my cap there either. Instead, he shrugged his shoulders, sucked his teeth, and headed out the door to work.

Love hurts, and then, you cry.
In Denver, Donny had *his* friends.
I had none.
He and his friends were in their 30s and up.
I was still in my mid-teens.
Donny and his buddies hung around our apartment swilling Coors Light.
Me? I wasn't included.
When they went out, they drank at the bars in LoDo (Lower Downtown – Denver), known for its nightlife.
I stayed in bed reading romance novels and sipped on "screwdrivers."
Echoes of my lonely childhood revisited.
Why did all my dreams have to be squashed? Torn between uncertainty and shame, I didn't mention my pregnancy to my family. I experienced deep feelings of melancholy when I wrote home and penned how hunky-dory life was, when in reality, my life was belabored with strife and difficulties.
I began to feel like I shared my bed with the enemy, that I couldn't speak to anyone about Donny's alcoholism and abusiveness. Whether because of pride or shame, I kept the pain to myself. I felt numb, miserable from the emotional, verbal, mental, *and* physical abuse. I hoped that my pregnancy might end Donny's cruelty.
I was in for a rude awakening.

Ducking from under a heavy rain shower, I scuttled to my apartment juggling a soggy grocery bag in one hand, fumbling for my house keys with the other. At that instant, Donny threw open the door like a crazed maniac. Startled, I dashed past him to get out of the downpour, chilled to the bone, soaking wet.

Before I caught my breath, Donny seized my arm and swung me around.

"You didn't know I was home, *did you?*" he spouted.

"What? No. Why should that—"

"Answer me!" He backhanded me.

I saw stars. "What's wrong with you?" I responded as boldly as I dared, tasting blood. "I didn't do anything!"

"You and *that guy* behind you, racing to come inside *here*, weren't you?"

"WHAT? *What* guy?" I racked my brain. *I never noticed anyone running behind me. Even so, whoever he was, he was probably trying to get out of the rainstorm like me—*

I never imagined what came next.

Donny grabbed the coffee table and hurled it at me. In a blur, I scarcely had time to turn away. The impact struck across my shoulder blade. I buckled and cried, "God, help me!" My head lowered as I anticipated another blow. I felt relieved to hear his footsteps leave the room.

Later that night, Donny reached out to me in tenderness, the best way he knew how; his way of expressing that he was sorry. He always became remorseful after one of his fits. We chatted and when I felt the baby move, I placed his hand over my bump. We rubbed my belly and imaged the baby's foot or an elbow. Donny mentioned how he'd always wanted a son named after him. He said he'd already fathered several daughters.

I played along and agreed with the idea of having a boy, lost in my own thoughts. I wondered what my mothering skills might be. I couldn't wait to show my pregnancy and wear maternity clothes. At that moment, I craved a big, fat, juicy cheeseburger, fries and a vanilla shake. I wondered what my baby would look like. And in the quiet, private corners of my mind, I wondered, *What if I gave birth to a girl? Would I become one more of those women who had a daughter fathered by Donny — and then dumped?*

Mary A. Pérez

CHAPTER 14: COLORADO'S BICENTENNIAL ADVENTURE

July 31, 1976

WE HEADED FOR Rocky Mountain State Park for a continued weekend bicentennial celebration, to enjoy the magnificent canyons' cool mountain air and breathtaking river valleys.

The afternoon breeze, mingled with the whiff of hamburgers sizzling on the pit, put Donny in good spirits, along with an ample supply of beer. He recounted old childhood and war stories while he guzzled one drink after another. I roasted marshmallows over the campfire, until raindrops drove us inside our van. We tucked into our sleeping bags for the night.

In no time, Donny's snoring commenced. As my eyelids grew heavy, I thought, *At least I'm not out in this wilderness alone.*

Sometime later, I awoke with a start, "Donny! Donny, wake up!"

"Hmmm?" my still-asleep, great protector mumbled, turning over.

I sat up and held my breath. I felt the van vibrate. The plunking sound of raindrops rattled across the rooftop, lashing at the van's exterior. I strained to listen for something else, feel something else, but wasn't sure what.

Only a case of bad nerves, I reasoned, starting to lie back down. *No! There it is again.*

"Donny, did you feel that? Our whole van shook!"

"Go back to sleep, gal," Donny muttered. "It's probably just a bear."

Just a bear? Better not be any bear out there!

Minutes passed. I lay back down and willed my mind to relax. The sound of rain soon lulled my unsettled thoughts and sleep overtook me. Before nodding off, I thought I heard rumbling in the distant.

Dusk turned to dawn, and I considered my night's fright silly. We ate a quick breakfast of hard-boiled eggs, leftover meat and orange juice.

"Shake a leg," Donny announced. "Time to go."

We left our campsite, cruising over mucky roads. Puddles and slushy trails made the roads treacherous and tricky. At one point, our van was stuck in the mud. Donny kept his foot over the gas pedal and accelerated. The tires sloshed and the van swirled, nearly tipping over.

"Jesus!" I cried out, thinking we were history.

Unruffled under pressure, Donny turned the wheel sharply to the right and back on the road again.

"What's the matter?" he said, looking at me as if I were a dimwit.

"Nothing," I huffed.

As we continued, we noticed massive trees toppled over; many bobbed along in the river. We heard helicopters. Soon, we approached park rangers rerouting traffic. I stuck my head out the window and overheard bits of instructions given to other passengers in their vehicle.

"... mountainside ... engulfed ... destroyed ... proceed with extreme caution ..."

The reporter on the radio described how a typical summer rainfall turned into a horrendous nightmare for hundreds of people. Many homes washed away in a flash flood. Cars vanished, buried under tons of debris. Roads had swept away along the canyon, broken concrete stuck out of the riverbank like foreign objects. It took hours to navigate our way back into town.

The morning headlines read:

"THE BIG THOMPSON CANYON FLASH FLOOD."

Many reported missing. *Dead.* Houses and businesses washed away, destroyed. An overwhelming thought hit me—we had been completely *oblivious* to the dangers the night before. What if we had camped near the Loveland area and Donny had brushed off my concerns in his half-drunken sleep, as he did the night before. Then what? We might have been one of those statistics. *So much for my "protector"!*

```
August 1976


. . . I am so glad Donny took
you to the mountains but was
far away from that flood in
Loveland. What a tragedy.
God bless you both, Grandma &
Grandpa
```

Financial struggles forced Ruben and his new girlfriend, Cheryl, to move from Dallas to live with us in Denver. Although our apartment was small, we improvised. At night, we placed a thin mattress on the floor for them. We got along well and enjoyed one another's company. The guys liked to play *Atari*, while Cheryl and I tried our hands at cooking and baking. I felt comfortable with another girl around, even more so being pregnant.

One October morning, we decided to take a break and drive up to the canyons along the scenic, snow-crested Rockies. We stopped to explore and take pictures. Our footsteps crunched on the powdery snow that covered the ground like a blanket. The cool, dry air turned our cheeks and noses red. We saw our breath when we talked and laughed. When we drank from the stream, the water tasted sweet and cold. I even made a snowman.

My nineteen-year-old brother, having never seen snow before, reveled in a snowball fight with Donny. We girls cheered for Ruben when he hit his target, smacking Donny upside his head, leaving a white ball of snow residue on his afro. A warning glower from Donny changed my mind. I began rooting for him. The guys kept going until Ruben knelt and covered his head, both hands in surrender.

I returned to work on my snowman, adding a swollen belly to mimic my own. Then, when my brother slid down the mountainside on a trashcan lid, I couldn't stop giggling.

I loved to laugh. Laughter—so rare during those days—made me forget my troubles. I wished time would freeze and the moment never end.

Even so, Mama's voice rang in my head: "If something is too good, watch out."

I looked forward to my grandmother's type-written letters.

She kept me abreast on family matters. I saved *all* her letters:

> . . . George left for St. Petersburg because he couldn't find work here. Your mother has many problems and is not doing good physically. Willie is not in school. Your mother wants to move again. I don't know why you people move around so much and then don't want me to give your addresses to anybody. Seems funny. May God bless you all and give you understanding.
> Love, Grandma

Grandma felt we *all* had some growing up to do still. Can't say that I blamed her. A few days later, I received more news from her, but this one shocked me to the core:

> Mary, Papa and I are in much pain. Our legs are so painful as we are in chairs resting and taking medicines. So many things we do not understand in this life, the shock will remain with us forever . . .

I rushed to a nearby payphone and made a long-distance collect call. My heart stuttered when I heard Grandma's details about their harrowing near-death experience:

"Oh dear, on our way to church, we were in the rear seat of Frances' car when out of nowhere, an oncoming car ran the red light!"

Their car T-boned; the front passenger died instantly. Frances, the driver, was in a daze while my grandparents remained trapped in the rear, with their legs pinned under the seat. Thankfully, help came and an ambulance rushed them to the hospital.

I recalled a Bible passage on how it "rains on the just and unjust." And I've heard, "Bad things happen to good people." I never understood that theory. I only knew my grandparents were good and was grateful that God had spared them from something worse.

Mary A. Pérez

CHAPTER 15: COMBUSTION

FOR ME, LEARNING to drive was a milestone. My grandparents never learned, nor had Mama. Although Daddy taught himself, he didn't get his license until he turned twenty-seven. The more I drove, the more confident I became; however, I was still without a driver's license.

After Donny agreed to let me drive, Cheryl and I hopped into the van to go to the store. Already late in the afternoon, we headed out. With the windows rolled down and our hair blowing in the wind, we stuck in our favorite eight-track tape, bobbing our heads to the beat of K.C. & the Sunshine Band, *Shake Your Booty*.

We took our time in the store. We browsed around perhaps too long, talked too much, and laughed a tad too loud. By the time we left, the sun was due west.

I decided to take a different route home and cruise along the outskirts of town. We sang, joked and giggled, but the jokes soon fell flat. We were getting farther and farther away from our apartment on Corona Street. The clock ticked and the dark closed in. Eventually, I managed to get us back home.

Once we arrived, Donny's cold, hard face made me dread what was to come. *Well, no use beating around the bush,* I thought. But my explanation on how we got turned around landed on deaf ears. Mr. Suspicious never believed a word I said.

A week before this we had stopped at a filling station. When the service man came out to greet us, Donny told him to 'fill 'er up' and went to find the men's room. I stayed in the passenger seat. While the attendant pumped gas, he craned his neck inside the rear window to admire the interior side panels upholstered in maroon and black, and the seats covered in plush velvet. The attendee said he hoped to get wheels like ours one day. Immediately, the thought crossed my mind: *If Donny comes out and sees your head in this window . . . talking to me . . . !*

No sooner did I have that thought than King Kong returned from the men's room with that look on his face. Before he made a scene, I tried explaining that the dude was admiring the van. Overhearing our conversation, the attendee popped his head out, knocking it against the window in the process with a loud *thump*. Once he filled our gas tank, he collected payment from my ever-so-glaring chauffeur, stuttered his thanks and scooted away.

Donny's extreme jealousy and obsession were continuous.

At the theater that same evening, after selecting our seats, Donny went for popcorn and drinks. Three boys around my age sat across the aisle. One brave soul moved in close.

Here we go again, I thought. *Dead boy approaching.*

Romeo sat next to me, leaning on the arm of the seat, grinning and jive-talking about the previews. Donny returned a few minutes later, hands full of snacks. In an instant, Godzilla emerged, with that all-too familiar "kill-murder-destroy." Flaming words spewed from Godzilla's mouth. He kicked the boy's leg and dumped the entire bag of popcorn over his head. Romeo mumbled an apology and limped back to join his snickering friends. *Poor kid.* He probably thought Donny was my father or something. I didn't say a word but Donny's gaze burned a hole through me the entire movie.

Now, after our long drive in the car, he looked at me the exact same way. His blazing eyes made me break into a cold sweat.

"You hear me?" He grabbed my arm. "You and her weren't driving around *lost*," he hissed, pointing at Cheryl who was walking in. "You two were fooling around with some pimple-face *boys*."

"No! That's not—!"

A ruthless slap followed his accusations. My entire face pulsated.

"Leave her alone, you psycho!" Cheryl yelled, pulling me away from Donny's clutches, "Think what you want; you never believe her anyway."

Grateful that Cheryl stood up for me, I held unto her as we ran in the bathroom, locking the door behind us. But I knew that if "psycho" had enough drink in him, that door wouldn't remain intact. With my mouth throbbing, and my lips numb, we waited, whispering, until we heard him leave. Then, we laughed ourselves silly when the bathroom door jammed and we couldn't have gotten out if our lives depended on it.

Perhaps Cheryl coming to my defense threw Donny off. At least he never again mentioned our getting lost when she and I went to the store.

Crash!

The sound of breaking glass.

In bed, my eyes flew open.

Thud!

Sounds ricocheted. Footsteps echoed in the distance.

Before the fog cleared from my mind, someone pounded on our door. I jumped, nearly coming out of my skin. Donny sprung out of bed before me. I heard voices.

"Fire —"

"What . . . ?"

"Your van's on fire!"

"—everywhere! Come quick!"

I followed the sound of the commotion out into the cold. Acrid smoke reached my nostrils and made my eyes water. The sight stunned me.

Our van. *Burning!*

The blaze rose higher and higher, engulfing everything inside. Dancing, reddish-orange flames mesmerized me. Transfixed with shock and disbelief, I stood too stunned to move, too numb to cry. In a blur, someone dashed by with an extinguisher. But it was too late. The interior was charred. White smoke billowed from the windows.

The night breeze scattered the ashes like my unsettling thoughts. Nothing doused the burning in the pit of my gut.

With eyebrows knit in anger, his nostrils flaring, and tight-lipped, Donny shouted threats to life and limb (and damnation) to whoever did this.

I couldn't calm my nerves. I had heard footsteps and wondered *who would do this? Someone with a vendetta against Donny,* I reasoned. *But why? Whose husband or boyfriend had he betrayed?* While mulling over my thoughts, I wrapped my arms around myself for warmth. I stood under the balcony of our apartment in that dreadful, clammy midnight hour. The cold evening draft filtered through my nightgown like icy fingers.

My eyes riveted over the one I cherished. As I looked at him looking at me, he told me nothing.

But his eyes told me everything.

Later, Donny accused someone at work. In his mendacious manner, he never admitted to any guilt or wrongdoing on his part.

How does he sleep at night?

Donny always came out on top one way or another. He said he'd go to the bank in the morning and purchase another van. He still drew interest from an account left to him by his mother after she died. Of course, he never divulged the amount to me.

Sure enough the next day, Donny nonchalantly came home driving a red Ford Econoline van. "I know how to survive," he boasted. "When push comes to shove, I'm smarter than the average bear."

Yeah, and I'm the nincompoop who puts up with you.

With his secret out in the open for the entire world to see and mock, I realized that if Donny looked like a fool who couldn't keep his zipper closed, wasn't I a bigger *pendeja* for tolerating his infidelity?

He knew I felt trapped with nowhere else to go. I often questioned his capability of loving anyone other than himself. Uncertainty dug deep—uncertainty about him, about me, about us. The one sure thing:

Soon, I was bringing a baby into the world.

Running in Heels: A Memoir of Grit and Grace

Mary A. Pérez

CHAPTER 16: MOTHERHOOD

1976 Thanksgiving Day

THE DAY FILLED with a hum of activity in the preparation of the holiday meal. Because Donny didn't want help in the kitchen, Ruben and Cheryl watched the Denver Broncos game over drinks. Three days overdue in my pregnancy, I sat and watched the way Donny handled the twenty-pound turkey. He stuffed her with a mixture of cornbread and spices and herbs sautéed in butter. After placing the bird into a pan, he wrapped her in foil to roast in a hot oven.

A pot of boiling potatoes sat on the stove. Soon a creation of potato salad garnished with sliced boiled eggs and tomato wedges rested in a bowl. Donny even mixed flour, eggs and butter in a frying pan with oil to make dinner rolls—something I had never seen done before. Lastly, he whipped up a bowl of cream gravy made with the turkey giblets. The aroma made my mouth water.

I ate to my heart's content. The men drank to theirs. After our feast, the apartment settled down. Earlier I felt a dull ache in my lower abdomen but hadn't mentioned anything to anyone. I had heard the term "false labor" and didn't want to bring attention to myself. Still I worried.

All the others were in bed. Determined not to pester anyone, I gingerly headed for the bathroom. When I awkwardly lowered myself in the tub to soak, the discomfort intensified. I watched the clock, realizing the pain occurred every five minutes.

Uh oh, I thought with a shudder.

I yelled for Donny. *No response.* After dinner he'd gulped down enough vodka and water to float a battleship.

I climbed precariously out of the tub and wrapped myself in a towel. At a snail's crawl, I entered our room, leaving a row of wet footprints behind me. Donny, in his drunken stupor, hadn't made it into bed; he lay out cold, sprawled on the carpeted bedroom floor. I sat on the edge of the bed and nudged him with my foot. *Dead.* I gave him a swift kick. *Nada.* I imagined the possibilities: We owned one car and Donny was the lone licensed driver. I'd take a chance, but wasn't in any condition to get behind the wheel. Neither Ruben nor Cheryl drove.

"Where's the help when you need it?" I muttered to myself, and put on a gown.

Shuffling into the living room, I turned on the overhead light. Ruben didn't move a muscle, zoned out from his own binge earlier. Half of his body lay next to his girlfriend on the mattress, half draped onto the cold linoleum floor. Cigarette butts in overflowing ashtrays, empty beer bottles and food wrappers scattered around them. Thankfully, Cheryl's head appeared from pillows and blanket as she stirred and peeped in my direction.

"Whaya doin'?" she mumbled, half asleep, shielding her eyes from the light.

"I have to get to the payphone. I think it's time –." A sharp pain snatched my breath and I bent over in agony.

Cheryl scrambled up from the floor mattress, and rushed

over. She helped me into my robe and, as she held my arm, we hobbled out in the cold, down the block to the phone booth, and called the hospital.

The pain heightened with our fear. Stopping with each contraction, I scarcely managed to plod back. When we returned, we tried to awaken Donny again, and this time we succeeded. I didn't know who looked worse: me with my face contorted with misery or him hung-over with puffy, red eyes and disheveled hair. At least he looked semi-conscious—or so I hoped—as I grabbed my overnight bag.

"Quick, gal," Donny ordered gruffly, slamming his car door. "Get in the car."

So much for chivalry. I managed to climb in with Cheryl's help.

"You gonna be okay?" she whispered, a worried look pasted on her face.

"Close the door, girlie," Donny barked at Cheryl, reaching over my rounded, thirty-seven-week belly to slam my door shut in her face.

I mouthed the words 'thank you' to her.

I'm certain Donny broke the law rushing to the hospital. We blazed over snow-covered streets. We zipped through stop signs and zoomed past red lights. Donny even risked our lives when he turned onto a one-way street and continued plowing unfazed. We ran over every bump on the road. Praise the good Lord; we finally arrived at the emergency entrance of St. Joseph's.

Before I knew it, my quick-thinking, so-called savior rushed on ahead and vanished through the sliding doors, announcing at the top of his lungs, "We're having a baby! We're having a baby!"

That's funny, I thought as I waddled in without any help from him, *I don't recall seeing <u>him</u> with a swollen belly.*

Once in my room, I hoped to relax. But Donny's erratic driving rattled my nerves. He said he needed coffee and remained in the waiting room.

Just as well, I thought. *He needs to sober up.*

But there would be no relaxation for me.

My youth labeled my pregnancy as "high-risk" and that added to my anxiety. I felt anything but calm when a nurse came in to prep me, whipping her razor around my privates. Next, she rolled me on my side and inserted an enema that helped to flush out the Thanksgiving feast I had gorged on earlier. *Shameful.* Lastly, she hooked me to an IV and a monitor that read my contractions.

Alone in my room, I waited for nature to take its course. After a single visit, Donny returned to the waiting room for a stretch on the couch.

The nurse checked in with routine examinations, poking me with her long, pointy nails. The labor pains were deep, sharper with each contraction. Time dragged on as the clock's hand ticked.

After six hours, I dilated to a three. "You still have a ways to go," she announced, leaving to make her rounds.

I stared at the TV, hearing the drone but not paying attention to the program.

Then, I felt a strong urge. Alone and frightened, my heart raced.

I pressed the button. No answer.

I pressed it again. Nothing.

I shouted. No one came.

In desperation I banged on the wall, yelling, "Anyone out

there? I have to push! I have to push!" *Doesn't anyone hear me? I . . . have . . . to . . . push!*

I pounded on the walls, about to put a hole through it. At last, a nurse ran in. Much to her surprise—and my anguish—she found me fully dilated and ready to pop.

Too much was happening at once. Oddly enough at the same instant, I felt like an ice cube. The nurse noticed me trembling and threw three blankets over me. She fetched Donny. They gave him a hospital gown, a cap, and a mask. After he followed them to the delivery room, they instructed him where to stand.

With my knees bent and feet in stirrups, I leaned forward with an assistant's help.

"Now push," my doctor instructed. "Push, hard."

I took a deep breath and held it, managing a couple of pushes, one or two deep grunts and a long groan, feeling the blood rush to my brain. "I . . . can't!" I gasped. "No more. I'm tired."

"Come on. Keep pushing. Bear down. A little more."

"Arrrrgh!"

"Shush. It's okay, honey," Mr. Macho-turned-coach drilled. "Stay calm."

"*YOU* stay calm! *IT HURTS!*"

"Humph," Donny snorted.

"All right, now give me one big, long push."

"It . . . b-burns!" *Lord, I feel like I'm tearing apart!*

"Okay, now *stop*. Stop pushing a moment."

Push-Breathe-Bear down-Don't push-Breathe! My mind zoomed from ninety to zero. *Oh, what am I supposed to do? Why hadn't Donny and I completed those Lamaze classes with the breathing techniques?* Finally, the answer came to me: In order to refrain from pushing, I needed to do a series of shallow breaths. Pant. Like a dog.

Donny watched the whole process bug-eyed and ashen-faced.

Some macho-man he turned out to be.

2:56 a.m.

Gorgeous. Chestnut hair. Almond-shaped eyes. Rosy cheeks. Ten fingers and ten toes.

At the ripe old age of seventeen, I delivered a beautiful, healthy 7 lb. 6 oz. baby girl. *My baby girl! Thank You, God.* With the ideal name for her—in memory of my beloved grandma and my deceased sister—I named her Anna Marie.

After three days in St. Joseph, it was time to go home. Surprisingly, Ruben and Cheryl were gone. A couple of days later, much to my chagrin, my brother's girlfriend confided to me that while I recovered in the hospital, my dear Mr. Wonderful got wasted and tried to forced himself on her. When she had slapped him, he supposedly came to his senses. The next day, they moved out.

How could he?

Of course, Donny denied everything. I never knew if that was true, or if he had blacked out and honestly forgotten.

Grandma wrote:

```
December 5, 1976

   Praise God and thank Him for
His mercies endure forever and
He can hear and answer prayers.
As soon as Papa started read-
```

> ing your letter and saying,
> "Great-grandparents," I started
> thanking God. Well dear, I can
> imagine all you went through
> but thank God it's all over.

No, it's only begun, I thought.

Determined to focus on all I had read on the joys of motherhood, I longed to feel and savor those joys. Instead, I underwent a continual feeling of emptiness, coupled with depression. I became acquainted with a common, postnatal condition called "Baby Blues." Although I had raised my baby sister, I harbored self-doubts about mothering, for the first time feeling like a baby who just had one.

My rude awakening: zero support from Donny. Things were supposed to be different. Wasn't he a daddy now? Instead, he'd come home with drink in him, turn the TV on and park himself on his chair. He was home all right—minus communication, interaction, or even a grunt, except for the snoring. I reached over and turned off the TV.

The dead arose. "Hey, I'm watching that!"

After giving Anna Marie her bath, I put her down for the night. I went back and stood in front of Donny again with my arms crossed, listening to his snores. I thought about how he didn't know or care about commitment, let alone fatherhood. He always said that babies weren't *his* department. *Yeah, just in making them*, I thought, while he continually stayed preoccupied with "other" things. Well, I needed to toughen up and learn my role. I now had a baby to love and care for, no matter what.

❖ ❖ ❖

Bittersweet sentiments flooded me as I read the surprising closing of a letter from Mama:

... I always did love you. Just had too many problems....

Mama's attempt at expressing her love for me was increasingly limited to pen and paper. Her words leaped off the printed page and squeezed my heart like clasped fingers. Akin to a castaway on an island sighting a boat ... Dare I hope for a rescue? Will there be a lifeline afloat in muddy waters? Is it possible that my own mother, at last, reaches for me and saves me from years of deep-rooted rejection?

I knew she loved me. But to see those ten words on a page stirred something inside. Never too old to crave my mama's love ... I couldn't contain the hot tears.

I focused my attention and savored the miracle before me: An innocent life at peace in her crib. A life I'd only known as bittersweet; a life filled with much adversity from being alone, cold, hungry, and frightened.

My mind was full of unanswered questions. Could I protect this child and keep her safe? As her mommy, I wondered if I'd always be there for her, and not fail or disappoint her. Would we have a close relationship? Would she always feel my love?

Uncertainty and fear sapped hope from me like a thirsty blood-sucking leech—fear that I'd wind up missing the boat, and like Mama, choke with failure and drown in the sea of regrets.

Maybe Mama will make a better grandma.

CHAPTER 17: LETTERS FROM HOME

FIVE MONTHS INTO my pregnancy, I wrote Mama to tell her that she would be a grandmother. I had hoped the news might help mend our strained relationship. I had hoped Mama might express joy and happiness for me. Moreover, I had hoped that she might see this as an opportunity for us to start over, to undo past hurts and disappointments.

I looked in the mailbox. Every day. Six days a week.

Weeks passed as my anxiety grew along with my round belly. *Finally!* In August, a letter arrived. I ripped the envelope open to read Mama's reply. After scanning the five, small handwritten pages, front to back, two main factors in her response trampled all my hopes: Mama failed to comment about the news of my pregnancy. She also neglected to mention anything about my approaching birthday.

```
August 2, 1976

   I feel like starting a new
life for myself but I'm a lit-
tle mixed up and not sure of
anything . . . It's hard to ex-
plain . . . I've had a nervous
```

> stomach lately, but I'm much better now. I'm going to get a checkup for myself. I would like a physical; the last time I had one I was 28. I say I am in my menopause . . . Maybe it's just a case of nerves. I feel nauseated and tired . . .

Everything in the letter was about her, of course, and it was clear she didn't take better care of herself than she did with any of us kids. I knew she procrastinated, but her going for over thirteen years without having a physical was too much to fathom. Then again, that's my mama.

A week later, a letter from Grandma read:

> August 10, 1976
>
> Mary, how I wish your mother wouldn't be infatuated so much with a man that can't do anything for her. The Welfare folks want to reduce her check since they learned that you were no longer living with her. George went back to Ocala, so your mother was unhappy all the time and wondering where she should go or move to with Willie, either to the country or somewhere—at least, this is her theme song. I am sorry for

> her. We want to help, but she
> doesn't cooperate with us. So
> long for now. God bless you
> both. Prayerfully, Grandma.

Two weeks later Mama confirmed my hunch:

> August 16, 1976
>
> I've been sick, nauseated, and
> dizzy . . . I have a lot of
> thinking to do and don't know
> where to turn. I'm so scared
> . . . the pregnancy test came
> out positive. I went into the
> bathroom and cried. I don't
> know what to do . . .

My heart sank. Once again, Mama—worried about her own dilemma—was unable to show any regard for my condition. I felt badly for her. And I still couldn't get over the irony that mother and daughter were pregnant at the same time.

My seventeenth birthday had come and gone uneventfully.

> September 1, 1976
>
>   Don't worry dear if your
> mother forgets your birthday.
> She has so many of her own
> problems that she can't think
> right, and you know, Mary, it's
> all her own fault. Your mother

> also forgets important events. I told her, "Remember Mary's birthday, Ruthie." She says, "Yes, I am going to send her a card." And she had money at the time, but she left things for later and when the time comes, she forgets and then, it's too late. Get me? Love, Grandma

As much as Mama's indifference hurt me, she wasn't going to change. She'd been that way as far back as I could remember. Still, I wished she'd get a grip.

From Mama:

> October 19, 1976
>
> . . . First time I heard a baby's heart beat . . .

"'First time?'" I shouted. "Did you not hear *my* heart beat?" I continued reading:

> . . . After the doctor put a stethoscope on my belly, I asked him if I was pregnant. He answered, "Are you?" I told him, "I don't know, I'm asking you!" Then, he said, "Well, I hear a baby's heartbeat." This is something I'm going to have to go through all alone; I don't know how. You have your

> husband; I have no one and no baby clothes. So, I'll probably won't be able to keep it. I don't know when I will be able to write you again, as you can see I'm in no mood to write. Too many problems.

I set her letter on my lap. Even after I left home, Mama's drama sadly continued, one mess after another. *Oh God, I still need my mother. But she can never give me what I need.*

> There was a conference room with student nurses helping us to fill out forms. You know, they want so much information: age, weight, illnesses, when was your first pregnancy and info regarding any other pregnancies. When she asked me who the father was, I just stared at her. I didn't even know who she was talking about! Then, she said, "The father of your baby . . . is he in good health?" I said, "What father . . . ? Oh!" (I had forgotten I was pregnant.) She must have thought I was 'nuts'!

Once again, I couldn't believe my mom's denial of her own condition, although she was already four months along. Then again, she did have a miscarriage before; unaware that she was even pregnant to begin with.

In her first mention about *my* pregnancy, Mama wrote:

> Mary, By the time you receive this letter you will probably have your baby.
>
> I hope you don't have a hard time. I still haven't bought anything for mine.
>
> Well, I don't have anything good to say about myself.
> Love, Mama

After a month's time, another letter arrived from her.

> December 21, 1976
>
> Congratulations on your beautiful daughter . . . Anna Marie is beautiful, whenever I look at her picture I say, "I love you." I like babies, if I was younger, but at my age, it's ridiculous! A boy should have a brother; a girl should have a sister. I wish I had a sister . . . I had an EKG . . . I hope the results come out all right. I will not know until Jan. Now I am taking different pills. I'm more scared and nervous than before. You're lucky—you didn't have to go through any

> of that alone, and all the time
> Donny was with you all the way
> and wanted the baby. You don't
> have any idea what I'm going
> through. It's my problem . . .

'I love you.' My eyes welled with tears as I read those three words. Why? Why was it easier for my mother to express love to someone she never met before, than to speak them to her own daughter? Wasn't I the one who craved to be her mother's rescuer, caring for younger siblings, while putting up with feelings of neglect? *Yes, Mama, no doubt, you do 'like' newborns . . . but they grow fast and soon develop minds of their own . . . and then what, Mama?*

As for me feeling 'lucky,' I thought, Sure, everything's peachy-perfect in my world. You really have no idea what I'm going through . . . if you only knew . . . My tears ran down my face as I thought, *Even if you knew, what could you do to help me when you can't even help yourself?*

I continued her letter:

> Take care of my granddaugh-
> ter. When you were small, we
> were crazy about you. I guess
> you know what being a moth-
> er is like now and what it's
> all about. Why, you never even
> got hit when small . . . So
> long again . . . I don't an-
> swer right away, too many prob-
> lems. Here I'm about to have
> a baby and haven't bought one

> thing. I don't have any way to get to the stores. George isn't one bit concerned; don't ask me about him. When he first found out, he told me, "That baby, you do whatever you want to with. Flush it down the commode! Kill it or anything you want!" He wants me to give it up for adoption. He said I'd be stuck with it for another eighteen years.

I shook my head. I wondered if the liquor did the talking, or if George was beyond doubt, nothing but a cold-hearted snake.

Grandma was too embarrassed and ashamed to admit the troubles and concerns of her heart to anyone around. Yet whenever she wrote to me, she poured her heartache through the words she typed on those pages. She shared all that my mama suffered and endured, never realizing that I, too, was living my own hell.

> January 31, 1977
>
> Mary, Please pray that your mother have a normal delivery and child and that she won't have any more babies, and that this one she'll give the best

> care to. She don't have space
> in her one room for a crib or
> even two children. I am so sor-
> ry for that daughter of mine.
> She never have been smart. She
> could have gone out with George
> fishing, to the movies, or out
> to eat without having a child
> from him. ¡Qué sinvergüenza!
> He's always broke.

Mama at forty-two gave birth to another boy. Jesse was number six. My daughter's uncle was four months younger than she was.

> March 10, 1977
>
> After seeing your mother,
> George went home happy from the
> hospital and called us. George
> talked to Papa and said, "Jesse
> is a 7 lb 4 oz boy and pretty
> as his father!" So, Mary, your
> mother and her son are doing
> fine.

Guess one look at his own flesh and blood made George think twice about 'flushing the baby down the commode.'

> March 14, 1977
>
> Today I already talked with

> your mother and said to her that when Papa sometimes asked Willie a question, he stares at him without answering. Your mother snapped and said to me, "Oh that's because he wants attention and you have made him *malcriado*." Papa told me, "That's the thanks we get from our daughter, by thinking we have spoiled our grandson."

¿Malcriado? I thought, *How sad for something as normal as talking to a child to be considered spoiling them.* And if anyone could do with some spoiling, it was Willie.

After being home a couple of weeks with Baby Jesse, Mama wrote:

> March 29, 1977
>
> I would have had an easier time if I would have taken the Lamaze classes and knew how to breathe and what to expect in the labor room.

I stopped reading. My mind screamed: *This is your sixth baby! You didn't know "how to breathe" or "what to expect"?*

> To me, Jesse is a special baby and the best-looking baby in the whole wide world! George has been buying him things

and he's bought him the cutest infant-size shoes I've ever seen. He seems happy with him . . . that's what he wanted was a boy. He said, "What can you do with a girl? You can't take them fishing or put them to work." Willie is very happy, telling me he wanted a brother to play with. I would have liked a girl to give you—the sister you've always wanted, but I can't satisfy everyone. If I was younger—I love babies. I envy you. You're young, just starting to live. No one is going to take Jesse away from me. George gets mad at me, but I know one thing—no one is taking my baby! He's a 'special' baby and if you see him, you would know what I mean. He's so loveable, just like your sister was. . . .

Mama comparing Jesse to Anna upset me. We couldn't bring my sister back; she could never be replaced. The sister I longed for was gone. *Forever.*

My grandmother fretted about the way Mama doted on Jesse while seemingly ignoring Willie.

Grandmother wrote:

Mar 23, 1977

> When you write your mother,
> tell her that a mother should
> not have a 'special' baby, for
> she should love both the same
> and perhaps give more attention
> to the one who needs more. . .
> My daughter needs counseling.

In my mind, receiving news from home about *la familia* was supposed to make one joyous, happy — warm and fuzzy all over. Instead, the letters reminded me why I *had* to leave at an early age and the reason I hadn't a stable home to return to.

CHAPTER 18: A DAY OF RECKONING

SOON AFTER OUR daughter's birth, Donny wanted to leave Denver and head back for Miami. I was more than ready to leave behind the country, however scenic, filled with such unpleasant memories for me.

After a tiresome three-day road trip to Miami, our pit stop was at my mama's place. Donny parked in front of her apartment. I went in while he waited in the van.

Eight-month-old Anna Marie straddled my hip as I walked to Mama's door and then knocked. Eager to see her face upon meeting her granddaughter, I imagined what Mama's first words might be. Surely, she'd say, "Oh Mary, it's good to see you. Is this the baby? How precious. Here, let me hold her."

I knocked again.

I envisioned Mama's reaction: *She'll find Anna Marie irresistible, want to embrace her and smother her with hugs and kisses. She won't be able to take her eyes off her.*

There was a rustle of movement from within. The door cracked opened.

"Hi—"

"Hope you don't have to use the bathroom," Mama said flatly. "It's broken."

I hadn't imagined *that*.

I rolled my eyes, mumbled a hello. As I entered the dingy apartment—stuffy inside with only a small oscillating fan for air—a familiar, stale scent reached my nostrils. I slowly browsed around me and took in the enormous piles of newspapers, junk mail, and soiled clothes spilling from the counter and sagging chairs onto the floor. Dirty pots and dishes were piled in the sink; the trash overflowed. A soap opera blared from the small black-and-white TV on a dresser.

Anna Marie motioned for me to put her down, but I didn't dare. I peeked at the unkempt bed. Four-month-old Jesse napped without an undershirt; curls around his face dampened with sweat. An empty baby bottle lay close by. One whiff from a bucket of soiled cloth diapers made me gag.

"Isn't he big?" Mama asked, her face beaming with pride. "Sorry, I don't have anything cold to give you."

"Didn't come for drinks, Ma." I shifted Anna Marie on my hip. "Look, we're tired from being on the road so long. We better go. Gotta get us a room." I pecked Mama on the cheek and made a quick exit from the awful, uninviting place.

I climbed in the backseat of the van.

"Well, how did it go?" Donny asked.

"Don't ask." I secured my daughter in her seat and folded my arms.

"I don't under—"

"My mother," I cut in, "doesn't have the foggiest notion what to say." I felt annoyed with myself for being such a glutton for punishment, hoping for something that wasn't there. I didn't expect a warm cup of *café con leche*. But it still would have been great to receive some warmth from her, especially for my child. "Can you believe she never even acknowledged her own granddaughter?" I brushed angry tears from my eyes. "We've traveled for hundreds of miles, and she never invited us in, let alone offered the use of her precious bathroom."

"You've got to be kidding me!" Donny shook his head in disbelief.

"Wish I was," I confessed. "She never said, 'Hello Mary, how are you?' or 'Good to see you,' like even a vague acquaintance. Couldn't even give me a drink. All she offered was a cold shoulder *and* she entirely ignored her granddaughter."

"So is that it? You ready?"

"You betcha," I choked.

As Donny drove the van away from the curb and sped off, I determined to let bygones be bygones and leave my childhood behind. But my heart felt like lead. My mind was consumed with the 'what ifs.'

Running in Heels: A Memoir of Grit and Grace

Mary A. Pérez

CHAPTER 19: MY TWO CENTS

IN THE SUMMER of '77, as I applied makeup to cover my black eye, I looked forward to my new job waitressing at a restaurant located in Skylake Mall on North Miami Beach. I was glad to see that the place wasn't a typical greasy-spoon diner.

The mornings welcomed aromas of freshly brewed coffee, combined with the lingering scent of bacon and pancakes from the cooking area. When the kitchen door swung open, dishes and pots rattled from within.

Considered green, an outsider, the new kid on the block, I was the youngest waitress there. But I didn't mind. I scurried about taking orders, my hair tied in a ponytail with a clip. I wore a short white dress, white shoes, and a black apron with deep pockets filled with chewing gum, a pen, an order pad, a couple of bobby pins, lipstick, a matchbook, and my daily tips.

I busted my tail for those tips.

The waitresses I worked alongside with were cold and snappy; been around a block or two. The diner was *their* turf, *their* bread-and-butter. The manager reasoned that anyone younger gave these older gals a run for their money. Instead, they had *me* running in circles. Those seasoned servers barked orders in gruff voices, as if I was their *esclavita*.

I was still learning the ropes and a tad bit overwhelmed. *I'll show them. I'll pull my own weight.*

By and by, I got the hang of things. I excelled in carrying a couple of plates in one hand, balancing two more on my forearm. The chef was Cuban, an older man, and took a liking to me. This counted for something. When you called out an order, it needed to be right, without any hic-cups. Correct orders produced happy customers. Happy customers tipped.

Weeks later, I won half of the waitresses over. Their hard lines softened. They gave me pointers about what worked and what didn't: how to clean my station properly, turn my orders in quicker, run the cash register; they even hinted about which customers liked what. The rest left me alone. I had enough trouble serving some regulars who dined.

"Hey lady," the voice of a girl no more than ten called out to me. "Yer gonna take our orders, or what?"

"Sure am," I chirped, trying to keep a positive attitude. "What will it be?"

Pippi Longstockings and her big sister had dined here before and sat at my table. The two redheads rode in a fancy car and wore designer clothes, boots, and multicolored chokers. "I'm-better-than-you" was etched on their powdered faces. I knew the older sister schooled the younger one on what to say.

"My usual bagel, the way I like it . . . burnt," Carrot-Top crooned, "with cream cheese, and orange juice over ice. Got that?"

I popped my gum and turned to Pippi. "And what can I get you?"

"Hot chocolate and three pancakes . . . ." Pippi grinned, batting her lashes. "And . . . leave out the batter," she whispered.

I ignored the snide remark and wrote down her order. "Coming right up."

Before I darted away, within earshot, little rich girl hissed, "*Spic.*"

My blood boiled. I bit down on my tongue until I tasted blood.

After the Red Hens ate and left, I cleared their table, half-expecting to find a hate note instead of a tip.

Nada.

"Oh Miss-sy," another familiar voice summoned, followed by the sound of snapping fingers.

This sunburned "Bubba," a construction worker, who wore a stained plaid shirt over a beer belly and blue jeans a couple of sizes too small, frequented the diner daily. Never alone. When possible, he waited for a table in my station.

To make my life miserable.

I walked over with three glasses of water.

Bubba held up a cigarette. "I need a light," he smirked.

Here we go again, amusing his friends at my expense. I'm so not in the mood. I reached for my matches, lit his cigarette, jotted down his usual order and took his friends' requests.

He was persistent with his demands.

"Bring me the morning paper willya, doll? The 'King of Rock 'n' Roll' died."

"More water."

"Another napkin."

I chewed on the inside of my cheek.

"Hey, my friend's coffee's gone cold."

"My ashtray's full. Make it snappy, kiddo. Haven't got all day."

Time to put this chump in his place in front of his pals, I mused. Slapping the bill down, I asked, "How come ya never leave a tip?"

Bubba's face turned a lovely tomato red. "Why should I?" he retorted. "You're not that great, girlie. How 'bout a little peck on the cheek?"

My own face turned colors; I stomped away and stuck a second stick of gum in my mouth.

They soon left.

When I returned to help clear their table, I noticed Bubba had left a tip, sitting neatly beside his plate.

Two pennies.

Who does this sinvergüenza think he is? I'm not a sangana. Can't he see I'm a hard worker, trying to do my job? I want to prove myself to Donny; want to make him proud. I have a daughter that I need to buy things for.

The next day, a new server worked the floor; he and I switched stations. *Ah, so young and wet behind the ears,* I chuckled to myself. *Yep, green as anything.*

In no time, the lunch crowd swamped us. *But wait. What's this?* Bubba strutted in with three of his pals, and headed for my usual station.

The newbie became flustered with taking their orders. They were now harassing <u>him</u>. *I must give my new coworker a hand,* I thought.

Newbie fumbled with the vegetables and the condiments at the salad bar.

"Here, let me help," I offered. "I know the way this customer likes his chef salad. Comes in here *all* the time."

Newbie thanked me for my assistance and moved on to the iced tea dispenser. By the time he came back, I'd finished the salad.

"There ya go," I said to Newbie, pointing to my creation. "Just the way he likes it. He's quite picky, you know?"

"Oh, th-thank you so much," Newbie replied, nearly spilling his drinks.

"*No problema*," I smiled. "Here, I'll take the salad to his table."

As I left their table, I heard *Dancing Queen* playing on the jukebox and felt a familiar tune of my own creep into my soul.

Several minutes later, a commotion stirred. "What kind of joint y'all runnin' here?"

Bubba's voice carried clear across the crowded restaurant. I turned to see my "favorite" patron, flushed red, gesturing forcefully between Newbie *and* the manager. He and his friends stormed out of the restaurant and never returned.

When the coast cleared, I approached Newbie. *Pobre muchacho, looking quite spent.*

"Those clowns, they're something else, okay?"

"Sure are," Newbie answered, wiping his glasses and the sweat off his forehead. "Weird thing though," he continued, gazing at me as if studying me. "After that one dude finished eating his salad, he claimed he found something at the bottom of his bowl."

"He did? What?"

"Two pennies."

"Well, I'll be doggone!"

Running in Heels: A Memoir of Grit and Grace

CHAPTER 20: NEW YORK, NEW YORK!

"I CAN'T TAKE it anymore!" I blurted out to Aunt Irma over the phone. Although I hadn't seen her in years, I knew from her letters she cared and would be supportive.

"Mary, are you okay?" she asked gently. "Are you hurt?"

I observed my reflection in the mirror and noticed a faded black-and-blue shiner peering back. I closed my eyes, deep in thought. My stomach wrenched as I came to grips with what I'd feared all along.

"He doesn't love me!" I sobbed.

Reruns from the past six months played in my mind's eye: Donny wrestling with his demons, becoming more violent, his fistfights, and the endless brawls with me on the home front.

Since he imagined himself slayer of dragons, superior to women, Donny trampled over me. He saw himself king of the castle. But I had begun seeing him as a knight who'd fallen off his high horse, the joker who chased after wenches who happened to prance along and beguile him.

Yet, I was still hopelessly in love.

"Never argue with a drunk," Mama had always said. Even so, the most difficult pill for me to swallow after long nights of havoc: Donny's lack of recollection of anything he had said or done the day before.

I remembered.

I carried the hurt.

With hardly any tenderness, affection, or communication between us, life dragged on.

How's it possible to feel lonelier now than I ever did as a child?

I didn't want to tell Aunt Irma all my problems. Not over the phone, anyway.

How do I explain the stirrings of my heart?

She somehow understood my silence. "*Mija*, come on up," she said. "We'll think of a plan once you and the baby arrive safely."

After Aunt Irma wired me the money, I called a cab to drive us to the airport. Before long, Anna Marie and I were in the clouds flying to New York, my birthplace, in the hopes of starting over. Tucked away in the belly of the airplane were our possessions, including my baby's stroller and crib. I'd left nothing behind. Not even a note.

Soon after our arrival, dusk fell. I put my sleeping baby in the back bedroom. After a glass of ice tea, I sat on the sofa. As we chatted, Aunt Irma shot rapid-fire questions out of her mouth faster than I could respond:

"How many times has he laid hands on you? Has he ever hurt the child? How do you plan to earn a living? What type of work can you do? How much education do you have? What are your plans for your daughter's future without her father? Do you love him? Does he know you came *here*?"

My heartbeat slowed to the rhythm of the clock on the coffee table. Reality slammed into me like a Mack truck. Haunting thoughts rattled my brain: *From now on, I will be a single mom. How can I ever provide for us? Will Donny find us? Does he miss us? Does he even care? Or is he out drunk, celebrating his freedom?*

Hours before, I had left the father of my child flushed with power and purpose. But now that all my earlier self-assurance crumbled, pangs of self-doubt gnawed at me. *God, are you there?* My soul cried. *Please. Please make a way for us.*

Though born in this fast-paced land of opportunity, I hadn't revisit this wonderful city as a happy-go-lucky traveler. Sadly enough, I returned broken and distraught. Returning to New York as an eighteen-year-old, single mom left me feeling inconsequential, like a nobody, going nowhere. Puerto Ricans living in this energetic city proudly called themselves "Nuyoricans," a conflation of "New York" and "Puerto Rican." Many accomplished musicians, poets and writers fulfilled dreams here. Hanging by my fingernails, I felt anything but talented or successful.

The next day, I caught the Fourteenth Street cross-town bus and headed for Union Square. Getting off at my destination, I hesitated at the curb. Memories from nine years earlier when my baby sister ran out in the middle of a busy intersection resurfaced. Her death, caused by a hit-and-run-driver, flashed in my head. I stood frozen, overwhelmed by the zooming cars, cabs and buses. I waited before daring to join in on the jaywalking with other pedestrians — strangers — dodging through the congested traffic, interchangeably accelerating and braking.

How do people exist in such an overcrowded city, with the hustle and bustle of multitudes on foot, galloping in opposite directions at once?

"The 'Big Apple' is giving me one 'big' headache," I said under my breath.

Each step took me farther away from my aunt's apartment, now home to my daughter and me. My feet hurt. I preferred being barefoot to walking in heels. My progress came to a crawl and my neck ached from gazing at the skyscrapers. *Is this what tourists do?*

Soon tantalizing odors from hotdog stands made my stomach growl. Even so, my nose couldn't keep another odor at bay: the reeking fumes from exhaust-spewing buses. I ignored the honking of yellow cabs driven by insistent individuals who preyed on out-of-towners. Then, when I boarded the nerve-wracking subway that took me to Thirty-Fourth Street, I imagined all eyes were peeled on the bewildered, pale-faced *muchachita*. I kept my eyes on the window, where I saw the image of a lost soul in the reflection: *me*.

For an entire week, I filled out job applications. But wherever I went, ten others fought for the same position. I got all the spiels: "Put a résumé together," "Don't call us, we'll call you," and "You're not experienced enough." Another interviewer saw right through me and said, "Loosen up, doll face. You look like you're trying to smile away a migraine."

My cue to leave and quit for the day.

Aunt Irma took wonderful care of my daughter. She affectionately nicknamed Anna Marie, "Boo-boo," because that was the third word she learned to say, after "Mama" and "Dada." But whenever Anna Marie reached out for my aunt, a strange feeling chomped at me. I soon realized that I had grown jealous of seeing them together. It worried me that my baby girl may grow to love my aunt more than she did me. Dreading the harsh reality that I'd be away from my daughter for a job, I doubted if I made the best choice in leaving our home . . . and her father.

Days later, as Aunt Irma was showing me how to make lasagna, the phone rang. As Aunt Irma answered, she quickly motion for my attention. The phone still to her ear, she looked at me with raised eyebrows. "Why yes, Donny," she said. "Yes, she is . . ."

My heart skipped a beat. *How did he find us?*

"Well, wait a minute. I'll put her on."

I wrestled with logistics: *Should I talk with him and hear what he has to say?*

"Nooo," I shook my head at Aunt Irma, "*No me importa.*"

She still held out the darn phone to me and sighed. "*Mija,* you two need to talk."

I gathered my nerves and took Donny's call.

"I want you to know I'm sorry," he said.

Should I believe anything he says? At least he sounds sober.

"I didn't mean to put my hands on you."

Remorseful, sincere . . .

"Are you ready to come home?"

I want to. But to what? "To the same thing?" I finally said.

"No, Mary Ann. Look. I'm sorry. I may not show it. I probably don't know how. But I promise I'll do my best to make it up to you, gal."

While he talked, intense emotions flooded my heart: *I have to believe him. Isn't a relationship worth fighting for? Isn't a child better off with both parents? Clearly, he wanted us back home. And frankly, I want to go back home.*

Later I learned that Grandma told Donny where we were. He convinced her that he loved his family and wanted us back home with him. She wrote me a letter that I had put aside:

    Mary, When I found out that
    you went far away with Anna Ma-

rie, it broke my heart. For I thought you could patch things up with your spouse and remain in your apartment till things smoothed out. *Por favor*, give Donny another chance and see if he changes his lifestyle without you talking too much and come back home. We all miss you. You have to realize that in our lifetime—from cradle to grave—there will be more than a dozen changes. These experiences are to learn more about life, especially when we don't live right. *¿Entiendes?* Love, Grandma

While Donny talked about goals, I mustered up some gumption and swallowed what pride remained. Before hanging up the phone, I decided to fly back to my man. Even though it had been fifteen days, I felt as if we'd been apart forever.

By the end of the week, with Anna Marie straddled on my hip, I was pacing and searching for Donny's face in the crowd. He had promised to meet us at the airport. Fear clawed at my heart as I thought, *He stood me up. He won't show. Or he'll be drunk, pick a fight with me and slap me in front of everybody for daring to leave him. Somebody will call the cops . . . !*

I needed to calm my nerves. Then, I noticed him. As if in

slow motion, he smiled and waved. Like a frightened child, I inched my way toward him. Our eyes locked. He looked older, tired, his jaw tense. As we drew close, he swept me into his arms. He kissed me and reached for our daughter, kissing her. *He misses us!* The first time—in a long time—he expressed love. As we walked to get our luggage, he promised to curb his drinking and never to hit me again.

He deserved another chance, didn't he?

I wanted to believe him.

I *had* to believe him.

Like the song by Gladys Knight and the Pips, "I'd rather live in his world than live without him in mine."

Running in Heels: A Memoir of Grit and Grace

CHAPTER 21: MY GUARDIAN ANGEL

DONNY DROVE A 70s Ford utility van that he had painted a glimmering shade of red. One afternoon, he arrived home in a baby-blue, two-door '73 Plymouth Duster.

"Don't screw this up, gal," Donny said, tossing me the keys. "I can't be around to drive you to work and to the sitters all the time."

Perhaps he sees me mature, a big girl now.

"So, it's called a Duster?" I asked, peering inside.

"This here is a muscle car. You and my daughter will be safe."

"*Our* daughter," I corrected, perhaps too quickly. Not wanting to ruin the moment I added, "It's great Donny, but can we afford this?"

I expected him to do things of his own volition, but never imagined in a million years he'd buy a car for me. I didn't want to get my hopes high, but I already relished the freedom and responsibility of holding a job and earning money. Now, I savored the idea of some independence.

"Shush, gal," he said with a wink. "You know I'm a wheeler and dealer.

Weeks later, one-year-old Anna Marie sat in the back of the car, half-asleep. I was late for my new job and had yet to drop her off at my dad's house.

Torrential rain unnerved me as I drove along the highway. The downpour hammering on the roof of the car echoed in my eardrums. I turned up the radio. My car's wipers were stuck on slow speed, hindering my vision and distracting me. Driving in the far right lane, I leaned forward, both hands clutching the steering wheel and wondered how late I—

Suddenly, the taillights in front glowed red. The driver slammed on his brakes. Automatically, I hit mine, but they locked up. The backend of the car in front loomed closer.

I cannot hit them! So, doing what any sensible driver would have done (or not), I aimed for the concrete divider, swinging sharply to the right.

My car plowed into that barrier. The tires screeched and drowned out the screams in my head. I skidded out of control at 180-degrees before stalling in the middle lane—facing on-coming traffic.

My world slammed to a stop.

The wipers still swished lethargically back and forth across the freshly cracked windshield. Music blared over the radio. My mind in a daze, I glanced in the rearview mirror. I was thankful that Anna Marie appeared unscathed, apart from the fear in her moist eyes.

"It's okay, Anna, don't cry. Mommy's gonna get us out of here."

I made a quick assessment of the wreckage: the hood had flown open; the front end was caved in, the right headlights busted.

I rolled down the window to stick my head out, and became drenched by pelting rain and the splash from a truck hurtling past.

Headlights from cars beamed as they swerved to miss us, terrifying me even more. Soaked and trembling with my nerves on edge, I thought, *Lord, how am I going to get the car off the road without causing a bigger accident?*

I wasn't even sure my car would budge.

Vehicles roared by, but one slowed and stopped. With headlights practically blinding me, the driver left his emergency lights blinking; he exited his car and made his way toward me, hunkering down from the rainfall. He scanned the inside my car, his eyes alarmed, yet warm.

"Miss, are you all right? Is your little girl okay?"

"Yes . . . yes, I think so," I scarcely heard my own voice say.

"Put your emergency lights on. Need to get you out of this traffic."

I nodded and watched my angel head back to his car and pull over onto the shoulder. When the coast cleared, he ran across the freeway and opened my door. I scooted over. He climbed in behind the wheel and proceeded to veer my Plymouth across three lanes, out of on-coming traffic and onto the shoulder. Finally, in reverse, he maneuvered my car to the off-ramp.

After prying the hood back down to shut it, I thanked my rescuer and climbed behind the wheel. Then I slowly headed toward Daddy's house, praying a cop wouldn't pull me over.

I'm sure my stepmother's heart came out of her chest at the sight of me driving a newly smashed-up car, with Anna Marie in the back seat.

Once my own fright wore off, I figured I'd be a carcass after Donny assessed the condition of his purchase—certain he'd call me every name in the book, slap me senseless, take the car keys away. Or maybe he'd throw in my face what a dumb broad I was, more of a headache than a help.

But to my amazement, I must have hit a soft spot with him. Imagining that his daughter and I bravely dodged a bullet, he didn't ridicule me. Donny knew I wasn't a reckless driver. I drove his van all the time, even though still without a license. The next day he put the Duster in the shop for much-needed bodywork and a paint job.

Three months after that collision and two months after my eighteenth birthday, the State of Florida pronounced me a five-foot-seven, 125-pound certified legal driver.

When I needed help the most, a total stranger — or perhaps a guardian angel — came to my rescue and showed me compassion. Something I would never forget.

Mary A. Pérez

CHAPTER 22: TEXAS OR BUST

AFTER OUR MOVE from Denver to Miami, we settled into a duplex apartment. The small amount of money we had saved quickly dwindled. Donny couldn't find steady work and my waitressing tips barely kept us afloat. Six months later:

"Pack your bags; we're moving," Donny announced out of the blue.

"What? Another move? Where to now?" I wailed and braced for the answer.

"The Lone Star State," he shrugged. "Jobs are booming in Houston." He left to tie up loose ends for our big move.

I put Anna Marie down for a nap and plopped on the floor surrounded by boxes Donny had gathered, waiting to fill. I wept instead of packing, wanting to pull my hair out in frustration.

What are we going to do in Texas? Live out on the prairie? Herd a bunch of cattle? Ride horses? Donny might think himself a cowboy, but I ain't no cowgirl.

I found myself talking to God, pleading with Him to change the circumstances, to help me survive one more day, another move—to Timbuktu for all I knew. Was it selfish for me to want my little girl to know the love of her great-grandparents? Was it wrong for me to want her to know her humorous grandpa and enjoy Gloria's pampering?

Angry. I threw things into suitcases and boxes. *Pointless.* Coming and going. *Didn't I move enough times as a kid?* As I fumed and tossed stuff around, an envelope fell out from my dusty Bible and dropped onto my lap. *A letter!* Written from Aunt Irma, after I'd returned from New York after my "great escape" from Donny. I sat cross-legged on the floor and re-read her letter, allowing her words to digest:

> I pray that Donny's heart will soften, so that he learns that our being imperfect beings that we are, we tend to make mistakes. Even with the best of intentions. May God put in his heart these truths, so that he'll be able to forget that you left him when you were hurt and so confused. And that the act in no way lessened the love you have for him.
>
> Mary Ann, may he ever remember that a woman is not to ever be mistreated by hitting, but to be held, respected, and loved as someone precious as a part of himself. As for you dear, please remember; no one wins in a fight. And having the last word in an argument is not important. We love you and miss you and Anna Marie.

Mary A. Pérez

```
God bless you,
Aunt Irma and your Uncle Jimmy.
```

I re-folded the page and tucked it away. With a fresh determination to put all self-pity aside, I went back to my packing.

Several days later, we arrived in Houston. With no job or promise of work, our funds ran low. We rented a room at a roach motel on Telephone Road. Donny eyed a couple of girls stalking the parkway and whistled at one. This wasn't a time to pick a fight, so I kept my mouth shut. After we signed in at the office and started to unload our van, a police car pulled into the driveway.

"Stay put, gal," Donny ordered and walked toward the cop. I worried that he had done something and failed to mention that "something" to me. After some time, the officer shook Donny's hand and waved at me, then drove off.

Donny walked back, wiping the sweat from his forehead with a paper towel.

"What was all that about?" I asked impatiently.

"Looks like we landed on the wrong side of the tracks."

"Oh, great. What else did he say?" I feared for the worst.

"We need to leave here as soon as we can. But until I find work, we'll just have to stick it out."

That evening, I watched my baby sleeping while my imagination ran wild with fearful scenarios. Once or twice, I peeked through the curtains to see some jazzy cars, the drivers in fancy clothes and hats. Whenever Donny went for ice, or to bring something in from the van, scantily dressed women sashayed near to ask him something or other. I felt relieved to see him brush them off, even though he thought their attention humorous.

The next day, Donny set out, resolved to find work, and told me to stay in the room with the door padlocked. He cautioned me to remain indoors and said he would return with grub. We had a few snacks, so I made do with peanut butter and crackers.

When Donny said he wouldn't come back without a job, I knew he wouldn't. Before dark, he returned with a bucket of fried chicken under his arms, announcing that he'd be reporting to work in the morning. This became the beginning of his career in the construction field.

Two weeks later, with the funds from his first paycheck, we moved to an apartment in Spring Branch on Old Katy Road.

We walked through the freshly-painted, two-bedroom, unfurnished apartment. Heavy, cream-colored drapes covered the venetian blinds on the tall windows. The moss-green wall-to-wall carpeting, dark brown bathroom and kitchen cabinets, and shiny mustard-colored kitchen appliances were all appealing. Our new apartment felt huge and inviting, so unlike the one-room efficiencies I grew up in.

"We'll be fine here; you'll see," Donny said. "All we have to do is rent us some furniture."

We decided we didn't need bedroom furniture right away. Instead, we rented a dinette set, a sofa bed, a chair, a coffee table, and lamps to sit on a couple of end tables. In the evenings, we camped on the sofa bed.

Anna Marie's room had a twin bed and a dresser. Her favorite toys, her rocking horse and an overstuffed teddy bear soon took up occupancy. Bookshelves overflowed with coloring books, fat crayons, and a variety of Little Golden and Dr.

Seuss books. Our daughter enjoyed giving tea parties with her bear and dolls sitting around a small table. Grateful that she had her own room, something I never had as a kid, I looked forward to making our new place a home.

"Houston," Donny explained, "is the largest city in the state of Texas, named after *General Sam Houston*, commander of the army . . ."

Mr. World Encyclopedia took us to NASA, Johnson Space Center, where we spent an entire afternoon. My feet hurt and I grew tired from pushing Anna Marie's stroller. The place was enormous, and a bit boring for my taste.

On our next adventure, we left Anna Marie with a sitter to go to Six Flags AstroWorld. As we strolled around, I thought, *All right! This is my kind of place.* We wandered along, deciding what ride to hop on. This time however, Donny's enthusiasm dwindled.

"We gonna ride that thing?" I suggested, pointing to the Texas Cyclone, the sky-high wooden roller coaster.

"You've got to be kidding me!" Donny snorted. He studied the curves and the highest incline, and shrugged his shoulders. "You can go on ahead. One of us has to keep our feet on the ground."

I had begun to realize our age differences, which up until this point, never really mattered to me. But the stark reality that Donny was twice my age only served as a reminder how often we viewed things differently.

"We can skip it," I sighed.

"You hungry?" Donny asked, changing the subject. "I bet you never tried funnel cakes, and when was the last time you had a candy apple?"

"Make mine caramel," I chimed in, my mouth watering.

I had to admit, Houston—the state where I first tasted chicken fried steak, jalapeño poppers and "puh-con" pie—offered much to see and do. Annual western trail rides began in central Texas. A three-week rodeo followed the event with the Houston Livestock Show & Rodeo. I don't believe they had rodeos in Miami. If they had them in Denver, I missed the memo. In Houston, cowboys with big belt buckles and big hats rode their big horses at these events, with greetings of "howdy."

When someone gave us tickets to attend an Oilers game at the Astrodome, I couldn't tell which of the two of us was more excited. After parking and much walking, we found our seats in the nosebleed section. Once the game started, we cheered whenever Earl Campbell, our favorite running back, with legs the size of tree trunks, scored a touchdown. This was a "Luv ya Blue" proud moment. I actually enjoyed myself, until Donny drank one too many beers. Instead of cheering, he barked like a hound dog, so much that I cringed from humiliation.

On another outing, we strolled on *The Strand*, in Galveston Bay's historical downtown, and visited the beach. The brown murky waters and sand were disappointing. Raised in tropical Miami, I missed her turquoise ocean and sugary-white sand between my toes. Having also lived in Denver for a year with occasional trips to the Rockies, I wasn't too excited living in a flat city with nary a mountain or a molehill to write about in my diary or in letters home.

Eventually, I adapted to the idea that Houston might become our permanent residence. Fields of bluebonnets in the springtime, magnolia trees, pecan trees, and the humidity became tolerable. I grew accustomed to "Tex-Mex" entrees such as enchiladas or fajitas accompanied with plenty of tortilla chips and salsa to snack on.

These geographical changes came as second nature to Donny. But changes never came from within. Even though we settled into our apartment, and work was steady, Donny continually tussled with the commitment of everything. I watched him float through cities, vocations, and liquor like a leaf in the wind. How long would Houston hold him? More important, I still wasn't sure if there was room for me in his world.

Running in Heels: A Memoir of Grit and Grace

CHAPTER 23: LET GO AND LET GOD

LONELINESS ATE AWAY at me. Insecurities consumed my mind. Donny came home whenever he wanted to. He expected me to ask no questions. The more I clung to him, the more he shrugged me off like a neglected child.

One evening, in the foyer of our second-story apartment, I stood by the window and watched Donny saunter away. I felt like my heart had split in two.

He paused, turned and glanced up at me, with that smirk of his. Like the proverbial slow twist of a knife lodged in me, his ominous grin cut and curdled my blood. His haughty expression loomed before my eyes, burning my insides.

I flung my fist at him to punch him in the face—

Glass! Shattered into a million pieces.

A glistening shard of windowpane sliced across the tender flesh of my forearm, smearing crimson blood across my skin. My fist had only gone clear through the window.

Donny raced up the stairs and wrapped a towel around my wound, berating me for being a harebrained fool. But I didn't balk. Even though he must have been more concerned with his own interest than in taking me to the emergency room for stitches, at least he stayed home that night.

After the swollen and jagged wounds closed, an uneven,

ugly scar served as a reminder of my moment of insanity.

I took inventory of my life, peeling back the layers of time:

At eighteen years of age, I went through the motions, trying to keep from sinking into the quicksand of "woe is me." My world was darker than a thousand nights. Like an afterthought, I received leftovers from the man I loved, whose concerns were about his own needs and desires when it came to intimacy. Even to the point of brute force. All the while, I hid behind a mask, afraid of letting others see my insecure, tormented self.

At home, Donny was there in body but was noncommittal and aloof. I never imagined in a hundred years that I'd run to the exact life I hated, staying with someone as drunk as I remembered my stepdads being. Just like Mama, I remained in a relationship of unrequited love with a noose tightened around my heart.

With the romance long dead in my own world, the unending drama left me empty. Another *Luke and Laura* soap opera episode came on the tube. I turned the TV off.

Lost in my thoughts, I longed for a friend close in age to talk to, laugh with, or share a cry with. Someone who'd share in the alleged joys of relationships, motherhood, and homemaking. Someone who'd listen to my heart, my doubts, my hopes, my secrets.

My mama failed to be that someone. I remember her glued to the TV, watching soap operas, and *Donahue*, with her fingertips red, stained from eating pistachio nuts back then. Her cares didn't center on children, house chores or cooking. My grandmother never sat in front of the TV during the day. She attended to the welfare of her household; she enjoyed keeping a tidy and organized house and preparing home-cooked meals.

I strove for merit in my role. As a parent, naturally, I desired to do better and to be better than the way Mama raised me. The more I strived for perfection, the more the odds were stacked against me.

Donny, a strictly meat-and-potato man, prided himself on his culinary skills. Me? I was a novice over the stove. Although I bought more than enough cookbooks and tried to follow the recipes, I still felt inadequate and couldn't escape Donny's berating. He hated pasta. He hated casseroles. I supposed he was hoping for someone barefoot in the kitchen. But what he got instead was someone barefoot and pregnant.

"What do you call this? Mush?"

Shut up and eat it, I wanted to say. "Tuna casserole, Donny."

"Are you nuts or something?" He dropped the fork on his plate. "Throw it to the birds. Don't fix this again for me."

Donny's sharp tongue bit. His every criticism stung, intensifying my failure-mentality and feeding on my low self-esteem. When he sent me to the store to buy a can of corned beef hash, he nearly slapped me for mistakenly returning with a can of corned beef instead. Then, the one day I proudly prepared his favorite pot roast surrounded by potatoes, onions, and carrots resting in gravy, he accused me of having a neighbor cook it.

Donny prided himself as the breadwinner. He carried himself grandly in the workplace. He received praises from those who worked with him, yet his life behind closed doors spun out of control. His public display of the typical hard-working, "family" man was anything but genuine and harmonious.

I knew enough to know what a family man resembled.

I'd seen my grandpa's example. I'd seen my own father's. I'd read enough books and even seen enough movies. But I didn't see much under my own roof.

Jerry—a slow-talking, chain-smoking beanpole with an Adam's apple that stuck out to kingdom come, gray eyes, and oily, stringy gray hair—parked himself on my couch, guzzling bottles of beer back to back. After kicking off his boots, he sat in dingy socks, his gangly legs crossed at the ankles. His feet stunk. Donny always needed to remind him to take a shower.

Jerry was Donny's drinking partner long before I arrived on the scene. He needed a place to stay. He moved in with us under the premise that he would pay his share of rent and groceries. He slept on a mattress in the master bedroom. *Our* bedroom. The room meant for Donny and me. We still slept out in the living room sofa bed.

Donny landed Jerry a carpenter position. After coming home from work in the evenings, Jerry's habits grew old fast. Filled with liquid courage, he didn't crave food but starved for action and mischief instead.

Jerry easily found havoc and trouble but never backed it up. He was a talking point—all mouth. Didn't matter, because he knew Don the Brawler would be there to charge in, come to his rescue and fight his battles. Donny never balked from accepting those challenges. They fed his ego.

"Where are you going now?" I asked Mr. Macho after he and Jerry talked quietly and started putting on their shoes.

"Not your business," Donny answered. "Don't stay up." With determination written on his face, Donny headed out the door. Jerry, in tow, wore the usual conniving look pasted on his.

Again, left alone, with no one to share my heart, I regretted that I never stayed in touch with old classmates or finished school. Although I had advanced to the tenth grade, I never went back, relying solely on Donny's moral and financial support. I regretted that, too.

I felt my prayers answered the day a neighbor knocked on our door. I recognized her immediately. *At last, someone my own age to talk to.*

Not much older than me, she was a friendly sort with deep-set, *café con leche* eyes, long espresso hair, and a tan complexion. She wore blue jeans and a T-shirt. The warmth of her smile cast away my shadows. Liz sold Avon. Even though I doubted I'd be able to buy any of her products, I welcomed her company.

With Donny engrossed in TV, she and I visited at the dining room table over coffee and slices of block cheddar cheese. We chatted about makeup and the latest perfume. After an hour, she dug deep when she peered into my eyes and asked, "Mary, do you know Jesus?"

"Well . . . I . . . I used to . . . as a kid," I stuttered and hung my head.

She proceeded to remind me of God's love, goodness and grace.

Liz was my neighbor who soon became my sounding board and best friend. She made me laugh and forget my troubles. She made suggestions about hair and makeup. We went window-shopping at the malls, grocery shopping, and we baked cakes together in her kitchen. Liz even introduced me to garage-sale hunting on weekends. In the mornings, we started reading our Bibles over coffee at her place, after our husbands left for work and her older kids had trotted to school. Our pre-school girls were close in age and enjoyed playing with each other.

Donny never said too much around Liz. Fine by me. He once labeled her a "Jesus freak" and usually made himself scarce whenever she came around. Also fine by me.

Before long, I started sitting in on Bible studies Liz held with other couples in her apartment. When I attended her small church, I felt a sense of belonging and serenity I hadn't known since living with my grandparents. As much as I longed to return to the God of my grandparents, I needed to overcome the stinking-thinking about myself. I never felt worthy enough; may as well have worn a sign over me that read: *Deflated, Dejected and Discouraged.*

After our devotions in the mornings, Liz led prayer. She prayed that I'd learn to "let go and let God." I wasn't sure how to "let go," let alone move on. Then, before closing our devotions, she always asked what my prayer requests were.

"I can't stand Jerry . . . he's a moron," I blurted one day. "When he's around, Donny drinks more. Jerry and him go bar-hopping and get into fights with other drunken bozos."

"What do you want God to do?" Liz asked.

"I don't know. Maybe Jerry needs to take a long walk on a short pier or something."

She smiled.

I felt foolish.

She then asked if I ever asked God to sever Donny and Jerry's friendship. I never thought about praying that way. She said she believed we needed to be a family in the privacy of our home without negative interferences from an outsider.

A woman of simple faith, Liz started praying for that specifically.

Weak in my faith, I hoped against hope.

One autumn day as the temperatures fell and the evenings grew chilly, Jerry wanted "female companionship." He borrowed my Plymouth Duster, and drove more than a thousand miles, all the way from Houston to Denver, to get that companionship. Once there, he landed in jail and the police impounded my car. Weeks later, Donny paid someone in Denver to get my vehicle out of impound to drive it back home.

Coincidentally—or by divine intervention—we never heard from Jerry again.

With Jerry out of the picture, tension eased, though we gave up our apartment and rented a smaller one. I didn't mind; at least Donny wasn't around his so-called friend and his bad influence.

I contemplated that my life might become easier once I settled down. Surely, after I "turned all over to God," life would be smooth sailing.

Not so simple.

Faded dreams of a "happily-ever-after" life filled with love and happiness sank like the sun below the horizon. Once again, I dreaded morning sickness.

Running in Heels: A Memoir of Grit and Grace

CHAPTER 24: IT'S OFFICIAL!

WHEN I TOLD Donny, "I'm pregnant," he sighed, shook his head, as if I—yet again—had made a mistake, and went back to watching his western on TV. Even though he sat at home, I couldn't have felt lonelier.

Excited about my grandparents' visit to our home in Houston, I longed for the warmth and security of their love, which I had always felt as a child. They arrived older, frailer than what I remembered; yet they came for me. On their first night out, we took them to a barbecue joint for a Texas-sized, chicken-fried steak meal accompanied by a loaded baked potato and banana pudding for dessert—so much food we doggie-bagged the leftovers. We joked about everything being bigger in Texas, portion size included.

Once home, I bathed Anna Marie and put her down for bed. After Grandma's shower, she sat out in the living room in a button-down housecoat, and Grandpa joined us wearing his comfortable plaid shorts. He and Donny talked about the weather and politics. Grandma and I caught up on family stories and recipes. After the men went to bed, we pored over several photo albums late into night. We poked fun of those losing their hair, those wearing funny hats and those giving dirty looks.

"Mary, who in the world is that lady bendin' there in

the back ground?" Grandma asked, pointing to a picture she couldn't make out.

"Don't worry, Grandma," I answered and laughed. "It doesn't look like you from behind." I loved joking with her to hear her laugh.

Donny genuinely showed a soft spot for my grandparents. He didn't mind doing things for them, especially cooking. He often grilled fish, knowing Grandma loved seafood. He prepared *Fungi*, a Caribbean dish of cornmeal, butter and okra. When I baked a carrot cake with cream cheese icing, that dessert instantly became my grandma's favorite—I could count on her to be my cheerleader.

I thoroughly got a kick out of watching Grandpa bonding with his great-granddaughter. He fed Anna Marie her breakfast, read to her, and took her to the playground. He affectionately pinched her earlobes, and made her giggle by rubbing his prickly chin on her cheeks until they turned pink from his whiskers. I saw myself as a little girl with him so many years ago.

But the special day for me was when four of us went to the Justice of the Peace, when Donny and I became husband and wife. With my grandparents serving as witnesses, at that instant, like the song says, I became "the happiest girl in the whole USA!" At nineteen, seven months pregnant with my second child, and at last, a wedding band on my finger.

After three weeks, my grandparents returned to their home in Miami. Saying goodbye saddened me. Once again, I knew I wouldn't have any kinfolk around for the birth of my next baby.

I hated goodbyes.

Eventually, church members reached out to me in love

and became *familia*. They prayed for our needs and even put "feet" to their prayers. Despite this, whenever someone gave me something—whether clothing, sacks of groceries, or money to help pay a delinquent bill—my proud and self-sufficient husband barked, "Take it back!"

Of course, I wasn't about to rob anyone out of their blessing. Besides . . . we *needed* those items. Therefore, I graciously accepted "alms" and (unknown to Donny) disregarded his prideful and unreasonable refusals.

Maybe if I give Donny a son, he will change for the better.

Running in Heels: A Memoir of Grit and Grace

CHAPTER 25: AND THEN THERE WERE FOUR

November 1978

MY MIND REELING, I tossed and turned and kicked off the covers. I struggled to get out of bed; for the fifth time that night, I floundered toward the bathroom.

"Where are you going *now*?" Donny demanded.

I turned the bathroom light on. "Need to go again, Donny."

"Didn't you *just* go?"

"I'm feeling a lot of pressure in my bladder." How I wished to erase the sneer from his face. "Didn't mean to wake . . ."

He responded by sucking air through his teeth and then flipped over, turning his back to me.

Unable to get a good night's rest, I had started cramping at 3:30 in the morning. By noon, the cramps grew stronger. By 3 p.m., the pain had become agonizing, but still irregular, followed by spotting. The instant Donny walked in from work I said, "It's time."

We arrived at Rosewood General. An attendant assisted me into a wheelchair. When I sat down, my water broke. *So much for dignity.*

Once I was in my room, the nurse who examined me discovered I was already dilated to six—the second stage of labor. Glancing down at my belly, I found the shape oddly lopsided, oval, no longer round. Much to my dismay, after the nurse's probing, she mentioned in a concerned voice that she felt a foot.

The doctor ordered an emergency X-ray. Apparently, at the last moment, my baby had turned and remained in a breech position. The X-ray also revealed the umbilical cord had wrapped around the neck. After the medical staff had prepped me and given me an epidural, they confirmed that I needed to have a Caesarean. This time Donny would remain in the waiting room.

During the birthing process, even though I was awake, I felt nothing from the waist down. I concentrated on trying to relax and comprehend what the doctors and nurses were discussing. A large blue drape blocked my view of the entire birth.

I couldn't keep my upper body from shaking. Even my teeth chattered, and the uncontrollable tremors caused my shoulders to ache, as if ready to fall off. Petrifying thoughts raced through my mind. I feared something was terribly wrong. When I heard someone say, "Here *she* comes," the "she" rang loud in my mind: *another girl.*

But why won't she cry?

Time stopped. I prayed. Felt like forever.

At last, wails from strong lungs pierced the room. My doctor smiled and held my six- pound- four-ounce baby. "It's a girl."

I reached out for her, anxious to see if she was all right. *She looks so small, red and wrinkled, not like Anna Marie when she was born. And she had one purple arm!*

After they cleaned her, they tied my baby's arm securely to her side in a makeshift sling with a receiving blanket. The doctor explained to me that during her delivery, my uterus contracted and clamped around her neck and face, thereby causing fetal stress from lack of oxygen. They made an immediate decision to extract her from inside me. But because my baby's arm rested across her face, in the process of being pulled out, her collarbone popped.

Throughout the delivery procedure, I knew the team worked on my baby girl a good while before she cried. I recalled hearing medical jargon, the sound of suction, and even a slap, but I wasn't able to make much sense of anything else. What a definitive moment when I finally heard my baby's cries. Not until then did I experience a wave of relief.

They gave me an outside phone line to give Donny the announcement of our daughter's birth. "'*She*' *was* supposed to be a '*he*,'" Donny repeated and chuckled to all who listened. "Foiled again," he'd say. By then, I had learned to ignore his snide remarks.

The next morning, my instructions from the nurse: get out of bed, walk across the room, sit in a chair, get back up, and toddle over to the bed again. Convinced that I resembled the Bride of Frankenstein with stitches from one side of my hip to the other, I felt certain that any movement would rip me open for sure.

I could scarcely breathe without feeling pain—and God forbid if I coughed, sneezed or laughed. Plus, solid food was out of the question because of painful, cockamamie bubbles rumbling inside me. I wasn't even allowed to sip drinks from a straw. Miserable in a semi-private room, my mouth watered whenever I got a whiff of what my roommate was eating on the opposite side of the curtain. Sometimes I smelled a juicy hamburger; sometimes I smelled a pepperoni pizza. Whatever visitors brought my roommate to snack on left me drooling.

I stayed in the hospital for five days. Once home, I still endured a great deal of pain and discomfort. I had no choice but to manage caring for my newborn and two-year-old Anna Marie alone. Donny needed to work, and we couldn't afford for him to miss any days.

As expected, I didn't have the luxury of help *or* rest. I didn't have relatives close by, and even if I did, my grandmother wasn't physically strong enough, and my mother remained emotionally incapable.

We named our baby girl Diana. She had straight, black hair and huge, round eyes, the size of teacups. She happened to be a fussy baby. Regardless of being fed, given a pacifier, changed, bathed, rocked, or carried around, she fussed and cried. And cried. And cried. Thinking she was colicky, our pediatrician even changed her formula a couple of times. I grew flustered, unsure what to do to soothe or comfort Diana. Her demands prevented me from enjoying her as I had with my first-born. Whenever possible, I avoided her. I wasn't able to get into the groove of things. Then, I felt guilty. (I didn't know then that this was the beginning of a few challenges in Diana's care and development.)

Liz always showed up when I needed her most. When she knocked on my door with a card and flowers, I'd been feeling sick and weak for a few days. My Caesarean incision had infected, and when I showed Liz, she gently placed her hand over the tender area and prayed for my healing. Instantly, I felt better. When I glanced down there wasn't any more redness.

Later that same year, I felt crushed beyond words with sadness. I learned that Liz and her family were soon moving to another state.

A baby changes everything. Or so I thought. Yet this didn't change my husband. I continued to hope that home life and love might be the magic potion. After all, we now cared for two small precious girls who depended on us. Wouldn't that soften any man?

Most days—and nights—I felt as if my prayers bounced off the ceiling. Maybe I didn't know how to pray. Perhaps I lacked faith. At least I still had grandparents who knew how to pray, and to encourage me as well.

```
Dear,
   We are happy with the bless-
ed event. And according to a
legend from our home country
in Puerto Rico, she is blessed
already for she came out feet
first. Love, Grandma & Grandpa.
```

Running in Heels: A Memoir of Grit and Grace

CHAPTER 26: GOOD AS GOLD

GRANDMA WANTED TO celebrate her fiftieth wedding anniversary surrounded by loved ones and friends. In a rare act of kindness, Donny drove us to Miami to fulfill her wish. We traveled with three-year-old Anna Marie and two-month-old Diana bundled in an infant carrier. Not an easy trip. Still sore from my C-Section, my baby's cries didn't help. Diana fussed halfway there, her cries piercing.

"Can't you do something?"

"And what would that be, Donny? Any ideas?"

"That's your department. I do the driving."

"Very funny. Can we stop now?"

"Not until a couple of hours; then, we'll get a room."

When the day we arrived to my grandparents' house, Donny said his hellos, settled us in and conveniently chose to "stay in the background" for the entire two-week visit. How? By hiding out with some old pals of his, drinking and fishing, and Lord only knew what else.

When the special day arrived, Grandma wore gold dangling earrings and a shiny, golden silk gown. Even though her hair scarcely showed any gray, she wanted to wear a wig. She was beautiful, happy; her eyes filled with love. Her minimal makeup consisted of lipstick, eyebrow pencil and light facial powder. Grandpa dressed sharply in a snazzy tie and a crisp navy-blue vest. He was handsome, standing tall and straight and proud in his spit-polished shoes.

The radiant couple celebrated their love and adoration for each other. Both were in their eighties, robust like two oak trees that stood the test of time.

Even though Grandma wished for a large family reunion at home, the event turned out to be small in attendance. Her only living sister wanted to attend, but she lived in New York and illness prevented her from traveling. Uncle Richie, also up north, couldn't make the trip and sent a card with a fifty-dollar check instead. Ruben arrived in good spirits. Mama and George graced us with their presence, with Willie and Jesse in tow. While George maintained his mean streak toward my mother, I kept up the pleasantries for my grandparents' sake.

I relished every moment: catered food, photos taken, children played as they wiggled and giggled. Stories were exchanged around the table. For one day, we resembled one big, happy, normal family.

After company left and Grandpa had gone to bed, Grandma and I talked in the living room. As Grandma rocked back and forth in her comfortable rocker, I watched how nimbly her fingers worked the crochet needles.

"Grandma, tell me about you and Grandpa," I said, reaching to hold the ball of yarn as she worked. "Tell me when you guys met and you knew you loved him."

"We went to school together as children." Grandma stopped her crocheting to adjust her glasses. "As he got older, he hated workin' on the farm. He ran away from home to join the Army."

"Didn't he tell you goodbye?"

"Oh *sí*, I watched him leave on a train, not knowin' if I'd ever see him again."

"Did he write you?"

"He wrote when he could. I wrote him many letters."

"And when he got out, he asked you to marry him," I said, smiling.

Grandma put her glasses on her lap. "*Pues*, I couldn'," she answered sadly. "Had to take care of *Mami*."

I started remembering pieces of her story, not all of them being joyful. "And didn't he walk out on you?" I pressed.

She continued with her crocheting, shadows traveling across her face. "*Si* After tellin' your grandpa I couldn' marry him just yet." She sighed and added, "*Y entonces* he up and left."

I pictured my grandpa young, impatient, headstrong—to have walked away from her—so coldhearted.

"*Pues, ya tu sabes*. After that I threw myself on the bed," Grandma paused, misty-eyed. "I cried for days, thinkin' how am I ever goin' to live without him? *Entonces*, I continued to pray for him, even though he had gone to marry another."

I mulled over her words, imagining the hole in her heart, along with the devastation she must have felt. Yet her faith in God never wavered. She maintained her love for a man who thought about no one but himself, whom she believed she had lost forever.

I knew that ache.

I sat still, pondering my grandparents' times together. Yes, Grandpa left to start a new life for himself, but eventually he returned, five years later, after his wife passed away. When Grandpa asked for my grandma's hand—yet a second time—she still wasn't ready. Grandma couldn't leave her mother alone. Grandpa grew impatient and left again . . . this time, to marry the sister of his deceased wife.

"I love no other man," Grandma said, "only your Grandpa."

"And years later the other wife died, too?"

"Too much sicknesses back then. Their only boy passed away, *tambien.*"

"I don't understand. After all that, you still married Grandpa?"

Grandma wiped her eyes with a tissue. "Love covers a multitude of sins," she quoted from the Bible.

I doubted I was capable of loving like that.

"Did children come soon for you?"

"I wanted a house full of children. *Pero*, your grandpa didn'."

"Why not?" I asked.

"*Ay mija*, havin' children wasn't so easy in those days. After some time in labor with my first one, once the baby started to come out, the nurse . . . she closed my legs and . . . "

"The baby died," I finished the sentence for her, knowing their first-born, David, had died, but then I understood the reason! "Why would she do such a thing?"

"The doctor . . . was out," she hesitated. "Away at lunch."

I thought about my grandparents' commitment and devotion for one another once they became husband and wife. I thought about their undying love, their sacrifices, and their dedication along with the hard work they shared throughout their lives.

They were simple, hard-working, Hispanic people. Together, they endured the Great Depression, the "Great White

Plague" of tuberculosis, and World War II. Their first son was stillborn. Their second child, my mother, underwent a horrific bout of scarlet fever. Through all that, my grandparents held onto their traditional values and principles and maintained their faith in God and commitment for each other. How I longed for a marriage like theirs. Imperfect, yet pure as gold.

Running in Heels: A Memoir of Grit and Grace

CHAPTER 27: NO GUTS, NO GLORY

THE SLIGHTEST CHANGE in Diana's routine would create havoc. She needed to be in her own crib to sleep regardless of how tired she was. If we were out and the hour passed Diana's bedtime, her fussing and crying would commence, growing louder and louder. Nothing could pacify her then, nothing would soothe her. Whenever she became upset, she would hum and rocked back and forth on her knees. Sometimes she'd bang her head. Other times she'd stand on her head. The child baffled me.

```
Dear, Concerning your baby
standing on her head: Be very
careful. In Puerto Rico when
babies do that they say it
means another baby is on the
way to make company with the
other one. Lovingly, Grandma
```

"*What!*" I stared in disbelief. "How can this be?"
"These things happen all the time . . . especially when *pre-*

cautions aren't taken," the doctor answered with a raised eyebrow, confirming what I did *not* want to hear.

Not now. Not *this* soon.

With a six-month-old baby, and our oldest just two-and-a-half, I was pregnant *again!*

At nineteen years of age, I got used to what others thought as they stared at a young girl with a swollen belly, a baby straddled on her hip, while holding the hand of a toddler. But I would never get used to my husband's indifference.

"Well, what's another one?" Donny said after the announcement to our newest addition.

Then, he added for good measure, "It *better* be a boy."

When he drank, my husband became an overwhelming monstrosity. One drink was one too many, ten never enough. The more I tried to be supportive, the more he was in denial, declaring, "I can quit anytime I want."

Emotions carved a hole in me like the machete Donny used to slice at the shrubs, vines and lurking snakes. I hated seeing my husband in a drunken stupor, losing touch with reality. But when he was sober and in his right frame of mind, I became goo-goo eyed, in love with him all over again.

The paradox of my heart.

One foot in front of the other — that's how I kept my sanity intact. Much too encumbered to mull over my plight, I tended to my girls and even began thinking about babysitting other children for extra income.

By then, Donny threatened much, delivered less. I tried to ignore his childish ways whenever he became too tipsy to do anything but slur and stumble about.

Except for maybe once . . . or twice.

I opened the door and knew full well what to expect. Glassy-eyed, with his newly grown mustache over a silky smirk, Donny was swaying back and forth. My Prince Charming had turned into a frog. He mumbled and staggered in. His pores reeked of booze and a sour odor permeated the air.

"Where have you been all night?"

A snicker and a sneer, his only response.

"You're drunk as a skunk," I said in disgust. I watched him trip over his own feet and throw himself on the sofa. "Do you know what time it is?" I persisted.

"Shut up, woman!" he slurred, rolled over and sprawled on the couch, out cold.

Enough is enough. I'll show him. I'll teach him if it's the last thing I do!

I went into the bathroom. Donny's shaving-kit beckoned.

Images of a masterpiece ran wild in my head. With purpose in mind and a razor in hand, I stood over my prince-turned-toad, still snoring. Most likely, he dreamt he was a young Nimrod, back in Antigua chasing skirts, for all I knew.

Ever so cautiously, I leaned forward and began to give him a wee bit of a trim . . .

Come morning, I sat across the kitchen table from Donny, my gaze fixed on his slouched frame, forehead glistening, eyes blood-shot, hands trembling with white knuckles as he gripped the coffee pot. *Suffering from another painful hangover*, I observed while he poured.

I glared, poker-faced, amazed by my own bravado. Suspense was killing me.

"How's your mustache?" I asked.

Nonchalantly, he brushed his fingers over his lip and

started to rise. "It's fine," he croaked, and downed his coffee. He refilled his cup and headed out, slamming the door behind him.

Oh well . . . I did try to clue him in. I went into the kitchen to make breakfast.

An hour later, I answered the phone to the anticipated call. "Hello?"

"I'll give you this one," my husband retorted. "You're getting to be a gutsy broad. I'm getting picked on here by all the guys at work."

I snickered to myself. "Kinda surprised you didn't notice anything this morning, Donny."

"Well, you got me. Have to admit, this *is* a good one."

I placed the receiver down and sat back on the recliner. A smile twisted the corners of my mouth as I replayed the events of the night before . . .

I'd bent to my task but had frozen when he stirred and muttered something. I backed away and ditched the idea of finishing. I left him asleep in the living room and crawled into bed.

Over coffee this morning, I figured he'd take a hint. Instead, he went straight to work with *half* a mustache.

I confess: such rare acts of sweet revenge gave a natural high.

CHAPTER 28: OH, BROTHER!

THE JUVENILE AUTHORITIES routinely asked Mama for my whereabouts, even before I had run off with Donny. Although I managed to escape the system, they forced my mama to attend many court-ordered appointments regarding the welfare of my little brothers. Of course, she blamed me. She said I was the one who snitched to the cops about Willie and me not having any food in the house to eat.

Willie, then almost nine, bounced between home and various juvenile placements. He was an introverted sort with the attention span of a fly. What Willie needed, Mama couldn't give him. She didn't know how. Being left on his own caused him to suffer academically.

Conversely, two-and-a-half year old Jesse, a thick, beefy child, was strong-willed and already dominated the household. Mama had him at forty-three; he was her baby, her golden boy who could do no wrong. She mollycoddled him big time.

Grandma continued to keep me posted regarding their status. She wrote:

```
Mary, These "people" are
keeping their eyes on your
```

> mother and the boys because she continues to be irresponsible in taking good care of them and can't take them by herself on the bus to get their vaccinations and keep necessary appointments. This only makes things worse for your mother and the boys regarding court. Others mention how she lives in a dump, is sloppy and doesn't cook for the boys. How she has so much clothes tossed all over the floor to wash. ¡*Imagínese eso!* I can do nothing to remedy the situation for my daughter. She doesn't want to be told anything nor take advice from anyone. *Pues*, she's always short on money, yet, wants to call a taxi to go places.

Of course, I could imagine what the boys suffered — hadn't I lived it?

After our earlier relocation from Hoboken to Miami, we changed addresses so many times that Grandma and Grandpa never saw with their own eyes what *my* living conditions were like with Mama back then. I don't think they truly grasped the idea that I, too, had undergone circumstances similar to my brothers'. Had my grandparents known, I'm certain they'd have stepped in sooner to rescue me.

To see with one's eyes is to believe.

December 1979

Willie was home with Mama for the winter holidays. I figured a change of scenery might be good and decided to send for him.

Donny, the girls, and I greeted him near the arrival gate at Hobby Airport.

"Willie, how tall you've gotten!" I stood back and noticed how pencil-thin he looked. His hair was too long. His outdated clothes hung from his frame. His faded sneakers had holes.

"Yeah." He grinned sheepishly; his eyes round, marveling at the sight of me pregnant.

I reached out my arms to squeeze him. "Well, give your sister a hug."

He awkwardly embraced me, his arms like flimsy noodles. I knew hugs didn't come naturally for him. Mama wasn't a hugger. I myself worked on giving them.

"No mushy stuff here," Donny said, as he extended his hand.

Willie giggled after Donny's hearty handshake and exposed a mouthful of crooked teeth. I introduced him to his nieces: thirteen-month-old Diana, fussing in her stroller, and three-year-old Anna Marie trying to hush her.

```
Merry Christmas! We take
pleasure to include a check for
$200 to help cover your ma-
ternity expenses. It's a good
thing we have no car, for gas
is going to $1.17 during the
holidays. Can you imagine? Well
```

```
          dear, do the best you can with
          what you have at hand, and keep
          on smiling and taking good care
          as you have with your girls,
          husband and home.
          Love, Grandma & Grandpa.
```

On Christmas morning, we gathered around the tree and I started passing out presents. Willie stared open-mouthed with the funniest crooked grin on his face. He and the girls made a racket with *oohs* and *aahs* as they each unwrapped gifts.

Donny stuffed a turkey in the oven, to go with my sweet potato soufflé, a green bean casserole, and a couple of pecan pies I had baked the night before. At mealtime, I watched my girls pick at their food while Willie gnawed on an entire drumstick, his plate piled high with cranberry sauce.

All in a Day's Work

Donny continued to advance at work. He supervised the renovation of an apartment complex after a huge fire. I was amazed that whatever he touched turned to gold. He started as a laborer, and advanced to a lead carpenter, then to a punch-out man and finally to the construction super on the jobsite.

Mr. Wonderful received praises and pats on the back. Me? I worked a thankless sunup-to-sunset job as a stay-at-home mom. My husband rubbed shoulders with the big wigs. I changed diapers and powdered baby's bottom. He read blueprints and charts. I read my children's expressions, fairy tales, and thermometers. He inspected buildings. I unstopped the toilet and wiped snotty noses.

When Donny said he would take Willie to tag along with him out on the field one day, I thought the experience would do them both good. Little did I know.

With the remodeling project neared completion, I knew that a handful of workers would be on the property applying the final touches.

Once there, Donny became preoccupied and Curious Willie, as was his custom, wandered away to explore uncharted territory. Alone in a recently painted unit and left to his own devices, he decided to become an artist for the day. With drop cloths, ladders, brushes and buckets of paint left unattended, he busied himself and began the task. Willie covered the freshly white walls and doors with a new coat of bright blue. By the time Donny discovered his master painting, Willie slouched in Donny's pick-up, seemingly taking a nap.

After some scolding, Donny ordered Willie to remain in the truck. Forlorn and dejected, my little brother learned an important lesson that day . . . or did he?

Willie grew restless. He needed to use the bathroom and went into another vacant unit. He had done his business before realizing there was no toilet paper in sight. He sat for some time with the seat's imprints on his tushy, before his search began . . .

"Say . . . er, Don," a carpenter nearby said. "Doesn't he belong to you?"

"Say what?"

"Him," another worker answered, pointing behind him.

Hobbling like a mummy, Willie emerged from the vacant unit, inching his way toward them with pants lowered at the ankles.

"He's . . . my wife's kid brother. . . " Donny muttered.

"You know . . . he's a wee-bit slow." He shook his head in disbelief and added, "And if I hear *anyone* snickering, they're fired!"

No one dared to say anything within his hearing, nor did Donny stick around to find out.

He and Willie headed straight home.

That evening, when Donny recounted his glorious day to me, I burst out laughing, wishing I'd been there.

"What's the joke?" he demanded. "Cackling like a hyena; you think that's funny?"

"Sorrrry!" I choked out, but I couldn't contain my laughter. With tears in my eyes, I went into the kitchen to prepare dinner. I overheard Donny make a loud sucking noise through his teeth, the way he did whenever agitated.

I took pride in having learned my way around the kitchen, and in cooking my pièce de resistance—my aunt Irma's three-layered-lasagna recipe. Even Mr. Picky asked for seconds.

I never imagined a wholesome family meal at the dinner table would lead to disastrous consequences. Willie shoveled in the food, even after he devoured a third helping.

"Willie, should you be eating so much?" I asked.

He glanced up; his mouth full, and hiccupped, wiping his chin with the end of his new shirt.

My girls giggled.

"You eat all you want, boy," Donny chimed in.

After dinner, I leaned over the kitchen sink, washing dishes. My back hurt, my legs were achy. A sickening noise came from the bathroom. I waddled toward that direction to investigate the obvious.

Oh, no! My dear, exasperating brother had barfed up his

lasagna. *Everywhere*. Pasta, red sauce and meat splattered the entire bathroom floor, the white walls, the cabinets and commode seat — every nook and cranny — except *in* the commode. For whatever reason, he thought to lift the toilet lid but *not* the seat.

Willie later confessed (to Donny) that he stuck his finger down his throat because he felt a "tickle." No doubt, that caused the explosive retching episode. I admit my thoughts were anything but saintly. My voice hit an unusual octave as I grabbed a mop and bucket from the back patio and pitched them into the bathroom. I stepped back and gagged, shutting the door. *Well, he'll have to clean that mess alone.*

Half an hour later, I grew worried when the poor child hadn't emerged from the bathroom.

The calm before the storm.

I took a deep breath and opened the door. "Willie, how are you . . . ?"

What in tarnation?

"Willie! Noooo!"

There he stood, frantically shaking the mop about in mid-air with hundreds of little black roly-poly bugs tumbling out. Why he never thought to carry the mop *outside* the house to shake off all those bugs hidden in there was beyond me. Then, seeing those things crawling and rolling in that nasty muck was the last straw.

I ordered Willie in the tub to soak. After sweeping the mess into a corner, I threw a towel on the floor and got on my knees to scrub my brother from head to toe. Also, I had the sole pleasure of cleaning the whole bathroom.

The sound of Donny's chuckling came from the living room.

After helping my brother into his pajamas, I tucked him in on the couch. I did my best to let him know that I was no longer upset, just tired. Too exhausted to bathe them, I changed the girls into their PJs.

"Get to bed, now," I announced. *Before I drop.*

"Awwwwww Mommy," Anna Marie whined. "Do we hafta?"

"We hafta?" Diana echoed.

I let out a sigh. "Yes, you hafta—I mean—*have* to."

"Ewwww! What's that smell?" Anna Marie moaned; her nose crinkled.

Diana mimicked, and pinched her nose, "Ewwwww!"

"Enough! Uncle Willie's tummy hurt and he's sick," I said, closing the door. "Now, everyone quiet!" I couldn't wait to drown away my frustrations under a steaming shower.

I let the warm water pour down over my bulging belly, glad, at least for another seven days before my due date. This week had been eventful enough already.

Three hours later, Donny rushed me to the hospital.

Once settled in a private room at Bellaire General, they inserted an IV in me to halt the labor pains. Instead of an epidural, I wanted them to put me out. "Out cold," I said.

I recalled the alarming sounds and dreadful thoughts that I had experienced while lying awake during my last C-section. I didn't want to relive that if I didn't have to.

After putting me under, they pumped my stomach because I had eaten such a large meal before going to the hospital. When I came to, my doctor wanted to know what I had consumed that night for dinner.

"Whatever you consumed," he said, "it sure included a great amount of meat sauce."

I'm certain my face turned three shades of red, thinking about the lasagna I had gorged on, and then having to clean up the bathroom after Willie's mishap. Lasagna wouldn't be the same for me.

New Year's night 1980, at 11:58 p.m., I awoke to the squalling of my new baby: another darling girl. My gorgeous angel came with black hair, black eyes, a cute pudgy nose and full lips. I named her Angela Renée. Thanks to Willie, she came eight days early. Angela and Diana were fourteen months apart.

"Four females in the house," Donny broadcasted to all before he went home. "I'll definitely have to get me some earplugs!"

He told jokes, like some young stud. I felt like a worn-out twenty-year-old.

My first night in the hospital, I couldn't get comfortable. Still in pain but druggy from the meds, I drifted in and out of sleep. Donny telephoned my room to ask about the baby and me, and to let me know that the girls were doing fine at the sitter's. Willie was staying with him. He then proceeded to give an account of his eventful day on four hours of sleep, which began in trying to wake Willie at 6 a.m.

"A funny smell reached my nose," Donny explained, sounding aggravated. "When Willie finally got up, he went straight to the bathroom and then locked himself in."

I started to say something but my tongue felt thick. I sipped some water.

"An hour later, he still wouldn't come out."

"That's weird," I mumbled.

Donny continued. "After I threatened to kick the door in, he opened it. I couldn't believe the stench that reached my

nose!"

Poor child had another "accident" during the night.

I heard Donny sigh. "Can you believe he tried to clean himself with a whole roll of toilet paper?"

"Hmmm. A bath would have been much easier," I surmised.

"I had to tell him to take a shower and throw his pajamas away. And I still need to unclog the toilet from all that mess."

A sound escaped me. I knew Donny would never touch Willie's soiled clothes. He had once paid a neighbor to change our daughter's diaper. But I couldn't resist. "You poor thing—"

"Don't mock me, woman!" Donny warned, and soon ended the call.

I couldn't laugh if I wanted to. I hurt too much. Then, I dozed off.

Five days rolled by too quickly, and it was time for Angela and me to go home. But since we lacked insurance, the hospital refused to release us without some form of payment. My outraged husband told them to go ahead and keep us as ransom; they weren't getting a dime from him. Eventually, Donny gathered his senses and, before he left, assured me he'd figure something out. After about an hour, the fear of abandonment crossed my mind.

If he leaves me now, I'll kill him!

I felt relieved when he returned, and shocked to see him pull wads of cash from his pocket. Where did the *dinero* come from? By selling *my* Plymouth Duster.

The week after my hospital stay, Willie flew back to Mama, I'm certain with enough stories to share about his three-week stay in Houston.

Mary A. Pérez

News from Home

February 24, 1980

    I was glad when I heard your voice over the phone and for telling me that you had gone to church this morning in spite of not having your car anymore. You never told me about having to sell your car.

    Mary, I talked to your mother, wish she and Jesse would go to Texas by plane to visit you. We'll pay for the tickets. What do you say? I can't offer no more, other than to take care of Willie who don't behave well. She says that Jesse don't behave either but I said, "He minds Mary and she will put all four kids down for a nap after lunch and then you two can talk and visit."

    Papa and I are glad to hear of your soon to be car, that '76 Pacer (whatever that is), that Don is buying from a friend.

> And congratulations for getting your voter's card so young. Look at your mother who is 45 and has never registered to vote. Not even her George. But you can hear him boasting that when he was 19 years old, he was married, had a car, a son, a house, and a yard growing vegetables and raising chickens. *Entonces*, look at him today, he doesn't even have social security insurance for his own son, Jesse, nor can pay rent for your mother, but drinks beer, smokes two packs of cigarettes a day, and makes your mother more nervous and the boys miserable. Your poor mother suffers. She wants a good man but don't know where to get one. Lovingly, Grandma

My grandparents had included a surprise gift in my letter: An unexpected check for $600. I called to thank them with tears of gratitude.

Soon I started to entertain the idea of Mama visiting us. I figured the trip a great idea for her to get away and have an opportunity to bond with her granddaughters. I still imagined she'd fulfill her role as a grandmother better than she had the role of mother. Maybe I should have learned sooner to hope for the best but prepare for the worst.

March 1980

As for your mother, I am sorry to inform you that I don't see her enthusiastic in visiting you. She is always full of alibis, saying she needs this, that, and the other. I asked her, "What do you say about the trip to Mary's?" She told me she don't know because she still needs clothes, shoes, and money, etc. She doesn't want to leave the house key with George, who she can't depend on, and he can't depend on her either to move around fast enough in getting the boys ready to go out at a moment's notice; she doesn't clean. . . Can you imagine? When is this *mujer* going to ever learn to do things fast and take an interest in her children? I am ashamed myself; anytime I hear someone say the same thing happened when she was married to your father. *¡Quéva!* I taught her and she watched me cook and clean every day. . . Blessings

> to the three girls, Donny &
> you. Love always, Grandma

When Mama started a letter to me, baby Angela was already one month old. Mama didn't finish writing that letter until Angela was five months old. (The letter barely included a mention—or a thanks—for taking care of Willie for the weeks he stayed at our home.)

> February-June 1980
>
> (Feb 1) I hope you are feeling fine. It's about time am answering you. I always say when the boys are sleeping then I'll write, but then am the one who's falling to sleep and put it off. Thanks for the picture of Angela. You're a lucky woman to have three daughters. About Willie, he had a nice time in Texas and lots of fun.
> (June 27) Well, I said I'll write you tonight even if it's late because tomorrow in the daytime I won't have time. As you know-let me change pens- Willie is over at Grandma's house. They couldn't go to church last month because of a riot and curfew here in Miami

and no city bus was running.
I go to court again; pray that
Willie isn't placed in that
home. Jesse remembers you. He
said that he has to write to
his "big sister." I don't know
where I put the card I had for
Angela . . . when I find it I'll
send it. Say hello to Anna Marie. Hugs & kisses to Diana &
Angela. Regards to Donny, tell
him I say hello and to take it
easy. I wish I had a phone but
the deposit now is $100 instead
of $50.
Love always, your Mother.

More news from Grandma regarding home:

July 1980

    Glad to hear your nice voice
on the phone and learn that everybody is doing well. Please
pray for your mother. She just
does whatever George says. Poor
daughter of mine is like she's
losing her mind and I myself
pray for her so much. I'm so
sorry, for she's my only daughter. George left 4 weeks ago
for an unknown place. He don't

> care for anybody, not even his own son, but is always in some kind of mood that I don't understand him. One minute he is nice and happy, the next minute he is grudging and fighting with your mother and poor Willie. I'm really sorry for them. Willie will be living in a Catholic Home soon and then go to a public school from there.

I felt relieved knowing that Willie had at least a chance to escape the pathetic home life that was more like a four-corner brick wall on a dead-end street. Maybe with the right help he would have structure and gain direction to survive in society. At least I hoped so.

Seven months after giving birth, I wrote:

> August 1980
>
> Dear Grandma and Grandpa,
>
> This month I turned twenty-one years old. I can hardly believe it! Thank you, again, so much for your token of love that I received in the lovely card. I also got a note each from Willie and Mama, and for the first time, Mama wrote 'I love you' inside. How about

that?

   Daddy called and we talked for 25 minutes.

   I don't know what you're supposed to do when one becomes of age. I don't feel any different. Sometimes I feel older, other times younger.

   Donny surprised me by arranging for our neighbors to baby-sit, and then we went to the Galleria to hang out. He gave me a heart to go with my silver charm-bracelet. He's always so full of surprises.

Love always, Mary Ann

Running in Heels: A Memoir of Grit and Grace

CHAPTER 29: GONE, BUT NOT FORGOTTEN

GRANDPA RARELY WROTE letters, leaving that task to my grandma. He was a man of few words, so whenever he'd say something, we all took notice. Whenever he wrote, it meant a great deal. A day shy of his eighty-third birthday, I received an endearing letter:

December 2, 1980

    Hello, Mary, this is Grandpa. I do hope by the time you receive this, you, my dear three great-granddaughters, and your husband are in good health. As for me, I thank the good Lord for all the years He has given me. Thank you for the birthday card you sent me. As for my age, I do not feel so bad. God is taking good care of Mama and myself. Praise His wonderful Name!

> I hope your husband is doing good in his new job. In the meantime, may the blessings of God be on you all. My love to everyone, Grandpa.

A month later, unexpected news from home:

January 1981

> Papa is in the hospital sick with Hepatitis, an infection of the liver. He is isolated in his room, because his illness is contagious. But your mother and I go inside his room to his bedside and talk with him, and hope God in His mercies spares our health.

I wanted to see my grandpa and started packing for the flight to Miami. A second letter arrived saying that his diagnoses had changed from hepatitis to liver cancer.

That same week, a wonderful couple from church offered to watch my girls, now ages one, two, and four. Donny, drinking heavily, agreed to stay behind and promised to "hold the fort." His words weren't reassuring; however, I made the plane reservations.

Two months later, a shocking announcement would blare on the news about an attempted assassination of President Reagan. The bullet had missed his heart by an inch and pierced a lung instead. But I had already had experienced a heartache a month earlier—the death of my grandfather still fresh on my mind.

I would never forget how an unsettling aura of death struck me when I walked into the hospital room. I shuddered and gingerly approached the form buried under layers of covers. The head of his bed was raised, the profile barely recognizable to me.

"Grandpa?"

A pale, thin face moved; eyes hardly opened. Those eyes, once sharp, were feeble and dull. Yellow papery skin hung loosely from bones. I reached for his hand. Large purple veins ran up and down them like a roadmap. Those hands, once strong and beefy, quick and nimble, felt cold, boney and fragile. The same hands that had once led, guided, and comforted me; that had embraced my grandma close by his side for more than fifty years.

Tears swam in my eyes. "Grandpa, it's me, Mary," my voice cracked. "Please hang on." "I'm . . ."

I leaned closer, straining to hear him.

" . . . trying," he gasped.

I struggled to keep my composure. I knew he was weary. To see him lose his dignity pained me, lying there so helpless, a prisoner in his own body.

Lost in my thoughts, my eyes roamed and paused on Grandpa's wristwatch on the bedside table. When I reached for the watch, my mind traveled back to a conversation— words I hadn't understood then. I was nine or ten years old.

Grandpa and Grandma, making their bed, were talking in low voices.

"Ana," he spoke with finality, "when the time comes, I

want to go <u>first</u>."

"You dun have to speak of dat." Grandma's broken but gentle voice came across—*crying?* "That's God's business," she added.

I continued to eavesdrop.

"Don't know, Ana," Grandpa continued. "All I know is, when the time comes, I have asked Him to take *me* home first."

I walked away that day puzzled and saddened.

Time.

Now holding my grandpa's watch in my hand, that conversation made sense.

Precious time.

Grandpa had buried two wives before he married Grandma; he never wanted to go through that experience again. I never doubted he loved my grandma dearly, and I understood that if she were to go before him, Grandpa wouldn't have been able to endure the loss.

He dozed off. I sat at his bedside, praying for God to hush the raging of my heart.

A friend had taken Grandma to her home for a warm meal and proper rest. Mama and I stayed overnight with Grandpa in the hospital. To my amazement, I observed Mama genuinely concerned, as she gently fussed over him and fluffed his pillows. She turned him on his side, rubbed his back, kept him covered, readjusted his leg if it dangled over the bed, and talked (non-stop) to him—telling him the time, the day, and the weather. Although Grandpa couldn't talk, Mama believed he heard her every word because they say the hearing is the last to go. She even said he nodded his head when she spoke.

A few days later, in Grandpa's final hour—while Grandma waited for her ride to the hospital—Mama sat with him alone. She promised him she'd take care of Grandma. *If only.*

February 3, 1981, exactly two months after reaching his birthday, my beloved grandpa sadly passed away.

"I kept socks on Papa to keep his feet warm," Mama later recounted. "In the end, his fingers turned purple. He breathed heavily until he stopped breathing altogether."

Grandma took the expected news with grace. I admired her quiet strength.

Truly, I would always miss Grandpa. In my eyes, *he* was a great man.

After Donny received word about Grandpa's death, he decided on his own to drive the 1,200 miles from Houston to Miami. When I opened the door to him, one peek at his drunken demeanor spoke volumes before he ever opened his mouth. He motioned for me to follow him out, all the while muttering what had transpired since I had seen him last.

Apparently, he had packed all our stuff in storage boxes, ditched our apartment, and tossed what wasn't boxed into the largest U-Haul on the lot. Seeing my things scattered in that U-Haul, and hearing that he had left most of our things behind left me in shock. But worse than that, he had done the unthinkable: He deserted our precious girls without telling them about his planned road trip or bothering to explain anything to the couple caring for them.

How will I ever be able to keep it together and be strong for Grandma in her time of grief?

Why me?

But the heavens were silent.

Mourners gathered at the funeral parlor. I tried conversation but inwardly still fumed over my husband's irrational behavior. *What to do?* I wondered. *Where to go?* Even within my own circle, how I wished we weren't so fragmented. I longed to see more unity—less division. *¡Qué va!* Thoughts about my clan and their idiosyncrasies ran fierce in my mind.

Uncle Richie had flown in early from New York. In no time, he and Mama picked up where they had left off as teenagers harboring resentment. They bickered over years of unresolved issues I couldn't understand.

Ruben and his on-again-off-again girlfriend sat in the far corner. One had to be deaf not to overhear all the profanity and brouhaha over a disagreement between them.

Soon the nauseating stench of beer filled my airway as George mumbled under his breath. He disregarded whatever Mama said to him.

What a jerk, I thought, shifting positions in my chair to escape the odor and the sight of him. I wondered if the drama would ever end. *Is there any sanity left in this family?*

Then, I noticed Daddy and Gloria sitting hand-in-hand, grieving silently. Cheeks glistened with tears. Genuine compassion. A silver lining—all hope was not lost.

I slid next to Grandma. "You okay?" I whispered, wishing I had something witty to offer.

Shadows shaded her eyes. Her face older, her creases deeper. Sorrow had stolen all traces of her vitality and youth.

"*Ay, mija,*" her voice cracked as she squeezed my hand. A lump filled my throat.

While I believed God was the source of her strength, I also knew we mortals needed someone with skin. Grandma was going to miss my grandpa terribly.

With my own marriage in question, I didn't think the grieving would ever end.

The funeral behind us, we gathered back at Grandma's place. The tantalizing aroma from the spread of food on the dining room table greeted us when we strolled in. Temporarily our troubles eased.

Donny, seeking to redeem himself, had cooked a large feast:

Baked chickens smothered in gravy; potato salad topped with boiled eggs and tomato wedges; baked beans mixed with brown sugar; cheddar cheese melted over broccoli, sweet, golden fried plantains sliced at an angle; buttery biscuits made from scratch; tropical fruit salad arranged inside a carved-out watermelon; and a moist pineapple upside-down cake topped with maraschino cherries.

The compliments rolled in.

George licked his lips. "I have to hand it to you, Donny. You're one hellava cook."

"I wanna little taste of everything." Mama smiled, holding up her plate already piled high.

"You cook as good as any woman *I* know," my brother chimed in, reaching for a second drumstick. His girlfriend shot darts at him with her eyes and whacked him across the arm.

Donny beamed, loading my mother's plate with extra helpings. "Ah, hush. No big deal. This was nothing."

"Notheen?" Daddy exclaimed. "Man, da first time I ever try to cook was when Gloria visited Puerto Rico and I stayed home by myself. I cooked spaghetti and I couldn' eat it." Daddy sucked on his chicken bone. "Man," he chuckled, "it was so mushy not even da dog wanted it!"

Laughter filled the air. My father and Gloria came to accept Donny, although initially unable to stomach him. Life had a funny way of moving on. I gazed at each one gathered around the table and paused on Grandma.

Reality slapped me in the face.

Sitting in silence, Grandma remained distant. She wiped an imaginary stain from her black dress. Unable to partake in the merriment, the sorrow in her gaze reflected the anguish of her heart.

I wasn't certain she'd be able to bounce back.

Homeward Bound

Donny and I quarreled all the way back to Houston. I think I did most of the arguing. I zeroed in on how he had abandoned our girls, ditched our apartment, and lost his job because he showed up "tipsy" one time too many. The more I expected him to reveal what his plans were, the less he made sense. Blood rushed to my face as our tempers flared. Sick with anxiety, I felt hopeless and angry.

Along the scenic highway, trees flashed past like my fleeting thoughts. I watched the mile markers zip by along with the stark reality that the rat race may never end. We had no jobs, no money, no home, and I had no earthly idea where we would live or what we were going to do.

Out of the corner of my eye, I observed Donny's hand tremble each time he let go of the steering wheel. He sipped from a can of beer hidden in a small brown paper sack, while dipping his disgusting Copenhagen between swigs.

We stopped to get a room for the night in Mobile. When

Donny went out for sandwiches, I wearily went into the bathroom to shower. Under the hot water, I stood crying out my frustrations until my face reddened and my skin wrinkled. When I came out, Donny was zonked on the bed, snoring.

Before sleep overtook me, I reached a conclusion: my girls and I would not dwell in the same house with him much longer.

In no way, shape, or form!

Running in Heels: A Memoir of Grit and Grace

Mary A. Pérez

CHAPTER 30: RUNNING IN HEELS

TAKING CARE OF my rambunctious trio, Anna Marie, Diana, and Angela, was a full time job. But the amount of work and energy needed to care for my middle child far surpassed the needs of her sisters. Three-year-old Diana was like three bouncing kids in one, spinning around me like a whirlwind. There was no slowing her down, no taming her. She had zero notion of fear or danger. She'd run out into the street, full speed ahead. She'd bounce and jump off beds, couches and chairs, not caring how or where she landed. The child loved climbing trees. She enjoyed dangling upside down by the back of her legs on branches — the higher the better.

Diana loved to compete, especially with her sisters. She determined to outrun and outdo anyone doing anything. The first time she saw someone do a backflip off the diving board, she said, "I can do that." She didn't care if she belly-flopped in the water. By day's end, Diana could do backflips, landing feet-first in the pool. Another time, after watching a girl do cartwheels at the park, Diana mimicked her perfectly. When she saw someone running and doing a round-off, Diana copied, landing on her feet with arms in the air, yelling, "Ta-daa!"

That episode nearly gave me a heart attack. But another Sunday morning is fixed forever in my mind.

"Hurry, girls. Time to go."

Once again, we were late for church.

"Is Daddy comin'?" Anna Marie asked.

"No, Daddy's going fishing."

"Go get your shoes on, gal," Donny bellowed from the living room, watching TV, barking orders, with a can of beer already in his hand.

"Can't find 'em, Daddy," Diana called from the closet.

"Well, has anyone seen *my* shoes?" I asked, kneeling as I peered under the bed.

"Ha, ha. Lookie, Mommy. I find 'em." Diana smiled from ear to ear, twirling with my high heels, one on and one off.

"Diana!" I couldn't believe that child. *Doesn't she understand we're late?*

Donny snickered. "Yep. That's *your* side of the family tree."

After enjoying some "me time" during the church service, I went to collect the girls from Sunday school. Parents clustered, waiting to claim their children. Laughter and squeals mingled throughout the building.

I bounced Angela on my hip, as Anna Marie dawdled behind. Before I got a tight grip on Diana, she shrugged off my hand and darted down the hallway, out the main door. My heart caught in my throat as she bolted for the parking lot. I sat Angela down and dashed after Diana, yelling over my shoulder to Anna Marie, "Watch your sister!"

Click. Click. Click. Click. The sound of my heels echoed on the tile floor while chasing after my daughter, and then a *ka-thump*, as I nearly sprained my ankle. I huffed and puffed on after her and when I finally grabbed her, she giggled. To her, the chase was just a game. I was out of breath, my mouth dry, my temper frayed.

Cringing with embarrassment, I dared not glance in anyone's direction, and ordered the girls into the car. Lost in my thoughts while driving home, I calculated how often I felt like a dope, running on empty, a complete failure. I didn't know how to help my husband with his drinking problem, let alone a daughter who needed special care and structure.

"Be quiet," Anna Marie whispered to her sister in the car. "Mommy's upset."

"Quiet," Diana echoed. She didn't like being told what to do.

Once, I had ordered Diana in the corner for spitting at her sisters. A minute later, I went to check on her. She stood in the corner, all right: upside down on her head, singing *Jingle Bells.*

Diana developed a number of pastimes that occupied her for hours. She loved balloons. She became fixated on them. She put her face to them. She smelled them. She ran her hands over them. She rubbed them against her cheek and darted after the one that floated away. When she chased after them, I often had to chase her and bring her back, kicking and screaming.

Diana also fixated on the color black. She'd reach for her black crayon first, coloring as hard as possible, and then run her fingers over her drawing to feel the texture.

She loved birds, especially black ones. At the park, I took my eyes off her for a second. When I looked up, she had vanished. Anxious minutes ticked by before I spotted her again. She was darting after a poor, skinny bird, mimicking its sound by squealing, *"BAWK!"* Once more, I had the pleasure of racing after her.

"Yep, *your* side of the family," Donny reiterated, whenever he heard or saw her behaving strangely.

"Your side!" Diana parroted at her daddy, grinning.

Now that's my girl, I thought.

My little bundle of energy adored her father's bronze skin and thought that if she sat out in the sun long enough, her skin might turn as dark as his. I'd call to her whenever I found her basking in the sun, hiding.

"Diana, you get in this house now, you hear me?"

"Nooo! Wanna be black like Daddy."

"Daddy's not black, he's brown, and you're *red* like a lobster!"

The child giggled. As much as I wanted to, I didn't smile, but stood firm and glared at her. She sucked air through her teeth, copying her father's annoying idiosyncrasy.

"Where did you get that habit from?" I stood with arms akimbo. "Your daddy?"

Diana jumped up and stomped past me, snickering. She headed for her next favorite pastime: to cool off and play in the bathtub filled with bubbles. "Wanna bath," she demanded.

As for Donny, sometimes he hung around for support, but mostly loopy-looped. Regardless, his favorite saying was, "I'm the man, you're the woman. The kids are *your* department."

My husband's liquor of choice: vodka chased with water. This gave me an idea, and I made a preemptive move. I poured half his vodka down the drain and refilled the bottle with water. My deed went unnoticed, and he was none the wiser. But Donny, a shrewd person in the wheeling and dealing department, agreed one day to have me monitor his drinking and say when he had enough. A couple of days later, the bottle still sat in the cabinet, scarcely touched. I thought, *Wow! He finally cut back on his drinking*. The instant I opened the bottle, the joke was on me. He had refilled the bottle with water. But some days I did get the last laugh.

"What are these here bumps?" Donny asked one evening after his shower.

"What bumps?"

"These bumps *here*," he repeated, pointing. "On my chest."

I blinked and leaned closer.

"Do you see them, or not?"

Can it be?

"Oh, I see 'em all right," I answered, swallowing a snicker.

"What's the joke, gal?"

Couldn't help laughing . . . Diana had given him the chickenpox.

Do What I Gotta Do

As fast as Donny made money, he drank it almost all away. His job performance suffered. He played hocky, having me call his boss to say he was too ill to work. Although we didn't starve, everything else fell short. I learned to improvise by preparing ground beef one hundred and one ways. We often ate bologna-and-cheese sandwiches with chips, or grilled cheese with cups of tomato soup.

Some women from church donated bagfuls of clothing and shoes for my girls. Sometimes I'd even find a cute outfit or two for me. Donny, filled with pride, usually roared, "Take it back," but by then, he may as well have been talking to the wall.

"Taking nuthin' back," I muttered, walking away.

To supplement our income, I babysat at home. Besides

caring for my own, I took in three others, sometimes four, on a weekly basis. Paid a week in advance, I watched one infant, and the rest were toddlers. Every penny counted. Amazingly, my husband never said *boo* about the extra dough.

"Desperate times, desperate measures," as the saying goes.

Whenever I hid money, Donny poked around the closet, and rummaged through my stuff until he found my hidden stash to blow on more booze.

My one weapon was my tongue. After I mouthed off, I scurried out of the apartment and sat on the curb. I remained in sight or he'd accuse me of all sorts of junk. All the while, I prayed for him to pass out before I dared go back inside. When he called me a belittling name one time too many, I lashed out. In the bathroom, I even shoved him backwards once. Tangled in the shower curtain, Donny had lost his balance and landed hard in the tub. With all the cussing flowing out of his mouth, I knew he wasn't unconscious, and I hightailed it out of there.

My great escapes were short-lived. Donny saw to that. In the evenings, he stripped off every inch of my clothing. After he had his way, I curled in a ball, whimpering as quietly as possible. Not until I heard his snores, would I crawl out of bed and bawl under the shower until I felt clean.

Mary A. Pérez

CHAPTER 31: MY GRIT, HIS GRACE

FACES. HARSH. AND GRIM. Countenances from every lifestyle. Frozen in time. The daunted old. The impulsive young. Uncertain of tomorrow. Unsure of today. Did they come from broken homes? Torn marriages? Abusive relationships? Addictions?

How did I get here?

As I waited in the line that stretched out the door into the hot sun, I swallowed what dignity I had left. When my turn came, the woman behind the window shoved stacks of papers my way.

"Next," she called out in a gruff voice.

"You know, I've never been here before. Just need some help."

She rolled her eyes. "Next."

I scuttled away to find a chair, and thought, *Lord, give me the grace to endure, or get me outta here.* Reluctantly, with trembling hands, I filled out the food-stamp forms.

I believed I was beginning to find the strength needed to make some changes. After all, it was what I'd been praying for all along. I believed I'd found an out even if it was only a temporary solution. Marisa, a smart cookie from church, and a thirty-something divorcée, owned a spacious three-bedroom home. To cover household expenses, she rented rooms to college students. Out of the kindness of her heart, Marisa took my girls and me in.

We camped out in the formal living and dining areas of the house, initially left unfurnished. Almost all our personal items and clothing remained in boxes and suitcases. We had our own TV and slept semi-comfortably on a mattress on the floor. I couldn't pay for anything, so I cleaned house, bought the groceries with my food stamps and cooked meals. The arrangement was our lifesaver.

Donny remained unwelcomed.

My hope and prayer for Donny was that, with us out of the way, he would seek help. But he continued to drink daily, losing touch with reality. He left us alone for a while, then would turn up drunk and make a scene in front of the house, arguing and talking crazy. All a sudden, he needed to be with "his" family. He parked his truck in front of Marisa's house and slept in the cab.

Liquor had reduced my husband to an obnoxious, annoying human being. With every drink, he shifted from a happy drunk to an angry drunk. When he didn't drink, random acts of violence lay dormant like a hibernating bear.

I pleaded with Marisa not to call the cops. She wanted nothing to do with Donny and didn't want him on her property.

One evening, Donny forced himself into the house and demanded that *his* family leave with him, "now!"

Mama's voice registered in my head, "Never argue with a drunk."

Marisa stepped in and voiced her objections; she and Donny had a shouting match. When he called her a derogatory name, she slapped him.

He didn't hesitate.

Donny picked her up by the legs and sent her sprawling over the sofa as if she were my daughter's Raggedy Ann doll. With face flushed and hair in disarray, Marisa's head popped up behind the couch, hissing threats.

"I'm calling the cops. Get out of my house!"

Thank goodness, her limbs are still intact!

I urged Donny out the door. I figured after three months, maybe the girls and I should go with him. I was, after all, still his wife. And he wasn't going to stop showing up.

During our separation, Donny had lost another carpentry job. But knowing we were returning, he snapped to attention and soon found a position as maintenance man at an apartment complex. His salary of $1,200 a month included free rent. We moved into a small two-bedroom, one-bath apartment. Our three girls shared a room and one bed, pushed up tightly against the wall.

Harried and haggard, I felt ready to throw in the towel, geared for the nuthouse. Brain cells overloaded, I went through the motions in complete numbness: dealing with Donny's alcoholism, caring for the girls, and keeping house while trying to maintain my own sanity.

Our daughters were four-and-a-half, two-and-a-half, and one. The doctors had labeled Diana everything in the book. As she got older, the prognosis changed: Pervasive Developmental Disorder . . . Autistic . . . Hyperactive . . . Schizophrenic . . . I wanted to scream, "Not my child!" Although there were undeniable complications at birth, another nagging question that haunted me was something I had read about Fetal Alcohol Syndrome (FAS). I couldn't escape the fact how her father continually drank, including at her conception. *Was this even possible?* I wondered. *And what about her hyperactivity?*

Diana's taxing mannerisms bewildered me. She shrugged off affection. If we tried to hold her hand, her fingers went stiff, resembling the shape of a starfish. The child saw the world through different lenses, not behaving or interacting the way other children did. She escaped reality by rocking or humming as early as ten months old. She avoided eye contact and looked either *through* you or *over* you. Depending on the circumstances, she'd throw tantrums or burst into hysterics, laughing at her own private jokes. And she hated anyone telling her "no."

Diana's inappropriate behaviors induced a response in me I didn't like. Because I feared my own reactions, I mostly kept her at arm's length. I tried convincing myself she'd grow out of those peculiarities and took her with me to different churches and prayer circles. But as time passed, I grew more short-tempered, feeling inept, at a loss regarding her well-being.

"No, not again! Not now!" I cried out in the bathroom. *I'll call Marisa. She's always been strong. She's got her act together.*

I reached for the phone and dialed her number. When she answered, I blurted, "The test is positive! I'm pregnant." *She'll lift my spirits.*

"Mary . . ." she began. "How in the world will you care for *another* baby?"

Then again, maybe not.

"What are you going to do?" Marisa squealed.

I thought, *If I knew that, I wouldn't have called you. Wasn't I the one who was supposed to get some reassurances, some guidance,* some support here?

"I . . . I don't know, I thought—"

"Mary, what *were* you thinking?" she shot back. "You *can't* possibly have another baby! You're only twenty-one; you already have three children, and now number four on its way? Your husband drinks too much, he works only when he wants to, you have a child with special needs, you guys don't have enough money . . ."

My mind swirled. I hung by a flimsy strand, all hope slipping. *Okay! Tell me something I don't know. Am I turning into my mother? Marisa's right: I. Can't. Go. On.*

Then, she added, "I'll help you. If you will get an abortion . . . I will help you pay for one."

So, that's it? The quick-fix solution to the problem . . . to end an innocent life?

"I . . . I'll have to think about this," I whispered. "Let me sleep on it and get back with you."

Did that answer come out of me?

I placed the receiver down, heavy with conflicting emotions.

I can't have another baby. But can I truly consider this the way out?

The girls slept in their room. Donny was—*Lord only knows where.* I sat alone in the dark, crossed-legged on the bed. My head ached. My stomach was tied in knots. Overcome with waves of hopelessness, my mind latched onto the memory of the only security blanket I had ever known: my grandparents' home. And I realized I was sinking. *Fast.*

What happened to my anchor of faith? My hope? Isn't God big enough to handle the mess in my life? I have to admit, I've been too busy for Him. Now that I need Him, does He still care? Then it occurred to me: *If I can't trust God now, then what's the point of going on?*

That instant, I prayed like never before and pored over my Bible. The Book of Psalms always comforted me and that night, before sleep overtook me, my "Ah-ha" moment came after reading Psalm 139:13: *For You created my innermost being; You knit me together in my mother's womb.* If God knitted together the unborn baby inside me, I wasn't about to take that life away.

Come morning, it truly felt like a new day. A fresh start. Resolute in my decision, faith sparked. God had always taken care of me before. I determined to trust Him to carry me now. *I believe, Lord . . . Help my unbelief. Give me the grace to endure.*

I reached for the phone and dialed Marisa's number.

"Thanks, but no thanks."

"Mary, think about what—"

"No!" I shouted. "I'm going to walk on and trust God. You knew my convictions. I thought they were yours too."

"Mary, I was only trying—"

"How?" I interrupted, pacing the floor. "By offering me an *abortion*? I came to you down and out for encouragement and prayer. I needed to hear 'hope' beyond my pain, but you didn't—you wouldn't—give me that!"

"Look Mary, you're still so young. I've been around longer than you—"

"You never had children," I protested.

"I married a jerk once too. They don't change." Marisa went on to explain that she was looking out for my best interest.

After long seconds of dead silence and nothing else to say, we hung up.

I thought of a lesson in Sunday school about Job who called his friends *miserable* comforters. They told Job to "curse God and die." They were supposed to be his friends; yet, those comforters increased his trouble.

Sometimes, it's best to keep your troubles to yourself.

Marisa and I parted ways. Our friendship ended that day.

Running in Heels: A Memoir of Grit and Grace

CHAPTER 32: INTO THE SHARK TANK

May 23, 1981

Dear Mary & Don,

   Hope you are in good health. Since Papa died, I've been so tired trying to squeeze myself and half of my junk in with your mother. It's not easy for me. I think I'm running out of patience, and this is no good for my health and the few years left of my life.
   Jesse's behavior is worse than Willie's, and your mother can't cope with him now. He's too demanding and she's too easy with him.
   I tire easily, and still have to do the cooking and stand the criticizing your mother makes.

> Anyway, I'm still breathing, with no one to go to but God. Well dear, let bygones be bygones, forgive and forget. Love and blessings, Grandma.

A RECENT WIDOW, my grandma soon fell under the burden of missing Grandpa's strength and guidance, while trying to tolerate my mother's endless plights and self-indulgence.

Mama's harshness and lack of consideration toward Grandma added fuel to the fire. I couldn't be of much help and felt at a loss. I had tried persuading my grandmother <u>not</u> to live with Mama, even suggesting that she stay with us. But Grandma felt sorry for her. Eventually, she bought a mobile home for the three of them: Mama, Jessie and herself. Although the trailer needed many repairs, she used her life's savings to buy it "as is" for $8,500.00.

> July 22, 1981
>
> Dear Mary,
>
> It's good to hear that you and the Trio girls are doing fine. My health, not so good, and my heart is broken as I face life without my beloved husband.
>
> I'll have to stay and take care of Jesse when your moth-

er goes to get her surgery done. They scheduled her a week ago but you know how easy she is leaving things for the last minute. First Willie was here for one week visiting. We watched the two boys closely for they fight like cats and dogs over their toys, etc. George took Jesse back and I paid for the gas for he had no money.

Pray for your mother and sons who are driving her to pieces till she gets exhausted and no desire to do anything but watch TV all day.

George is *muy buchipluma*; sometimes he's good, but other times he's easy to get mad and go to the bar to drink and smoke. I gave money to him for gas ($1.35 a gallon) and twice he took me to church. He don't care to join me because he needs his beer and smokes. Your mother and him are too nervous and don't agree with many things.

Glad you have started working nights to help your household. Take care, dear.
Love to all, G-ma.

I mused over that funny word Grandma mentioned in her letter. *Buchipluma*: a Puerto Rican phrase meaning "someone who promises but doesn't deliver."

I knew many *buchipluma*s in my life.

On Bended Knee

Tired. Bone tired.

At Rice Food Market, on my feet six nights a week, I worked the cash register, sacked and lifted heavy brown bags loaded with customers' groceries from five o'clock until closing at midnight. By the end of my shift, my feet had swelled. My back ached. But the job provided health insurance and a six-month maternity leave with pay. This was an answer to my prayers; God had provided.

I normally didn't get home until one in the morning. To my good fortune, I worked directly across the street from our apartment on Bissonnet. A teenage neighbor watched our daughters for a couple of hours and fed them before Donny arrived home. I'd leave work at break time to check in on him and the girls in the evenings.

Too often, I'd find my husband draped across the couch out cold.

"Donny . . . Donny . . . ." I stood over him shaking his arm. "Dammit Donny, wake up."

"What? I *am* awake!" he spat, and turned over.

"You're supposed to put the girls to sleep before passing out. Remember?"

"Theyrslumppnng . . ."

"What—? You make me *sick!*"

I stormed away to check in on the sleeping angels. Before I opened their door, I heard whispering and giggling coming from the kitchen.

I never imagined how I'd find my girls entertaining themselves. On the floor amidst pots and pans, they sat with the refrigerator door open. Five-year-old Anna Marie pretended to cook. She mixed her sisters a concoction of whatever she found in the fridge: raw eggs, ketchup, Pepto-Bismol, mayonnaise, grape jelly—and Lord knew what else—stirred in for good measure. I got home in the nick of time. *Good Lord, I think I even smell beer in the mixture!*

I wanted to quit work. However, I needed to hold on for those maternity benefits.

A few nights later, I discovered the two youngest girls precariously hanging out the window of our second-story apartment—fearlessly leaning on their bellies, legs flaying in mid-air. My heart swelled in my throat. I was concerned for their safety but didn't want to frighten them and caused them to keel over the windowsill. And I happened to be extremely skittish of heights.

¡Calmete! I told myself. *You don't want a repeated episode of having your baby early.* I held my breath. I snuck up behind them, grabbed them and pulled them in.

Repeatedly finding the girls unsupervised and unattended became too much to bear. They deserved better. They didn't need to see their father's belligerent drunkenness. They didn't need to hear their parents fighting, name-calling, and screaming. What they needed and deserved was a non-hostile environment—a safe refuge filled with love, security, and encouragement. And as their parents, we failed to give them that.

I imagined what our neighbors thought about us whenever uproars detonated through the walls of our apartment.

One evening I found out.

A couple of police officers knocked on our door. I wasn't too surprised, but by then, all was calmed. Donny, in a drunken coma, had passed out.

The cops noticed I'd been weeping; however, I hadn't any visible bruises. I had never pressed charges against my husband before. Call me stupid. But I wasn't going to then either. After some specific questioning, they gathered that I needed help. They asked if the girls and I had any place else to go or relatives close by. Naturally, I thought about fleeing to Miami, but even if we were to get there — then what?

Seeing our substandard living conditions, they handed me a Child Protective Services' calling card. They strongly advised I take the girls in for a routine medical examination in the morning. How many times had my mother dealt with them when I was a kid? I knew there was nothing "routine" when CPS got involved.

Early the next day, I bathed and dressed my girls in their prettiest dresses. I silently brushed their hair into pigtails, making ringlets with my fingers. I listened to their chatter, blinking away tears, and savored the opportunity to admire their beauty and uniqueness.

"Mommy, where we goin'?" Angela asked. "Put dis ribbon in my hair."

"Lookie, Mommy, I can tie my own shoes." Anna Marie grinned.

"Ouchie! Don't pull my hair, Mommy."

"Balloon?" Diana asked, thinking we were going to the store.

"Mommy, are you sad?"

"Your tummy is gettin' big again, Mommy."

I silently prayed for our quick return from CPS.

An hour later, we reluctantly walked into the clinic. There weren't any other kids or parents in sight. I wondered if they had opened just for us. I rang the bell, took a questionnaire to fill out, and plopped in a chair. My girls busied themselves exploring their surroundings, investigating all the toys and the books a-plenty.

The waiting room was kid-friendly but cold like a funeral home. Cushioned chairs lined the walls plastered with billboards regarding child safety laws. Small toys were scattered on the gray linoleum, bookshelves were crammed with picture-books and stuffed animals. A small fish tank rested on the counter, and a yellow Legos table sat in the middle of the room. Above the sign-in window hung a large round clock.

I wanted to flee but rang the bell again.

A petite, white-coated woman emerged behind the counter. She looked outdated, wearing glasses too large for her narrow face, and an exaggerated smile. She held a clipboard in her hand and glanced down, skimming the pages.

"The gang's all here?" she inquired.

I nodded. "Yep."

"Right on time. I will be calling your girls one by one to go into the examining room."

"Do I get to go in, too?" I asked.

She answered with a phony grin. "Won't be necessary." Then, she turned and called in a sing-song voice, "Anna?"

She and Anna Marie disappeared behind the door. I glanced at the clock.

I flipped through pages of a magazine. Diana tossed onto my lap a picture-book she wanted me to read. Glad to occupy some time, I made up the words and pretended to read to her.

Minutes passed before Ms. White-Coat, with her fake smile and tone, returned. Chewing gum, Anna Marie skipped by and joined her sisters.

"Diana. You're next," Ms. White-Coat chirped. Diana glared at her suspiciously, but when White-Coat produced a piece of candy, Diana's face lit up. They vanished behind the door.

My mind scrambled as I paced.

What questions are they asking Diana? She won't understand nor will be able to answer properly. They'll trick her or have her repeat whatever they want her to say. What if they ask if her Mommy ever spanks her? Or takes things away? Or sends her to her room?

I wanted to drill Anna Marie about what Ms. White-Coat had asked, but feared the room might be bugged.

I stared at the clock, unseeing. The second hand turned, and it felt like eternity between each *tick-tock*. I peered out the curtain and watched an ant crawl along the windowsill, carrying a big crumb in its mouth. It looked like far too heavy of a load for such a tiny thing. I could relate.

Diana wasn't kept long. The door burst open, and she scampered out with a balloon in her hand and a grape Blow Pop in her mouth. I smiled. She's no dummy; she got what she wanted. *I hope Diana gave Ms. White-Coat-Goodie-Two-Shoes a run for her money.*

"Okay, I guess we were finished anyway," she said, out of breath. "That leaves you, my dear. Angela, right?"

My baby girl held onto my leg, shielding her face. "Mommy, no," she pleaded.

"It's okay, Angela. Mommy will be right here waiting," I said.

White-Coat held a doll and, in her fake-sweet voice,

coaxed my daughter to going in with her.

    Once the examination ended, another woman came out to talk with me. She introduced herself with a last name I couldn't pronounce. I read her nametag: Gretchen. She told me that the physicals went well. The tests came out *clean* and she saw that my girls were *happy* and that I cared for them. Yet, account of our history of alcohol use and domestic violence, she deemed our home an *unsafe* environment for the girls.

    Here it comes. I held my breath and stared at the floor.

    "We understand your dire straits; however, due to your present condition" — I cradled my belly — "and financial situation, you have expressed you haven't any other place to go. For this reason, we must remove the girls from the home *today* into a more stable and suitable environment."

    A wave of nausea washed over me.

    She rambled on. "Before the girls can return home, you must provide a safe place for them to return to, or . . . if your husband moves . . . ."

    My mind was spinning, and I couldn't focus on her words.

". . . recommendations . . . ,"
". . . counseling . . . ,"
". . . seek professional . . . ,"
". . . proper care . . . ,"
". . . unfit . . . ,"
". . . temporarily . . . ,"
". . . so sorry . . . ,"

    Stability, I thought. *Where were these jokers when I was a child?*

    My baby kicked. I went back to the waiting area, feeling light-headed.

"Girls, Mommy has to go away now." On bended knee, at eye level, I struggled to control my queasiness and hide the devastation in my voice. *This is the darkest day of my life!*

"You will be staying at another place for a short time until you can come back home again" I felt my composure slipping, and didn't want to say too much and alarm them.

"You'll have fun." A tear escaped my eye. "Remember, Mommy loves you so much." I felt I might freak out at any time, bawl in front of them and never stop.

"Give Mommy a kiss. Mommy will see you again soon. I promise."

Anna Marie focused more on the toys in her hands than on what I struggled to convey. She nodded when I gave her a kiss and a tight squeeze. Diana repeated, "Bye-bye," hugging her balloon instead of me.

But my two-year old, Angela, clung to me tightly. She wouldn't let go and began to cry hard. Somehow, she understood. She felt my pain.

After kissing and hugging the girls, I trotted away as quickly as possible, leaving them behind with a CPS worker. Sobbing in the elevator, I couldn't breathe. My heart had been ripped from my chest. I saw black spots, and felt like a drowning child again, greedily grasping for air; but this time, CPS sharks encircled me. I cradled my belly, holding my unborn child in the safety of my womb.

They won't take this one away from me! I was five-and-a-half months pregnant.

I numbly attended a brief court session and had to consent to temporarily relinquishing custody of my daughters to foster care. I went through the motions of that ordeal alone, but my memory of the details remained a blur. When I arrived home to the empty apartment, the quietness jarred me. I imagined my girls' voices and giggles. My head echoed with one resounding thought: what a failure I was.

"Where are the girls?" Donny demanded after he came home and looked around.

"Where do you think they are?" I growled. The look of shock on his face drove me onward with rage. Before he uttered another word, I lashed out, "CPS took them so they can be someplace *safe*. They have a right to a healthy, normal childhood I never had. You're not going take that away from them!" I ran from his sight, locked myself in the bathroom and bawled my eyes out.

"Mary, come on," Donny pleaded. "Whatever it takes, we'll get them back."

He almost sounds like he cares. "Go away."

"You're going to get yourself sick. I promise I'll make it up to you."

"Leave me alone."

"You're going to have to come out sooner or later." His voice trailed away.

"I can't stand you!" I shouted.

But I hated myself even more.

```
October 14, 1981

Dear Grandma,


   There is no joy in this let-
ter. You haven't heard from me
in a while and I know you sense
something isn't right. Even
though miles separate us, God
```

has always given you an extra sense toward me and my household. This blesses me so much! Because I know you pray for us.

Well, things haven't been right for a while. You know by now, my husband has his set of problems. I've tried to hide it, and maybe even protect him. But my thinking I can depend on him has made me fall on my face time after time. It has come to the point to where it isn't just "his" problem but a "family" problem. Because everything he does affects us.

I don't know where to begin. But it boils down to this: our girls are temporarily in foster homes—I pray, no more than two months. In the meantime, Donny is receiving alcohol treatment; there will be therapy and family counseling. I must try to switch into the day shifts at work, and then I will be able to place the girls in a free daycare center that they will provide. The hardest part of this all was taking that first step—and now we must continue to go forward from there. In many ways, Donny has failed, but so have I. I must believe it's not too late to re-do and re-live, and to make amends.

Pray that Donny gets his life in order. That he settles down and comes to his senses. That the Lord will give me the strength to remain by his side and give him what support I can give him . . . that Donny may learn to be the head of our home as God intended for him to be . . . and that we as parents learn the responsibilities involved in raising our children, properly, pleasing to God.

I've always said, even though I didn't have a normal, happy childhood, my kids—including the one in my belly—have a right to have one.

I believe, with God's help, we will be able to give that to them. I've placed it in His hands, and whatever lies in the future.

Hoping to hear from you soon.

Remember I love you. No matter what. ~Mary

Running in Heels: A Memoir of Grit and Grace

CHAPTER 33: BOY, OH BOY!

I MISSED MY girls and longed for the day of their return. I kept myself busy by sorting through their closet, hanging and re-folding their clothes, smelling their scent on their little pillows, re-arranging the toys and dolls in the room they shared.

From early on, Donny always wanted a son. This had now become a strong desire in me as well. Whatever the gender, I believed God had a special plan for my unborn baby. After my ultrasound, they told me the sex. Not wanting to give Donny the satisfaction, I withheld the news from him.

The months whirled by with scheduled, one-hour, weekend visitations with the girls at the CPS center. CPS wouldn't allow visitations at any other location. My girls were split up and lived in three different homes. I never met any of the foster parents.

During those times, the hour hand on the clock flew by. The goodbyes were killing me with each passing week. Anna Marie usually got teary-eyed. The separation didn't faze Diana, one way or another. But my baby girl, Angela, bawled and held onto me with a death grip. She had always been clingy. Donny even declared that she loved me more than she did him. All I knew was that she and I held a special bond.

Back home, my thoughts centered on the coming weekends when I'd be able to hold my girls again and gaze into their lovely brown eyes. Every day, I worked hard at keeping my job as a grocery store clerk, becoming bigger and heavier with child.

Customers came and went, filling their shopping carts to overflowing with food and drinks. I couldn't get over the way many complained about not having enough time in their day to shop for gifts and new outfits for upcoming parties. *At least they have the funds to have those luxuries,* I thought. As I rang up one customer's groceries, I heard her tell another customer that she felt cheated at her in-law's Thanksgiving meal.

"Can you believe there were no mashed potatoes on the table?" she asked.

I hurriedly stacked items into grocery sacks and watched her stuff rolls of cash into her purse, without even offering me a "thank you." Her words echoed in my head: she would prepare her own traditional meal with all the holiday trimmings once she got back home.

There would be no such festive cooking under my roof this season. With the girls gone, the atmosphere in our apartment felt hollow and abandoned. I missed the laughter and chatter.

I trudged on. With the dreaded holidays at last behind, January 4 rolled around, my final day at work.

I continued to write Grandma hoping to persuade her to come and stay with us after the baby was born. And I bitterly watched Donny devise new ways to continue with his drinking and escape detection. *So much for his alcohol treatment.*

Then, I received wonderful news that Grandma would soon arrive from Miami. But not until after she had arranged for the trip did my mother decide that she and Jesse would tag along with her. I welcomed the visit, feeling both relieved and worried. I knew no real help would come from Mama. I anticipated that her bickering would bring out the worst in me.

February 23, 1982

My consciousness slowly swam up through the wooziness of the anesthesia.

"Wake up. You have a healthy, bouncing boy."

Oh boy! A *son*. His hair was fine—golden brown—eyelashes long, lips full, and he had a slight dimple in his chin. Yep, he definitely was all boy. One look at his privates confirmed the obvious. After having three girls, I didn't know what "he" was supposed to feel like. But once his solid bulk cradled in my arms, I *knew*. And I knew what to name him; surprisingly Donny didn't object.

I kissed my son and whispered, "Hello, Daniel Michael. I'm your Mommy."

I shuddered at the thought that months earlier, I might have gone through an abortion. That day God had given me the strength to make the fateful decision not to abort my baby.

This pregnancy was my last, the caboose. I had signed the forms to have my tubes tied. Because I had my babies so close together, the doctor warned me that my uterus might tear in the process. Thank the Lord there weren't complications.

"You did good, honey," Donny crooned, patting my hand. "Thank you for my son."

"Why don't you thank *God*?" I retorted.

Later in my hospital room, the nurse came for Daniel. Donny soon left for the night. Alone, I thought about my household and did the math. Anna Marie, the eldest, was five. Diana and Angela were barely fourteen months apart. My husband was thirty-eight, and I, a frazzled twenty-two-year-old who had baby number four.

I contemplated the future. My marriage had been a journey on a long, difficult, and bumpy road. Without the prayers, love and encouragement from others, we wouldn't have lasted. I remained hopeful, but rough waters were still ahead.

Day Three: Grandma, Mama and five-year-old Jesse visited me at Memorial Southwest. My heart swelled with pride. I heard a hundred questions asked about Daniel as they fussed over him. When my eyes grew heavy, Donny took my visitors to the apartment for them to settle in until my newborn and I returned.

Day Five: The shock of my life. The nurse traipsed in to change my dressing, holding an odd-looking tool that resembled a pair of pliers. She then peeled—with my skin still attached—the wide tape from across my abdomen. When I glanced down, I saw my incisions surgically stapled; however, someone forgot to forewarn me. Seeing the row of tiny metal fragments piercing through my skin, it was difficult for me to refrain from freaking out. I twitched when she cut, pulled, and tugged at each one of those blasted pieces of wire with that instrument.

Hours later, homeward bound. I hoped to enjoy a much-needed rest in my own bed, and to be able to tune out my mother's unending drone.

May as well have hoped for the moon to turn blue.

"Mary," Mama began, "you have to be careful to hold the baby's head . . . "

"Yes, Ma. I know. Not my first—"

"He's still hungry. You see, I used to put cereal in the bottle . . ."

"And that's why Jesse was overweight!" I shot back.

"You shouldn't lay him on his back."

"Well, how else am I gonna change him?"

"Did you burp him?"

"Didn't you see me?"

"This piece of string on his forehead will cure his hiccups."

Calgon, take me away!

After a few days of being home from the hospital, our daughters had their big homecoming. They'd been in foster care for almost five months. We had met all the requirements to have them return to our care. Back home. Where they belonged.

Our small, two-bedroom apartment soon became a whirlwind of activity with the nine of us. Volumes of commotion and excitement filtered through the walls. All gabbed at once. The girls clustered around their new baby brother with glees and giggles, showering him with smooches and snuggles. Each carried suitcases and tote bags packed with extra clothing and toys that had been given to them. Before long, bags toppled over; opened suitcases strewn about, every item taken out for show and tell. My out-of-town visitors brought numerous bags themselves, and oodles of trinkets and gifts for the girls' homecoming reunion.

In no time, activity in the apartment picked up where it had left off months before.

"Owww!" Anna Marie squealed. "Stop pushing! Mommmmy!"

"Girls, did you wash your hands before you touch the baby?" I wearily asked.

"Move, lemme see, too," Angela grumbled.

"All right, one at a time."

"I was here first," Anna Marie retorted.

"No, meeee," Diana whined, followed by a gurgling sniffle.

"Ewwww! Diana, go blow your nose," both girls cried in unison.

Shortly after, a sound like a trumpet's blare carried from the bathroom as Diana blew her nose.

"My turn now," she demanded when she stomped back. "My baby."

Before long, the girls were bouncing off the sofa, walls and ceiling, running with their five-year-old uncle about the place.

"Okay girls, Jesse, enough! The baby has to sleep." *Me too*, I thought.

Soon, quarrels from the kitchen convinced me that Mama still didn't like to cook but liked arguing over what to cook and how to cook.

"It tastes like water," my mother-turned-chef griped. "You need to add more salt."

"Everyone can put more on their own food," Grandma answered.

"That's not the way I saw *Julia Child* do it," Mama insisted.

"Well, do it yourself then, since you always have to criticize."

My mother, so full of opinions, didn't know her way around the stove. Mama's negativism drained me. Her incessant yakking whenever she attacked Grandma grated on my nerves, so much so I often wanted to crawl under a rock. I remembered what the Psalmist wrote: *Oh, if I had wings I would fly away like a dove!*

I felt hot to the touch. By the end of the week, pain from my incision intensified. Each time Grandma came to check in on me, Mama lagged on her coattail—not out of concern or the desire to help, but to hear what *we* were saying. When Grandma returned to the kitchen, Mama followed, continuing her jibber-jabber, nitpicking with Jesse or the girls, directing traffic with "do this," "don't do that," "don't touch that," "leave that alone," "can't you keep still?"

She never offered to lend Grandma a hand with me, the meals, the kids, or in the feeding, bathing and changing of Daniel. Instead, she stood in front of the TV, watching soap operas, making useless comments.

On the last week of their visit, as I rested in bed with Daniel, I heard two-year-old Angela turn on the light in the bathroom so that she could use the "potty." I smiled to myself and thought, *such a proud moment*. With the bathroom door left ajar as Angela was doing her business, Mama barged in and rifled through the medicine cabinet. When she found whatever she needed, she flicked off the bathroom light . . . and bolted.

"Unbelievable," I said to myself, closing my eyes. *Mama has left my child sitting on the potty in the dark!*

"Graaaama! Turn the light on, Gramma," Angela called out in the charming southern drawl she had picked up from her foster parents.

Oblivious to her calls, Mama continued gabbing in the kitchen with my grandma.

"Graaaaama! Turn the light on, Gramma," Angela called, louder still. "Graaaaama—"

I shot straight up in bed and screamed, "Dammit, Mama, can't you hear your granddaughter calling you? You turned off the damn light on her, and now she's sitting in the dark, trying to use the bathroom!"

There I said that, I remember thinking. *I blew a fuse, and I'm sure a stitch or two as well.* "And now," I moaned, "I'm gonna lose my Christianity because of my mama!"

Physically, mentally, and emotionally drained, I lay defeated, wallowing in tears and disgust . . . with myself, with my own mother, with the whole "out of control" dysfunctional feeling.

Donny arrived home from work and rushed me to the emergency room. For that moment, he was my hero.

My incision was red and hot to the touch. The doctor announced that the infected area had begun to re-open. He prescribed extra-strength antibiotics, complete bed rest and quiet.

Rest and quiet. Are you kidding me?

My visitors stayed for one month. As much as I wanted my grandmother to remain with us longer, I knew she couldn't. She promised to return solo next time.

I figured Mama wouldn't come again anyway; her hands were full with Jesse. He was Mama's baby; she had him at the age of forty-three. His father, George, lived a discontented life, drifting here and there, boasting that he couldn't be tied down; he was his own man. Willie was living in a boys' home, so Mama tended to little Jesse, who needed her. He tugged at her heartstrings. As lonely as she was, I believe she needed him, too.

At two, Jesse had been a chunky boy. Mama still fed him milk from a bottle, often thickened with baby cereal. When she decided to put her foot down and not give in to his demands, he threw a fit—tossing the empty bottle across the room, barely missing her. As usual, she relented and gave the bottle back to him filled with milk. Once, when Mama swatted him on his bottom, he tearfully regarded her and wailed, "I thought you loved me!" Now, at five years old, Jesse never got whacked, even when he needed it.

Lost in my thoughts one evening, as I put baby Daniel to bed, I wondered what manner of young man he'd become. *Will I spoil him? Cater to his every whim? Or allow him to learn from his mistakes? Will I be able to look him in the eye? Show him right from wrong? Will he become responsible? Loving? Respectable? Will I be able to love him enough to let go?*

I silently prayed for wisdom, and pushed a strand of golden-brown hair from Daniel's forehead. I loved the different shades of light brown in his curly coif—so different from the black hair of his parents and sisters.

"His hair . . ." Donny warned, interrupting my thoughts, invading my heart, "had better turn dark."

Running in Heels: A Memoir of Grit and Grace

Mary A. Pérez

CHAPTER 34: ON BORROWED TIME

I JOLTED AWAKE from a sound sleep on the recliner to someone banging. *They'll wake Daniel from his nap!* I glanced at the clock and wondered why Donny hadn't come home for lunch yet. Before I answered, someone yelled out my name. When I swung the door open, Sergio, the apartment complex painter, stood with a terrified look on his face.

"*¡Andale, Señora!*" Sergio motioned for me to follow. "Your husband is . . . *no bueno!*"

"What's that?" My legs automatically moved as I followed him down the stairs. When we exited the building, I noticed a crowd hovering around the corner from my complex. Someone lay on the ground, someone who had fallen or gotten hurt—

Donny!

Shocked and in disbelief, I ran and dropped to my knees by his side. Donny's eyes rolled back, revealing the whites. His head swayed from side to side. Deep grunting noises escaped through clinched jaws. His entire body thrashed about on the hard concrete. His stomach heaved in and out. Choking, he coughed up blood. I lifted his head. Someone had jammed a pencil in his mouth so that he wouldn't bite down on his tongue, but he'd bitten the pencil in two.

"Donny! Donny!" I cried, but he couldn't hear me. I

rubbed his arm, whispering the name of Jesus in his ears.

My eyes traveled across the crowd that had swarmed around, their curious faces peering down at us. "What happened?" I demanded.

"Dun know what to think, Miss," Sergio answered in broken English.

I glanced up, waiting for more details, but he stood wringing his cap in his hands and said nothing.

"*¿Qué más?*" I blurted out.

"We walkeen, *pero* he estopet to hold onto somteen . . . ," Sergio uttered.

"Yes, yes, go on," I broke in.

"*Y entonces*, I asket him, 'Somteens' matter?' *Pero*, you know *Señor* Don, he say, 'no, it's noteen.' Then, he jest fall *aquí* . . . hit head, *pero muy duro*. I jell for help."

"Has anyone called an ambulance?" I cradled the back of Donny's neck. My hand felt warm and wet, sticky with blood. Donny began to jerk his head from side to side.

"*Sí Señora*," Sergio nodded. "We do dis."

"So where are they? Why don't they come?" I didn't understand all that happened, but I knew that Donny needed medical attention. Now.

Petrified and helpless, I shot up prayers. *Not this, Lord. Not this.*

"We take him *ahora*, Miss. Put him in *mi troque*."

My girls weren't home from school yet. I thanked an elderly neighbor who volunteered to look after them. Soon a van backed up toward us. The rear doors slammed opened. Four men got out and my heart skipped a beat as I watched them hoist Donny into the back of the van. I jumped in beside him.

"*¡Vamanos pronto!* Let's go, hurry!" I cried.

Only when we pulled away did the nosey spectators disperse.

Caught in mid-day traffic, I thought we'd never get to Memorial Southwest Emergency. When we arrived, the men reached for Donny to carry him out. That's when he came to, with his fists swinging. His wide gaze flickered with panic. He had the look of a wild man. I'm sure he didn't know who these strangers were or what they were trying to do. I called his name, hoping he'd recognize my voice. Not until his eyes refocused did he become semi-coherent.

The men helped put Donny on a gurney and a hospital attendant rolled him through the doors. I followed closely behind. A balding doctor stopped me to go over a list of routine questions:

"Has your husband been in an accident?"

"I'm . . . not sure. I know he fell."

"Is he allergic to anything?"

"I don't think so."

The doc nodded to himself. "How old is your husband?"

"Thirty-nine."

He nodded again. "When was his last physical?"

"Possibly . . . a year ago."

The doctor eyeballed me, adjusting his eyeglasses. "Is he on any medication?"

"No." I turned to where they had taken him.

"Did you see what happened?"

"It looked like he was having a seizure or something."

Doc looked down and scribbled on his pad. "What time did this incident occur?"

"Maybe fifteen, twenty minutes ago."

"Does your husband take any drugs?" he asked narrowing his eyes.

"Of course not! I mean . . . well . . . he drinks. And he has one kidney." I thought we'd never get to where they were treating Donny. "Please, I need to see my husband."

I followed an assistant across the long, fluorescent-lit hallway. Groans came from a patient in a room nearby. My skin crawled.

The nauseating odor of antiseptic permeated the hallway. I imagined doctors probing and poking Donny behind the drawn curtains. I couldn't shake the dreadful image of him looking like a corpse only moments before.

What if?

A dozen X-rays later of Donny's head, neck and chest still didn't satisfy the doctor. He ordered more tests.

They think he took drugs.

Except for the after-effects—a throbbing head and a deep bleeding gash—Donny's fall remained a total blank to him. He remembered nothing.

After some time, I mentioned to a nurse that we couldn't afford a large hospital bill and that my husband was a veteran. Soon afterward, an ambulance transported us to the VA Hospital for hours of further testing and evaluation.

The VA doctor pushed the curtain aside and scurried to another area. Donny lay dressed in a hospital gown, his eyes burning with dread and apprehension. He looked stricken and pasty from all the convulsing. Dry heaves were forcing him to spit in a basin that he held with one hand, while gripping the guardrail with the other. His hands, once so powerful and steady with their beefy knuckles, now trembled and shook with each task.

I turned away and prayed: *Lord, please drill into his head the severity of this. Have him realize that alcoholism is a choice—his choice. Have him see the bigger picture: he must stop drinking . . . before it's too late.*

The doctor finally emerged from behind a door across the hall. His rubber-soled shoes squeaked across the floor as he made his way toward us. He began to read disquieting jargon from the chart in his hands. Fears swarmed my head as I struggled to follow his prognosis. His eyes bore down on mine while he mentioned something about the second stage of alcoholism. *Or did he say the third?*

" . . . your husband's body went through withdrawals," the doctor's voice faded in and out, " . . . convulsions . . . DT seizure . . . "

Seizure? My mind went back to days gone by in what had become routine. I recalled the numerous "heebie-jeebies" (Donny's terminology for whenever he had the shakes). When that happened, he'd "nurse" his condition by downing a "cold one" before heading out.

This morning, however, he drank nothing.

The doctor went on to explain the meaning of DT. He said that because Donny skipped his usual morning swig, he had a detox seizure. From what I understood, Donny's body screamed for alcohol like a drug addict screamed for a fix.

I struggled to comprehend why this was happening now. "On occasion," I began, "My husband puts himself 'on the wagon' and doesn't touch a drop of liquor or beer for days, or even weeks." I blinked back tears. "And nothing like this ever happened before," I added, avoiding Donny's gaze. The stern set to his face warned that I was saying too much.

The doctor nodded his head. "Understand . . . ," he began cautiously, "this is the severe stages of alcoholism." He turned to Donny and warned, "It is imperative that you stay off the juice. With one kidney, you are at the point of your life where you need professional help that requires close supervision. We have an excellent program here, but it takes weeks to monitor daily habits and activities, provide education, counseling...."

Donny lay with arms crossed, brooding. "I can't just stop working."

"Sir," the doctor said sharply, "there are high risks here and there are no other alternatives. I recommend that you get specialized help and begin treatment here. But this is entirely your decision."

I needed to make him understand.

"Donny . . . you need to do *something*," I pleaded. "You could have easily died today. You don't have control."

He pursed his lips and kept silent. I dared not say more.

After a number of sutures and further examinations, we wearily returned home at three in the morning.

The next day about twenty neighbors and friends visited, all wanted to know what had happened. I knew how to gloss-over Donny's true condition by stating that he merely needed to rest. He did so by taking antibiotics and a pill to help him remain docile while not drinking.

A week later, Donny returned to the VA for a physical, a neurology test and more meds. Even though they had a wonderful alcohol treatment program, Mr. Pull-Yourself-Up-by-the-Bootstraps refused to become an in-patient. Instead, he opted to receive treatment as an out-patient and take a disulfiram called Antabuse. That tiny pill wasn't a cure for alcoholism but supposedly made one violently ill if he drank alcohol after taking it.

Donny had to avoid using aftershave, cologne, or mouthwash. He couldn't eat anything that contained alcohol. Period.

Thankfully, weeks went by with some measure of peace. I monitored my husband daily, while he took his medication before he stepped out the door. But I couldn't shake off the thought that in a matter of time he'd tire of the whole accountability thing, or somehow blame me if it didn't work.

"Woman, are you trying to kill me?" Donny blurted out over the phone. *Now what is he talking about? Trying to kill him, indeed! If I was trying to —*

"The *lunch* you made me! You packed a Sarah Lee pound cake in there, right?"

"Yeah? So what?"

"The cake . . . has *vanilla extract* in it!" Donny shouted. I held the phone away from my ear.

"They had to rush me to the emergency room today," he screamed. "Out in the field, I thought I was having a heat stroke or heart attack or dying or something. I couldn't breathe. Felt hot and dizzy and started throwing up!"

That's when I realized I had neglected to read the ingredients on the package. The cake included vanilla extract that had *alcohol* . . . enough to make Donny ill on Antabuse.

Lesson learned.

Days overlapped one another and I found myself having to remind Donny to take his daily pill. Then he began taking them in intervals. That way when the weekends rolled around, the Antabuse's effect would have worn off and he could resume drinking his bottle of vodka to his heart's content. I felt I was fighting a losing battle.

I couldn't compete with *that* mistress.

Running in Heels: A Memoir of Grit and Grace

Mary A. Pérez

CHAPTER 35: MRS. C

WE AFFECTIONATELY CALLED her Mrs. C. In her sixties, with remarkable zeal, she possessed a charismatic and a gregarious personality. She was a Bible teacher, an author, a missionary, a powerhouse, a woman of great faith. She exuded genuine friendship in a Godly persona and took me under her wings. She held many prayer meetings in her home, and often prostrated herself on the floor on her face interceding on the behalf of others. She became my lifesaver, my spiritual mother. Throughout the years, I counted on her for spiritual advice and much-needed counseling.

On one dreary afternoon, the sky, along with my hope and faith, grew overcast. Suffering from battle fatigue, I sat in Mrs. C's den. I told her I was sick and tired of being sick and tired.

"I can't take it anymore," I confessed, wringing my hands.

Patiently, unassuming, and non-judgmental, Mrs. C handed me a tissue and gave me time to release the dread and pain in my heart.

"I've tried everything. Done all I know to do. Yet nothing seems good enough."

"Has he stopped hitting you?"

I sighed, much relieved that he had. "Oh, yes."

"Mary Ann, you know he loves you, in his own way," she

began, "but you have become 'weary in well-doing.' In your mind's eye, you've conceded it's not worth it."

She honed in on my sentiments. I hung my head in shame.

"You *know*," she insisted, "it *is* worth it all."

At that moment, I wished I were stronger and smarter and that Mrs. C wasn't so wise and couldn't read me so well. "But shouldn't this be a two-way street?" I suggested.

"Are you and the kids better off without him?"

I figured she knew the answer before I did. "We . . . we have nowhere else to go."

"Are you better off without him?" she repeated, and handed me the tissue box.

"I can't afford to do anything else."

"Are you better off without him?"

No," I whispered and wiped my nose.

I felt weak, inadequate as a Christian wife, struggling to maintain a measure of peace and sanity in my household with four children, tending to a man wrestling with his demons.

"Then, go home and be the best wife and mother you know how to be," she said.

Sometimes, it's easier to talk the talk than to walk the walk.

"But first," she added, "I want to pray for you."

That woman knew how to enter the Throne Room of God in her prayers. Electricity surged through my entire body when she touched me as she prayed. Before I left, she handed me her book, *Wives, Unequally Yoked*. I figured reading couldn't hurt; plus, the title intrigued me. I'd already devoured *The Total Woman*, by Marabel Morgan, the pages worn and underlined with yellow marker, much like my Bible.

I didn't leave Mrs. C's company the same way I arrived. Resolved in my heart not to become bitter, I determined to be better and left strengthened, with a made-up mind.

Mrs. C suggested that I study a passage in the Bible that read: "In the same way, you wives, be submissive to your own husbands so that even if any of them are disobedient to the Word, they may be won without a word by the behavior of their wives, as they observe your chaste and respectful behavior."

I had to admit this wasn't easy. I'd used my tongue as a weapon more times than I cared to count and didn't know if I could keep my mouth shut. But with renewed determination, I worked on dropping the holier-than-thou attitude and praying for my husband more. This time, I prayed not that my life might become easier, but that Donny might become whole: physically, spiritually, and emotionally.

Running in Heels: A Memoir of Grit and Grace

CHAPTER 36: FROM THE INSIDE OUT

"YOU PROMISED."
"Me plenty vex, ya know."
"When are you gonna quit drinking?"
"Gimme time, woman." Donny slurred.
Time? Hadn't I given him my youth?
Seven years of my life?
Four children?

Three months' time passed in cycles. Donny's use of Antabuse turned out to be a ridiculous fiasco. He went from taking a daily dose to taking the prescription sporadically—a premeditated plan for the next drink—especially when weekends rolled around. Three steps forward and two steps back; Donny wasn't fooling anyone but himself.

At times, I felt like the bigger *pendeja*. I thought he had gotten that hairy wart off his back. But I came to the conclusion that if he was ever going to get genuine help in beating alcoholism, he first needed to admit that he had a drinking problem. Second, he needed to accept help from a power greater than himself—beyond himself—to change for good. He had tried repeatedly on his own and failed each time. Nothing came easy.

❖ ❖ ❖

Another blackout. I lost count on how many there had been. I still endured the cheap shots, the name-calling, and the lunges he made toward me. If he hadn't stumbled or fallen, there is no telling what damage he'd have done to me. Of course, Donny continually denied his behavior, even when presented with evidence. Like the time when I took him to the closet and pointed to the ruined clothes and stained carpet. He looked grim, silent.

"Still think I'm making this up?" I said, pointing to the evidence, still damp.

"I can't believe—"

"And," I shot back, "you tried to choke me in your sleep, again."

A couple of weeks later, Donny stumbled in with brows furrowed over bloodshot eyes. "I'm ready," he slurred. "*Now.*"

My heart dropped to my feet. Hadn't he tried to go on the wagon to dry out before? But after a dry spell, the sickness and the shakes always brought him to his knees. Then, he'd break down and drink again.

"You hear me, woman?" he said, swaying, his face pale. "Close your mouth and let's go!" He tossed me the keys, grabbed his can of Copenhagen, and headed for the door, adding, "Before I change my mind."

"Yes, yes, I heard you, Donny. Wait up," I said, slipping on my tennis shoes. "I'm shocked, that's all."

"Well, it's time, and I know when I'm licked."

At last, an admission. *An answered prayer.* After arranging for our neighbor to watch the kids, I drove Donny to the VA Hospital.

That night alone in my bed, I felt a tiny sliver of hope and

I wept with relief.

The next day, the apartment manager looked both surprised and delighted when I told her that Donny started treatment. I was stunned when she said, "Mary Ann, he's a good man; he just got a lot of baggage." She patted my hand and continued, "And you are such a strong, young lady. Now dear, don't you worry about the rent. You take care of your family. I know Don is a fine handy man. He can do some repairs around here when he gets out."

February 1983

Four weeks had passed since a tired and torn Donny had admitted himself into the VA Hospital. In the visitors' lounge, we watched our curly-locked, eleven-month old son tottering down the hallway, his sisters giggling, skipping after him.

My husband looked sharp, the tremors gone. Determination to beat his demons was etched on his face. His eyes danced as he shared with me his daily activities, which included counseling sessions, group discussions, and AA Meetings. He spoke of his extracurricular activities: crafts, woodshop, oil-painting-by-numbers, ping-pong matches, and board games.

"They even have an indoor pool and a bowling lane here." Donny chuckled. "We eat plenty and drink all the cans of Sustacal we want throughout the day."

Those balanced beverages, filled with nutrition, helped replace the sugars from the alcohol he once consumed. They tasted like milkshakes.

My husband beamed and continued, "We have church services, too. I'm reading the Bible you bought me."

I felt God smiling down on that one.

On Valentine's Day, I baked a couple of homemade, heart-shaped chocolate cakes and took them to the VA. On one, I wrote in pink icing, "Jesus Loves You" and on the other, "Free In '83."

A month later — after nine lingering weeks — Donny came home. Without warning, he hugged me.

"I always wanted to thank you for sticking by my side, woman," he murmured.

My heart turned topsy-turvy.

Donny did a great deal of work for the apartment manager and that kept him busy. Within a couple of weeks, he landed a new job with a construction company that did mostly insurance repair work. He quickly climbed the ladder, becoming the *el jefe*, head honcho there. He gained respect, completed major renovation projects and gained much favor. When it came to work, he was gifted, having a photographic mind. Soon he earned the title of general superintendent. He told others what to do and demanded perfection. Everyone wanted Donny as a friend and team member. They knew he wouldn't hesitate to give them the shirt off his back.

Of course, many — even those he worked closely with — didn't know the "old" Don with the drinking problems and a wandering eye. I cringed whenever someone offered him a drink or gave him a bottle of booze for a holiday gift. I was both relieved and proud when he declined the offer, or dumped the contents down the drain when we were alone.

Although Donny was becoming a workaholic, working long weekdays and late weekends, things were far better than they had ever been. Our house became a home. I had a responsible husband and the children a reliable daddy. When we attended counseling together with Mrs. C, I believed my husband was turning into a new man inside and out; his rough demeanor started to soften. I no longer flinched whenever he came close after a disagreement.

Still, I had yet to get used to the "new" man, as he turned forty. The Bible says, *love conquers all.* I believed with all my heart it had been worth it.

Part 3

Back home with newborn Daniel, and happily re-united with my girls, Anna Marie, Diana and Angela. Their little uncle Jesse wanted to sit in for this shot.

Mary A. Pérez

CHAPTER 37: TRANSITION

WHILE DONNY WAS still in the VA Hospital, a wonderful family of five frequently invited the children and me to their home. Susan and I knew each other from church. Her husband—Fred—born and raised in Germany—made me feel comfortable. After Donny completed treatment, they invited us over for dinner. Our husbands finally met. We all shared a delicious meal and the men engaged in small talk.

My husband, the pursuer, sought after Fred's friendship, offering his help with carpentry projects. They quickly hit it off and talked among themselves freely. They spent most weekends on Fred's aluminum boat fishing or hanging out at his lake house. They knew the struggles of alcohol and often shared stories about the victories and failures during their alone time. They discussed work, God, or family matters. Sometimes they simply shared a comfortable silence. Their understanding and respect for each other grew.

Friendships blossomed. Bonds strengthened.

We wives were pleased. Susan and I often shared laughter mingled with tears as we prayed for our husbands, our children, and our community. We shared a common goal: We wanted so much more unity in our home. We celebrated as our families shared meals, barbecues, beach outings, and church activities.

Soon after, another remarkable friendship developed. Donny met Ronnie, one of the sweetest men I knew, married to Carolyn, the sweetest woman I knew. Known for being a "completed-Jew," Ronnie loved Jesus and shared the love of Christ with others. Not one to reserve his affection, Ronnie never shied away from giving Donny a couple of his bear hugs whenever they crossed paths. I believe that since Donny had no siblings, Ronnie's warmth filled a void in him and made Ronnie the big brother he never had. There wasn't anything one wouldn't do for the other.

Donny had always been a giver, but spending time with Ronnie taught him true compassion. My husband had a heart after all, and he had begun allowing others to see it.

Carolyn assured me that Ronnie was also learning from Donny about the willingness to take risks. Our husbands were worlds apart, like salty pretzels and sugar cookies. To our amazement, we saw them caring for and loving the other as true brothers in Christ.

It's been said that God works in mysterious ways. While watching Donny's uncommon friendships with a German and a Jew, bonds that would last a lifetime, I witnessed a feat that God alone could accomplish.

A year later, Donny surprised me by driving home in a blue Chevy Citation X-11. "My gift to you for putting up with me for the past ten years," he said. That same summer, we rented a van to head out to Miami on a mini-vacation. We planned to visit Grandma, then living with my mama and little Jesse in a run-down trailer that needed many repairs. Donny brought along his carpentry tools.

As expected, we found the place cramped, untidy and stuffy. Grandma had warned us about the "messy" condition, and that she received no help from Mama. At first sight of the place, a flood of unpleasant memories poured in on me. But since we were there to uplift and encourage my grandma, I determined to remain focused on the mission at hand.

Donny completed several household repairs: the floors, the plumbing, and the rotted walls. He tinkered with broken appliances and whatever else needed attention. Known for having a green thumb, he worked in her neglected garden, cut the overgrown shrubs, and even fixed the lawnmower to mow the yard.

Over the next couple of days, the children spent some long-overdue, quality time visiting their grandpa and Gloria in their home. While my daddy played games with them, scenes replayed in my mind of when I was a youngster and he used to play with me until I squealed with giggles. Daddy loved children and didn't mind becoming one himself. Watching him then with my small stair-steppers made me laugh with tears of joy, and I realized how terribly I had missed him.

He had a new above-ground pool in his backyard. The kids, which included my now teenage sister and brother, did somersaults, flip-flops, and hold-your-breath-under-the-water contests, and played Marco-Polo. Donny barbecued chicken and steaks on Daddy's grill and Gloria served her famous *arroz con gandules*.

We visited my paternal grandparents. My grandpa was *Don Angel* (pronounced "Annhel"), and my grandma, *Doña María*. Upon our arrival, we politely greeted them the way Daddy had taught us to, by asking for their blessing in Spanish:

"¿*Bedición?*"

"*¡Dios te bendiga!*" they answered, opening their arms, smothering us with bear hugs and wet kisses.

Abuelo was born in 1908 and *Abuela* in 1907. Both were born in Utuado Puerto Rico and married in their early twenties, ultimately having ten children. *Abuela* stayed home attending to her brood while *Abuelo* supported his family as a farmer. (Rumor has it he made a little Moon Shine too). On twenty-five acres, he tended to bananas, tobacco and coffee crops. He raised chickens and goats and even owned cows that he milked.

Daddy favored *Abuelo*; everyone said those two could be brothers. While there, I got to visit with my four aunts and a couple of uncles, and met a number of cousins for the first time; again—all on my daddy's side of the clan. They all had animated personalities, sharing savory family recipes, hilarious stories and laughter in full volume.

The next morning back in Grandma's trailer, the ambiance was much more somber. Although my past with Mama still existed as a painful memory, the entire week that Donny and I scrubbed house helped to ease the pain I carried. Each spick-and-span corner and repaired pipe in that dreary trailer helped unclog the hurt and mend the wounds.

That weekend, as we cruised along Florida's Turnpike, my children were napping in the back. Donny sat silently at the wheel, concentrating on the road ahead. Music played softly on the radio. I lay my head back and closed my eyes. Before I dosed off, my thoughts centered on *familia*. I relished the love and the bonding between all my relatives— those in Miami and those in the car near me as we drove home to Houston—more than I ever imagined possible.

Mary A. Pérez

Moving On Up

We needed bigger wheels for our clan, so we decided to hunt around for a used van. After walking the car lot and feeling disappointed, our eyes zeroed in on a new full-size, 1985 Dodge Ram Van. It came fully loaded, with four captain chairs and a rear seat that opened into a bed. We traded in my car. As we drove home, the children jammed to a Christian hip-hop rapper named *D-Boy* on our new cassette tape player.

A couple of months later, to my horror, we found the driver-side window of the van busted. Past the shattered glass, we noticed wires dangling from the steering-column. Someone had tried to hot-wire the ignition. The person either didn't know what he was doing or was frightened away.

We knew we needed to move to a better neighborhood.

A realtor friend had the perfect house in mind, one situated in the ideal location—on Pecan Meadow Drive. She took us on a walk-through. We immediately fell in love with the wall-to-wall carpeted, one-and-a-half story house—with its high ceilings, four large bedrooms, walk-in closets, three baths, an opened loft, and fireplace. A cedar-fenced-in yard with a covered patio added to the curb appeal. My gang loved seeing an inviting playground down our block that included swings and a slide. Even more to my delight, our subdivision sat in a wonderful elementary school district.

Days later, when we signed the papers to lease the house with the "option-to-buy," I felt the kiss of heaven upon us. For once, I believed that my children could live a life I never had.

I loved my kitchen with its cinnamon oak cabinetry. I pictured us having meals around a grand dining room table, looking through the oversized window to a well-manicured yard. Since all the bedrooms were spacious, we decided to make the one upstairs the master. Yes, for once, we could all spread out and enjoy some comfort in this 2,074 square foot home.

Children grow fast. All you have to do is blink. You'll wonder where the time flies. Cherish those moments. This sketch drawn by yours truly, May 1986.

I wasn't used to living in such roomy quarters. I found myself worrying that if danger arose, I may not be able to see, hear, or reach my kids in time.

The week we settled in our new home, an electrical storm rattled the windows and my sense of security. The rolling thunder and flashes of lightning, accompanied by gusts of wind, made me jittery. They reminded me of hurricanes during my childhood in Miami.

When morning came, Donny, usually the first one up, didn't find me asleep next to him. When he got out of bed, he discovered the children and me on the hallway floor in a nest of blankets, pillows, stuffed animals and favorite toys, away from the windows in the house. His loud snort awakened me. The kids slept on as I got up to start breakfast, wishing to wipe that all-too-familiar, smug expression off Donny's face.

The days were generally good ones. I visited neighborhood garage sales and found my dream dining room table: an ornate clawfoot table with eight matching upholstered chairs.

My husband worked hard and steadily and no longer drank. He planted a vegetable garden, spent more quality time with the children and joined me in taking them to church. Together we attended Christian entertainment shows such as *The Power Team* and *Carmen* concerts when they came to town.

I had great plans for our kids. Diana, Angela, and Daniel were involved in soccer, gymnastics, and violin. Anna Marie took piano and guitar lessons. One morning, she got the surprise of her life when Donny had a driver deliver a new, upright piano to the door. Private piano lessons in our home soon became part of Anna Marie's routine.

I wanted to do something for myself. That autumn, I took a GED class in the evenings and pored over my textbooks. After three months, I completed the course. My heart swelled with pride the day my certificate arrived in the mail. I couldn't wait to show Donny.

"What are you going to do with that thing?" he snorted. "Hang it on the wall?"

His words, laced with sarcasm, snapped like a rubber band. Before the ink on my certificate had dried, I stashed my GED away in a drawer.

Meanwhile, my grandma kept me abreast of her five chaotic years since she had moved in with Mama and Jesse. But her health was failing. When Mama and I talked on the phone, I pleaded with her to ask for Grandma's forgiveness for the ill treatment and the harsh criticism she had caused her to endure over the years.

"Because, Mama, if you don't," I cautioned, "you'll only have regrets and then it'll be too late to do anything."

"I love my mother," she confessed.

"I know you do."

"I should have told her more often."

"Yes, but she knew. Let go of 'should've, could've, would've.' Ma, tell her how you feel *now*."

Before we hung up, my mother assured me she would have that talk.

I couldn't bear the thought of losing my beloved grandma. She had been more like a mother to me. She was truly a Godly, unselfish human being. She suffered so much, mentally and physically. While my grandpa had always taken great care of her, after his passing, Grandma hadn't a soul to depend on. Yet she never stopped doing good deeds for others.

When my grandma talked about buying a mobile home for her and Mama to live in together, I balked at the idea — and for good reason. When the trailer started falling into disrepair, Grandma quickly ran low on resources, both physically and financially. Even so, she continually tried to clean and organize to make the place livable. Every day she stood over a hot stove, preparing meals for my mom, little Jesse and herself — even after her own health deteriorated.

Grandma often spoke with Mama regarding her illness, insisting she wanted to be at home and not in a hospital when the time came for her to die.

I prayed that when God took my grandma home, He would help me to relinquish her. I didn't want Grandma to suffer anymore but still found the letting go difficult. I knew I had to, I knew I needed to, but I didn't know how or if I could.

A horrific day for our country. In shock, I watched the Space Shuttle *Challenger* break apart and burn just seconds into its flight. Five men and two women tragically lost their lives for the good of all humanity. They lived their dream by serving others. I may not have known them personally, but they died as heroes.

Three months later, on April 3, 1986, sickness reduced an eighty-eight-year-old unsung Puerto Rican woman to skin and bones as she lost her bout with cancer. She wasn't affluent. Refined. Or famous. But she was loved. Adored. And my heroine.

When Mama called me and told me about Grandma's final moments, sobs stuck in my throat. She expressed how she had sat at my grandma's bedside, terrified, while listening to her breathing in short, laborious rasps.

"Your grandma's parting words were, 'God is calling me now,' and then she gazed up at the ceiling." Mama spoke dolefully. "So, I asked her, 'How do you know?' But she didn't speak anymore. She closed her eyes and I held her close."

My mother's trembling voice was broken by sobs. "I . . . told her that I loved her. And I said to her, 'you carried me for nine months.'"

I pictured that heart-rending image of Grandma's gentle countenance and Mama struggling to convey her love to her. And I thought, Oh Mama, she carried you longer than nine months. My insides ached, knowing that in her heart and prayers, Grandma carried us all.

My grief came in waves. Looking back, I know God spared me from becoming hopelessly morbid and consumed with anguish. Grandma wouldn't have wanted that. Knowing she no longer suffered, I believed her final heartbeat didn't mean the end but the beginning.

I wanted to celebrate her life when I journeyed back to help with her memorial.

Once a plump woman, Grandma had lost so much weight in her final days. She had always loved a simple white Easter dress that belonged to me and requested that when the time came we'd bury her in it. My dress fitted her perfectly then. I also asked that everyone wear white instead of the customary black garments at her funeral.

White carnations—Grandma's favorite—covered her opened casket. I stood, my eyes caressing her still face, now so thin. Vivid images of her life jumped in my thoughts. I saw her on her knees pleading to God to be merciful to her loved ones. I recalled her many prayers of gratitude for another day. I pictured her lips mouthing words as she read her Bible, with her index finger pointing to the sentences across the worn pages. I could still hear the sound of her soft voice calling my name. I remembered the merriment of her laughter after listening to one of my silly jokes. Hot tears blinded me and I couldn't blink them away.

In my mind's eye, Grandma came to me.

I could hear her.

Feel her.

Touch her.

Her love, her hugs, her kisses embraced me.

We honored her memory and her passing from this life into the next.

A gentle breeze blew the heat of day; the sun hid behind the clouds. The scent of rain permeated the air.

As it started to drizzle, my heart comforted. Grandma always considered it a good omen if it rained on the day someone laid to rest.

Before long, her coffin lay in a crypt next to her cherished husband, my grandpa.

At last, Grandma's labors had ended. Thank God, she hurt no more.

Mary A. Pérez

CHAPTER 38: *MAMA MÍA*

"I WAS BORN *where*?"
"I told you, Mary . . . Bellevue Hospital."
"But, Mama, why *Bellevue*?" I asked. "Isn't that a hospital for *crazy* people?"
Old suspicions of being switched at birth suddenly flared back to life. "Is there something you're leaving out?"
"No, no," Mama tossed back. "Your father worked in the hospital kitchen washing dishes. With you born there, he figured that way he'd see you every day and be near."
"Lord, have mercy! Mama, are you *sure*?"
"Yes, Mary." She cackled. "You know, when they brought you to me, I was so tired. You were more than eight pounds. Your head was too heavy . . . ," Her thoughts wandered off. "Did I tell you about the time I almost dropped you . . . ?" And she rambled on . . .

After Grandma's passing, we took nine-year-old Jesse to live with us in Houston. Mama had a rough time staying alone in the trailer after that. She couldn't sleep and she wasn't eating right. She grew fearful and kept thinking she heard something, saw something, or felt something. She left lights on in every room.

"We can send for her," Donny suggested.

"It won't be so easy for me, Donny. It'll be like opening up old wounds."

"You'll be fine."

But I wasn't convinced I'd be 'fine.' I feared facing Mama. She always had a way of stirring up negative emotions in me, emotions I would rather have left buried and forgotten. I didn't want to feel like I took a step forward and two backwards.

A couple of months later, we sent for her by plane in the hopes that she'd get some rest and sanity in our home.

"What are you going to do at your daughter's house?" a neighbor had asked her.

"Sleep for three weeks," Mama answered.

She arrived like a lost sheep, frightened and unsure of herself. I wanted to make her feel welcome and comfortable. At least in my home, things were more orderly and cleaner than what she was accustomed to, even with five rambunctious children that included Jesse.

Donny enjoyed cooking and received plenty of praises and adoration.

"It's all so good," Mama would say with eyes wide at the spread before her.

"You sure do like to eat," Donny teased.

"Well, I just don't know when I'll eat like this again."

Mama's appetite was enormous. I recall Grandma saying of Mama that she never cared to learn how to cook, but when it came to food, she could sure eat like a man. In her later years, I guess Mama never forgot what it felt like to go hungry. I knew I never would, remembering myself as a child, hungry enough then to steal cold cuts meant to feed stray cats.

After dinner, Mama and I went into the living room. She sat on the recliner.

I wanted to share an article with her. "Hey, Ma," I said and plopped on the ottoman. "Let me read something to you."

"Oh, okay," she chirped.

I started reading aloud. But by the third paragraph, when I glanced up, her head hung, her mouth gaped. Mama had dozed off in the middle of my reading. For one reason or another, it had always been difficult to share anything pertinent with her. I tiptoed out.

That evening we sat in the park watching the children play. I had been contemplating whether I should return to work but knew I lacked proper skills. I turned to Mama hoping for some insight and asked if she ever held a long-term job.

"Oh, I did a bit of housekeeping and the groceries for some people."

"Ever work for a company? You know, clocked in, clocked out?" I asked.

"Well, I worked as a finisher in a clothing factory for eight months. After the seamstress completed her work, I was supposed to cut the threads sticking out of fabrics"

I chuckled because Mama had a habit of fetching scissors whenever she saw a dangling *hilo* from materials. "But why only eight months, Ma?" I pressed.

"Oh, I don't know. Guess I wasn't needed any longer."

"Any other jobs?"

"Well, I worked three months at another factory."

"Doing what?" I asked.

"After they finish sewing doilies that covered furniture, I folded and boxed them."

"What happened that you worked there for only three months?"

"Someone did something wrong and when the boss questioned me, I wouldn't squeal. So he fired me."

As I watched the kids on the merry-go-round, I thought about how incredible it was that my mother had only held two jobs in her lifetime, for a combined total of eleven measly months.

I remembered a conversation I'd had with Grandma about Mama's education.

"Your mother was a fair student," Grandma had mentioned. "She never put much effort in her studies." She also said she believed that Mama suffered with an inferiority complex, even before she left home to marry my father at twenty-two. "She didn' finish her third year high school," Grandma had explained. "*Asi que*, I paid for her to go to a special business class to learn typin' and secretarial work."

"So she has office skills," I replied, surprised.

"*O sí, pero*, when they sent her to work in an office she was too afraid to go by herself."

"What?" I was shocked. "Let me guess. She didn't want to go without you, right?"

"*Imagínite*," Grandma said and laughed. "She wanted me to go with her, but naturally the instructor said no. So, this was the end."

Grandma's eyebrows rose and she added, "She took up sewin', but she never completed those courses *tan poco*."

Mama's Critters

Mama felt more at ease with animals. She unintentionally loved them . . . to death. And sometimes accidents occurred for "plain lack of common sense." That's what I had heard Grandpa say.

Mama had a pet terrier named Lucky when she lived in New York. Known for his sweet disposition and playfulness, Lucky was everyone's favorite dog. Those were the days when neighbors gathered and visited on the rooftops, more often than not during warm weather.

Unfortunately, Lucky did not live up to his name. While playing on the rooftop with my mother and uncle, he chased after a ball, leaping over the ledge, and plunged six stories.

Another time, while cleaning a fish bowl, Mama inadvertently dumped all the goldfish down the drain. Then there were the black guppies that Grandpa had bought her. Mama thought that guppies thrived in salt water. She sprinkled table salt in the fish bowl for them. Alas! She soon discovered them floating on their backs.

Turtles naturally develop bubbles in their nostrils, but Mama thought hers had a cold. She put a few nose drops in each nostril to cure him, only to notice the unfortunate creature had drowned.

Someone gave Mama a beautiful canary. The bird sang expertly and sweetly and Mama enjoyed feeding him from her hand. But one day, her feathered friend lay lifeless at the bottom of its cage with a bloated stomach. Mama had fed the sweet thing to death.

Before they divorced, Daddy had given Mama three lovely colorful parakeets. She sometimes let them out of their cage for exercise. They'd fly around the room and return to their cage, until someone forgot to close the windows one morning. As they flew away, one by one, Mama watched on helplessly. Guess who had forgotten to shut those windows?

Even in adulthood, Mama continued a trend in caring for animals that led to a comedy of errors. Pre-teen Willie had a pet mouse named Pee Wee and kept him in a cage. The white, soft creature had bulging, pink eyes. After they placed Willie in a boy's home, Mama had the sole responsibility of caring for his furry friend. When time to clean Pee Wee's cage, she first needed to get the critter out. Not an easy task. Pee Wee ran in circles. When Mama grabbed him, the frightened mouse continued to wiggle and squirm in her hands. Determined to keep him from escaping, Mama held onto him firmly. As she coaxed him and stroked his head, at last he calmed. She then got the shock of her life when she realized that she talked to and petted one poor dead mouse.

Then there was a kitten. George found a scraggly kitten to give to Jesse. The problem: Kitty was a fleabag. The poor thing was miserable and covered with fleas and Mama wanted to help. One afternoon, to his horror, Jesse witnessed his beloved kitten yowling, hissing, flipping and flopping. Foam came from the mouth and with one last shudder, Kitty quieted, closing her eyes forever.

"What did you do to my kitty?" Jesse squealed at Mama.

How do you explain to a kid that you were trying to help rid Kitty from her fleas by spraying roach spray all over her?

When it came to newborns, Mama amazed me. Throughout the years, I watched how she was infatuated with my siblings when they were infants. Yet once they walked and had minds of their own, she didn't know what to do with them anymore. Mama loved us, but I think she was at a loss at what to do with us.

Her visit with us lasted seven months. Mama was rested and stronger than she'd been when she arrived. She accompanied me to church and to various fellowship groups two or three times a week. That had become my anchor in life, and I wanted to share the experience with her and have her feel the same. We read the Bible together, and we prayed. I determined to forgive Mama and accept her for who she was.

The way Grandma always wanted.

During that time, Mama decided to make Houston her permanent residence. Donny and I agreed to find her an apartment and help her relocate.

Surely, Grandma was smiling down on us.

Mama flew back to Miami to tie up loose ends, including her rocky and unhealthy liaison with George. Finally, she began sorting through Grandma's things to see what she wanted to keep and what she wanted to donate to the church. But, the pack-rat that she was, she struggled to part with anything. Everything had sentimental value to her. Several weeks later, we returned to help her sell the trailer "as is." Thankfully, we had a bite from a buyer who wanted to live near his family at the same trailer park. He offered cash. What an answer to prayer! Once Mama signed the papers, Donny left to rent a U-Haul.

My patience soon unraveled. Mama wanted to hold on to everything, whether she had any use for it or not.

"She has way too much junk," Donny said, getting frustrated, hauling yet another piece of heavy furniture into the U-Haul.

"What do you want me to do? She won't listen."

"Leave it to me," he said. "You keep her busy."

When Mama wasn't looking, Donny either tossed out or

avoided putting numerous of useless items into the U-Haul altogether. I had to agree it didn't make much sense to hang on to a couple of rusty box fans, or a dresser with wobbly legs, or a TV set with a blown-out fuse, or one more flimsy lawn chair.

But she was on to us. Nonstop she squabbled, trying to put back whatever she found. I warned her that if Donny's patience ran out, we were *all* in trouble. She didn't like to see him upset either.

Days later, we moved her to her own apartment in Houston, tired but relieved.

When he first came to stay with us, we were optimistic for Jesse, knowing he'd thrive on a little stability. He attended family outings that included church, swimming lessons, camp-outs and Vacation Bible School during the summers. At school, he took part in basketball, gymnastics, and track-and-field events, and discovered he was a natural athlete.

Jesse turned out to be a goofball who loved to joke and make others laugh—including me. By the time he turned twelve, his mischievousness was anything but amusing. He had become a troublemaker, mixing with the wrong crowd; school became a joke to him, and he wanted nothing to do with rules and regulations.

"Face it, Mary Ann. Your brother is out of control," Donny said for the millionth time. "He's turning into a hoodlum."

Though I didn't want to hear Donny, I knew it was true. Jesse's defiance had indeed gotten out-of-hand in school, and we didn't want his rebelliousness around our kids. They admired him, thinking him "cool," wanting to mimic his behavior. We decided he needed to go back to Mama. After all, I wasn't his mother, and we'd already done everything we knew to do for him, yet he still wasn't happy or appreciative.

Once Jesse returned to live with Mama, he took over in no time. He'd come and go as he pleased. He'd kick the door until she didn't dare lock him out. Once inside, his music rocked the floorboards and blared through paper-thin walls, causing neighbors to complain.

The apartment managers eventually evicted Mama and Jesse. We helped them move to another apartment complex. In no time, history repeated itself. They were evicted again. My teenage brother hadn't changed, and Mama didn't do anything differently.

Definition of insanity: Doing the same thing, expecting different results.

Jesse's rebellion became Mama's constant agony. Yet I knew she continued to tolerate his behavior, cater to his every whim as she had done when he was a baby, and treat him like an unruly pet.

"Mama, what are those bruises on your arm?" I asked after picking her up to go grocery shopping one day.

"What are you talking about? You know how I bruise easily."

"Jesse did this to you, didn't he?"

"No, no. You're trying to cause trouble. I bumped into the wa—"

"Stop covering for him, Ma!"

"Nothing happened," she insisted. "It was an accident."

Obviously, Mama lived in denial, a place she found familiar, comfortable. I could not deny their problems; neither could I help them. Now they lived in the same town with us, a constant and hurtful reminder that their move from Miami—although I had hoped otherwise—served to bring more drama.

During those four years, I found myself on a perpetual journey on a road called Forgiveness. I continually exercised forgiveness with my husband, then my mother, and so on. A breakthrough came in trying to understand Mama's idiosyncrasies when I realized she was an emotional train-wreck *before* I came into the world. She had always been unable to see the sun for the rays, and had felt powerless to change her circumstances. Although childlike in her thinking, I believed she did the best she knew.

I was certain of that.

CHAPTER 39: HAPPY BIRTHDAY!

DONNY APPEARED COLLECTED. Contented. Even civil. He hadn't touched a drop of liquor in years. Six and a half years, to be exact. In his work, my husband was productive and proficient in expressing directives. He had made strides to undo some of his wrongs. I was proud of him for that. Even so, since his sobriety, he wasn't much of a gabber. At least he wasn't with me. We practiced communicating and sharing our feelings. We went on more dates. But opening up remained difficult. On occasions, I'd see him eyeing me as if studying me, but he wouldn't say a word. Afraid of what he might say, I pretended not to notice.

Donny spent more time with the children. He played soccer with Daniel and attended Cub Scout events; he even took him on fishing trips. With the girls . . . well, he'd break down by giving them money to buy what they wanted. Once he had the dough, it seemed easier for him to give his money than give his time.

Overall, he had come a long way. I had started to trust again.

One night, Donny came home with his charming, dimpled grin and told me to get dressed. He hinted he had a big surprise in store. I couldn't decide what to wear, and my new perm hadn't curled tight enough. On top of everything else, I had a cold sore at the corner of my lip that I tried concealing with makeup.

"Don't become like your mama," Donny warned. "Late for everything."

"Oh, for Pete's sake." I groaned, changing outfits for the third time.

"Sur-prise!"

I entered a closed section of the restaurant with my hand over my mouth, my heart beating out of my chest. Donny had arranged a birthday bash for me with twenty of our close *amigos*.

I surveyed the faces. We had bonded throughout the years at weekly Bible studies and during church functions. We'd been in one another's homes countless times. In truth, Donny and I been to *theirs* more. I still had self-doubts, feeling inept at playing the proper host, ashamed that my furniture was too plain, my dishes mismatched, or that I had more Tupperware than actual drinking glasses. But once in their homes, I felt welcomed and accepted.

Enthralled by the festivities, delicious food, and the warm gathering, I lay aside my worries of inadequacy and concentrated on the night before me, never wanting the moment to end.

After the waiter served cake and coffee, my friends sang "Happy Birthday." When Donny patted my arm, I leaned toward him, fully aware of his mischievous eyes and dimples.

He handed me a card and I began to read what he had written. At the bottom he scribbled, *The Eagle Has Landed*, which I read aloud. I chuckled along with the others, not quite knowing what that meant. Donny then placed a small box in my hand. My heart froze. All eyes fixed upon me.

I fumbled to open his gift: a diamond ring to go with my gold wedding band!

We had been together for fourteen years. We had four beautiful children, and more than six years ago, Donny had stopped drinking—cold turkey. Throughout our marriage, turbulent storms roiled and raged internally as they did externally. There had been bumpy roads with potholes the size of those found in Houston's streets. But through those seasons I had learned resiliency and forgiveness, even when everything in me wanted to give up and seek revenge.

No longer was I motivated by fear. I truly believed that prayer and my faith in God were the glue that held me together thus far as a woman, wife and mother. I believed faith had succeeded in holding our marriage together and now I was starting to enjoy the reward of my perseverance. I thought the worst was behind us.

I was thirty years old.

Ten months later, events set in motion by Hurricane Hugo revealed that I was only in the eye of the storm.

Running in Heels: A Memoir of Grit and Grace

CHAPTER 40: STORMS STRIKE – 1990

LESS THAN A month after celebrating my birthday, Hurricane Hugo devastated the South Carolina coast. Donny trailed the violent storm with the company he worked for, anticipating at least two or three years of disaster work. Before he left for Charleston, he assured me that frequent flights home wouldn't present a problem. He expected to be busy, and that was a good thing: Steady work. Steady income. Frequent flights home.

"No problem," he had said.

I believed him. But soon after, my doubts resurfaced.

Ring.

I reached for the phone. "Hello?"

"Hi," Donny's voice answered flatly. "It's me."

My heart pounded in my chest. "When are you coming home, Donny?"

"Not anytime soon."

"The kids are asking every—"

"I'm going to wire you some money for them," he blurted.

"Donny, you said you were coming home more often."

"Don't nag me, woman. I'm very busy here."

I closed my eyes, feeling the beginning of a migraine. "Well, it's been more than two months. Christmas is around the corner."

"You have no idea what I do for a living."

"*What?* You promised me. You promised the kids."

"Look, I'll come home when I'm ready."

"'Ready?' Why are you *talking* this way?" I studied his features on the family portrait on the wall, searching for clues. *Is it happening again?*

"I'm the one getting the short end of the stick here," he barked.

"*What* are you talking about?" A cold sweat came over me. "You're acting as if you want to pick a fight over the phone."

"Let me talk to my son."

"Working this way was *your* idea, remember?" I switched ears on the phone. "*You* said it wouldn't be a problem flying home twice a month."

"Put my son on. I don't have time for this."

He might as well have slapped me. I called Daniel to the phone and, still flustered from our conversation, went into the kitchen for a cup of coffee to calm my nerves. Donny's indifference sounded too familiar, too distant, too cold, an unwelcome voice from the past. I couldn't help questioning what he had done for my birthday—was it all for show?

Three Weeks Later

"What are you doing? Gimme that." I grabbed the Copenhagen from his hand before he could open it.

Big mistake.

He backhanded me.

My entire face numbed.

My mouth.

Heart.

Without saying another word, he turned the music off.

Hot tears rolled down my face. Dread crawled in my gut. I glanced at the kids from the side view mirror. They sat with their mouths opened, too stunned to speak.

When Donny quit drinking, he had stopped hitting me.

Until now.

As soon as we got home, we marched in the house and locked the door behind us, leaving the kids outside to play in the cool of the day, while Donny and I exchanged heated words inside.

My husband had begun to make old excuses for his absences: Too busy. Too tired. Too late.

I was losing heart.

We were losing him.

Again.

Donny, having returned to Charleston, purchased roundtrip airline tickets for Daddy and Gloria to visit the kids and me for an entire month. I warmed up to the idea of their early summer arrival, and of Donny's unexpected and generous belated Christmas gift to me.

Once my out-of-town guests arrived, I resolved to lay all marital melancholy aside. My daddy always knew how to make fun times and fond memories. In no time, my kids were having a blast, playing ball with him, swimming in the pool, going to the park. They played silly games and loved to straddle his shoulders as he whinnied and galloped about like a horsey—the way he had done with me as a child. I found myself enjoying the activities.

"You make one great *caballo*," I said watching Daddy trotting along the playground.

"Giddiup," yelled Angela from his shoulders. My daddy answered by whinnying and stomping his feet like a horse. The kids giggled, and Diana and Daniel pranced around like horses, too, anxious for another turn.

My kitchen instantly became *la cocina de Gloria*. She familiarized herself in my pantry and, soon, the wonderful aromas of Puerto Rico were wafting through the entire house, whetting our appetites.

"Gloria, what are you making?" I asked, watching her pour a batter mixture of spices and shredded meat into a frying pan.

She smiled and answered, "*Bacalao Frito.*"

I never figured I liked codfish before, but did it ever smell good as she fried them in her special way. I couldn't wait to try one.

Mama visited frequently. She spoke fluently in Spanish with Gloria, yet never took the time to teach me the language. Nonstop, they gabbed like old girlfriends. Daddy sat smack dab in the middle of them, looking back and forth with a comical, flabbergasted demeanor, feigning keen interest in their gossiping. I had to laugh.

Three weeks flew by, and one Saturday afternoon we loaded up in the van and headed for the airport. I drove around the terminal and parked at the passenger pick-up area. Donny stood near the curbside waiting with an overnight bag. As soon as the kids spotted him, they bounced out of the van and ran to greet him.

How I miss him, too.

I thought about the long hours my husband worked and

all the heavy responsibilities on his shoulders. Once home, I figured the rifts and miscommunication between us would surely dissipate. I hoped we could mend our unraveling harmony and rekindle the fire.

Might as well have hoped for a blizzard in hell.

After Donny greeted everyone with warm hugs and kisses, I expected mine.

I waited. And waited.

A cold greeting was what I got.

"Hey, you gonna kiss me, or what?" I suggested, walking toward him. What did I lose, my dignity? That was already shot.

He mumbled something and pecked me on my cheek.

Since our so-called conversations on the phone, Donny's demeanor hadn't changed one iota. Distant, preoccupied, as if miles away; his aloofness tore at my heart. I said nothing more. Not wanting to ruin my parents' visit, I put my mask back on.

I was certain Daddy and Gloria saw past the charade and into my heart.

Donny's week back was rather cordial; in fact, he acted more like a guest. With out-of-town family present, I knew we should talk but kept my comments to myself.

The morning sun hadn't yet risen, but I couldn't go back to sleep. I heard Donny downstairs making coffee and then making a phone call. I found this odd because it was still too early for him to check in with his boss. My suspicion grew. I quietly picked up the extension in our bedroom, putting the phone to my ear.

"Hello?" a sultry voice on the other end answered.

I felt the color drain from my face.

"Hello, baby . . . ," he answered her above a whisper.

My insides knotted. I threw the phone across the room. What happened next wasn't admirable. I stomped to the loft overlooking the living room, and glared down at the two-faced monster as he hastily ended his call. How I wished I had a brick to chuck at him then.

Since words were my only weapon, I used them. I used them well. To cut, slash. To hurt him as he had hurt me. I pitched a conniption fit: screaming, cursing. I stormed back into our bedroom. But words weren't enough for what I was feeling. In an instant, one sweep of my arm sent the entire contents on my dresser across the room: a hand mirror he had given me, perfume bottles, a picture frame of us — the "happy couple" — another taken with the kids, a collection of sentimental knick-knacks, now all shattered into a thousand fragments.

Like the hell around me.

Along with my heart.

My hopes.

Dreams.

"Look, it's not you. It's me," he said, charging in. "I'm not happy."

"*You're* not happy? Oh, I know. I can't make you happy anymore. I'm not good enough for you now, except to get your leftovers!"

"You don't understand me."

"Don't you turn this on me," I lashed out. "You're the one who hasn't been faithful, remember?"

"I work hard for a living—"

"And I don't? You know I don't sit around. I keep a tidy house. I take care of the kids, wash their clothes, cook their meals, and take them to all their activities—"

"I can't talk to you."

"But you can talk to *her*?"

He said nothing.

"Who is she?" I demanded. "I'll claw her eyes out!"

He turned to go back down the stairs.

"How can you do this to me again?" I threw my wedding ring at him.

Donny stormed out of the house. I felt ashamed knowing Daddy and Gloria, within earshot in the guestroom, had heard everything. With the children fully awake, my parents tried to console them in their room and instructed Anna Marie to keep the younger ones quiet. By the time I went downstairs, Daddy was on his knees praying in Spanish by the bed. Gloria was sitting next to him, tears in her eyes. I listened to the prayer, forgetting to move. Daddy, also crying, glanced up and reached out his hand toward me. I went to him and collapsed, sobbing.

Tomorrow they'd fly back home.

Today was Father's Day.

They didn't know what to say. They didn't know what to do. Daddy and Gloria departed the next day heartbroken and devastated. None of us spoke much or could hold back our tears on the way to Hobby Airport. When we kissed and hugged to say our goodbyes, words stuck in my throat. Daddy wrapped strong arms around me. I was a few inches taller than he but, at that instant, felt smaller. If only I could stay in his arms and be a little girl again.

That same evening, Donny flew back to South Carolina, or rather, back into *her* arms. I felt devastated. This was unlike the flings of his past, and that soon became obvious. Days later, I would scan through our auto insurance papers, shocked about a new vehicle added to the policy. Neither Donny nor I owned a white two-door Camaro. That was when I got a clue about Big Spender's lavish four-wheel gift for his mistress. Then whenever we spoke on the phone, the emotional outbursts between us raged as viciously as Hurricane Hugo had hit.

To my disadvantage, I'd been too dependent on Donny. I'd been a stay-at-home-mom for more than a decade and knew I hadn't played it smart and prepared for the what-ifs. I decided to go on a job hunt and stopped at *First City Bank*. To my surprise, I knew someone who worked there and would put in a good word for me. My brief employment history involved handling cash, so I figured working at a bank would be ideal, as they offered great benefits. After filling out an application, the branch manager interviewed me. Within a week, she called and hired me as a drive-thru bank teller.

The Big Bang

"Whatever happens," I warned, "don't come out." I quickly instructed my kids to lock the bathroom door as a precaution.

Donny had called, his words slurring, saying he was in town, around the corner and coming over to talk. Minutes later, he barged in, smelling strongly of booze.

We sat in the living room—he in his favorite chair, I on the couch. I sat rigid, my arms crossed, and glared into his bloodshot eyes, waiting for him to speak.

Crickets.

I crossed one leg over the other and glared at him quizzically. "Do you love her?"

"I don't know." He cleared his throat. "I feel something for her."

"You *what?* How can you say that after all we've been through, Donny?"

His voice rose. "I didn't plan this, okay?" He readjusted his cap for the third time.

A nervous habit.

"It . . . just happened," he stammered.

"You didn't see this coming. Before you knew it, *poof*, she appeared." I answered sarcastically and added, "What do you know about love?"

He stood, wobbling. "Aw, come on, baby," he said, his tongue thick in his mouth.

"'*Baby*?'" I snapped. "Since when have you ever called *me* 'baby'?"

He shrugged his shoulders. "Okay, honey. Let's just go to bed."

"You must be out of your ever-loving mind."

He stood in front of me and held out his arms. I needed to get away from him. Couldn't stand the sight of him, the scent of him. "You're pathetic. Don't touch me."

I sprang up, stormed past him, and climbed the stairs two by two. I heard him stumbling behind. At the landing, I turned and glared down at the demented, lunatic stranger who was supposed to be my husband. In an instant, he was inches from me.

"Get away from me. You're drunk!"

He stopped and muttered something about taking eight-year-old Daniel back to South Carolina with him.

My blood boiled.

"Go back to your *puta*," I spat. "But you're not taking my son with you!"

"Woman, you don't tell me what to—"

His hand rose—to slap? *No! Something's in—!* A chill ran up my spine.

Boom!

Fire belched from the barrel of his .357 magnum, exploding inches over my head.

"You crazy bastard!" I screamed, my body trembling.

Plasterboard . . . a gaping hole . . . ears ringing. On the landing, I had crumbled to the floor. Although I didn't believe he meant to kill me, it shocked me to the core. With no more fight left in me, I kept from blurting out, relieved to see him stumble back down the stairs, as if he surprised himself for pulling the trigger. He threw himself on the couch and thankfully passed out.

My thoughts jumped back to a story Mama had told me of when she and her man were in the kitchen and how she had feared for her life. He threatened her by saying, "Where do you want *it*?" alluding to the stabbing he would inflict if she didn't shut up. But Mama had said that he only talked that way because he had drink in him. I wondered. *Had I been in denial about Donny's behavior, just like Mama?*

I tiptoed down the stairs, and rushed to where my children hid, to comfort them, while trying to calm the beating of my own heart.

CHAPTER 41: THIS TOO SHALL PASS

DONNY'S DRUNKEN SNORES echoed from below. I closed the bedroom door. As my eyes grew accustomed to the dark, the silhouettes of my children came into focus. Two were asleep on the floor; two were on my bed. It had been a long and frightful night of questions mingled with tears.

While I hoped the eye of the storm had passed, rough weather lingered over the horizon. I knew what I needed to do but didn't know how. Self-doubt wore down my resolve. I had tried leaving Donny before with one child, but now there were four children.

I couldn't bear the thought of raising my children the way my Mama had raised my brothers and me. Fragmented. Bleeding. And wanting.

Questions and concerns tormented me. *Should I call the police? They may take my kids from me again. Should I leave, walk away and never look back? Where does one go with four children? And one with special needs?*

It had taken a great deal of effort to get the proper help needed for Diana. After numerous tests and evaluation at M.H.M.R.A. (Mental Health and Retardation Authority), and DePelchin Children's Center, she was now on several meds and rode on the mini school bus every day to attend those special-ed classes. I racked my brain: What would I do for income? After not working for so long, would my new job be enough *to pay the bills*?

The next morning, I heard Donny shut the front door behind him. He stayed gone for several days after that. *Better this way,* I thought, as I gained a sense of sanity. I needed to save some money, develop a plan.

One day at work, I sensed something amiss and drove home on my lunch hour. As I turned into my street, Donny's blue pickup sat parked in front of the house.

Why would he show up now, when nobody's home?

A cold sweat drenched my back. I noticed his personal belongings tossed in his truck, as fear, and then panic crept through me. My insides turned into a knot; I felt I might throw up. In an instant, all my preconceived plans washed away.

I morphed into that insecure, lost child again.

I barely remember parking the van or going in the house. I spotted him immediately; his back turned, closing a suitcase. "Donny, stop!" I groped for words. "Don't do this! Let's . . . talk."

He faced me, his eyes hard, cold. "Hush, woman," he said flatly, stomping toward the door. "Need time to think." He shouldered past me without stopping.

I followed him and pleaded, "No, not like this. We'll talk to someone, work something out."

He threw an overnight bag in his pickup, opened the door and got in. "You think you're all grown up," he snarled.

But I only felt like an abandoned child.

"Donny, don't leave me," I begged, as he rolled up the window. Yet before he started the engine, I crawled in the back of his truck like a fool, not caring my blue dress stained, or my pantyhose ripped, or my white heels ruined.

He climbed out; strode toward me. For a second, I became hopeful . . . until he grabbed me up by my waist and yanked me out.

I threw myself at him, my arms wrapped around his neck, sobbing, calling his name.

"Donny, Donny . . . don't . . . do this." *He's sober, why can't he hear me?*

With both hands, he forcefully took my arms. Peeled them apart. Shoved me back. He left me standing in the street as his Ford sped away. Tears clouded my vision.

I choked out his name, "Donnnnny!"

He never looked back . . . never . . .

Three Days Later

"Mom! Mom! Are you all right?"

How long have I been sitting here re-living the nightmare?

"Yes, Anna Marie, I'm fine." I wiped my eyes with a tissue. I still couldn't believe how he cast me aside like an oily rag. After he had taken off, I ran into the house, grabbed the phone to call my spiritual mother, Mrs. C, blubbering, "He's gone! He left me! What am I gonna do?"

She had rushed right over. Held me. Rocked me.

"This too shall pass," she whispered.

But I didn't think it ever would.

Locked away in my thoughts, I remained in bed since then. I needed to be strong for my kids, but couldn't quite come out of the funk.

"Mama, you need to eat something," fourteen-year-old Anna Marie insisted, bringing me a bowl of warm oatmeal.

Studying my gorgeous daughter's almond-shaped eyes, admiring her long lashes, I wondered if she'd ever find a devoted husband and be the one to break the cycle of failed marriages and torn relationships. First was my mother's — too many to count — and now my own.

She helped me sit up. "Thank you, Anna. It looks good."

Dizzy.

"How are the kids? Diana giving you a hard time?"

"Not yet," she smiled. Perfect teeth . . . *he* had paid for her braces.

I took a spoonful of my oatmeal and gagged.

"Mom!"

"Anna, I can't. Take this away, please."

She handed me a glass of juice. "Drink some, Mom. I'll be right back."

My head was propped on the pillow, replaying the hellish roller coaster scene of the past five months: *his lies . . . the children asking for him . . . cold bed . . . 'babe' . . . her voice over the phone . . . the pain . . . seeing them together . . . 'babe'. . . my knuckles smashing her face when she came too close . . . his eyes of steel . . . my tears . . . "I'll end the affair," he had promised . . . I believed him . . . more lies . . . drunk again . . . the glint of a gun . . . the blast . . . a hole in the wall . . . into my bleeding heart.*

"Mom . . . ," Anna Marie came in, interrupting my thoughts. "Here, try this." She held out a plate of buttered toast, waiting for me to take a bite.

"It's good," I said, chewing slowly after taking a nibble.

"Okay," Anna said, studying me with a worried look. "I better go check on the others."

I willed the toast to stay down and eased up from the bed. My legs felt like rubber as I crept toward the bathroom to wash my face. I scanned the reflection in the mirror: swollen bags under the eyes, sunken pale face, and a much older thirty-one-year-old glaring back. Then I glanced at a blue bundle, soiled with the smear of truck grease since that fateful day, still crumpled on the floor. It was my dress, *his* favorite outfit, now a cast-off. Dumped. Forgotten.

Like me.

After one quick snatch, I thrust the dress into a trash bag and felt a sense of satisfaction. I took a deep breath and went downstairs to see to my children.

¡No Más!

Eight months after Donny's desertion, he pulled into the drive-thru window at my new job. "Hey, good looking," he greeted me. Said we needed to talk, urging me to meet with him.

My co-workers gloated with amusement.

"Gonna take an early lunch," I said, flinging my purse over my shoulder.

I stood in the parking lot with the strength of a palm tree whipping about in a hurricane. *Who is this man?* I asked myself, gazing over his features, searching for a connection. *Who does he think he is, coming here now, bombarding me with platitudes?*

Miles had separated us: he crossing several states, I blocking the gateway to my heart.

Until now.

"You've lost some weight."

"So have you," I observed.

"I've come back," he said, his eyes moist.

My own eyes dampened. "Why, Donny? Why now?"

"Been doing . . . some thinking." He pulled out a can of Copenhagen from his shirt pocket with a trembling hand. "I was crazy, needed to think—"

"Yeah, and gone AWOL to 'think' for almost an entire year!" I exclaimed, crossing my arms. "Never pegged you for being so slow on your feet."

A grunt was his response. He pinched a clump of black snuff and dipped the tar between his lower lip and gums. After sliding the tin can back into his shirt pocket, his dark gaze bored holes through me. "I want you and my kids," he finally answered, in a slow measured voice.

"You threw me and our children to the wolves, remember?" I huffed back, looking away.

"How can I make it up to you?"

"It's not about *us* anymore, Donny." I turned to face him. The sun made him squint.

"So, you're all grown up now." His voice mocking me, jabbing at my resolve. He pulled on his cap to shield his eyes. "Don't need me anymore?"

Where was he when I needed him? Toying with my heart, treating me like an outcast. How many times had he trampled on my hope, forever taking and giving only when it benefited him? I'm not junk! Last I heard, God don't make junk. No more pain. *¡No más!*

"You hear me?" His face flushed. "I don't want a divorce."

D.I.V.O.R.C.E. Those seven letters—deadlier than any four-letter word. Surely, God hated that word, too. "Oh, so you're all through with your affair?" I scoffed.

"She's not what . . . ," his voice trailed off.

"Trapped in your own web, Donny? She did to you what you did to me?" Beginning to feel a lump in my throat, I dug in my purse, searching for gum.

"Don't want to talk about her; I want to talk about us," he hissed.

"Really? Well, I'm *not* the same woman you left behind."

He spat tobacco juice on the ground. His eyes narrowed. "I'm *still* your husband."

"Think of the kids, Donny. They miss you."

"They don't!" His voice rose. "They love *you* more than they do me."

"If you think that, Donny, then you need to reach out to them more." We stood at the side of the building. I scanned the surroundings to see if any "rabbit-ears" eavesdropped nearby. Relieved there were none, I continued, "You know, you sure haven't acted like you're married. In fact, ever since you left, you haven't sent a dime for the kids. We didn't know where you were, and you certainly didn't care if we were alive." Beginning to feel a headache coming on, my head pounded with every beat of my heart.

"I never stopped loving you," he muttered.

Or I you, but I knew better than to say the words and choked them down instead. "I'm through, Donny. There's nothing left to give."

"You belong to *me*, you know," he said, his voice rising again.

"*Excuuuse* me?"

He moved in closer, touching my arm, "Mary Ann . . . . "

"What, Donny? What?" I shook him off. "More lies?" Hot tears welled in my eyes. "How can you ever be trusted again?"

"Look, I was wrong—"

"Leave me alone!" I choked back the tears. "Go on back to whatever you do and whomever you do it to. I need to get back to work."

I trotted away and left *him* standing there dumbfounded. This time, *I* didn't look back.

Hadn't I given him the best years of my life? Yet he spun my emotions like an unending cycle of a broken clothes dryer, wringing the life out of my happiness, hopes, dreams—my actual existence. He never considered that if he made his bed with dogs, he'd get their fleas. Now, he wanted to traipse back home and pick up where he broke off.

How much can one take? Did he think I'd welcome him with open arms? For more leftovers? Tears burned in my eyes. *God, forgive me, but I promised him nothing in return.* I wasn't about to let him back in my home, in my bed, or in my heart to only break it again.

How many times had I repeated the pattern I'd seen in Mama and hated? *I'm not my mama!* I won't live in denial anymore with a victim's mentality.

Donny's last fling was the end of the road. I put up with his lies and more lies and cheating for the first eight years of our life together. Then for the next seven years, I thought he'd changed and we might enjoy domestic bliss. But no.

He knew I depended on him for *everything*. Then when he went to work out of town, he forgot about God, forgot about me, even forgot about his own flesh and blood—dismissing all four of them.

Until that phone call days later.

Oh, I knew my heart. I might have given him another chance. But then he said he wanted me but '*couldn't* leave the poor girl; not now, not right away.'

Later, I learned the 'poor girl' was five years younger than I was. And pregnant. I remember thinking, *How can they build a life together after they've caused me such misery? How is it possible that they can find happiness when they destroyed mine? And not merely mine, but they've uprooted the lives of our children, and turned them upside-down. Now he's starting a new life — and family — with her?*

Enough was enough. I visited a Christian lawyer. A few months later, after signing the papers, our fifteen-year marriage ended in divorce.

Sometime after, I heard that she had lost the baby.

Then I heard she cheated on *him*.

Running in Heels: A Memoir of Grit and Grace

CHAPTER 42: THE CATCH

MY KIDS AND I hadn't a choice but to move from our two-and-a-half story home to economize—downsize everything. I had a huge garage sale—sold Donny's tool chest, power tools, generator, ladders, fishing poles, tackle box—nearly gave everything away. A man's bargain. They came from miles around and couldn't believe my prices.

The week after, a handful of men from church loaded my boxes and furniture into their vehicles to caravan to a different residence. Twenty minutes later, we arrived at a newly rented, small three-bedroom house in Sharpstown.

I had a new job and a new address.

I kept my same phone number and, shortly after the move, Donny called me. Drunk.

"Hey, baby," Whenever he drank he slurred, in his intoxicated, high-pitched, singsong voice. "I found somebody who loves me . . . !"

I heard a familiar giggle in the background. I instantly recognized *her* voice.

"What do you want, Donny?" I stood impatiently with the phone at my ear, curious of what the call was all about.

"*Natasha* says 'hello.'" More giggling. "I'm gonna be a married man again, baby. So you can't flirt with me anymore—"

"Cut the crap, Donny. I haven't got all day."

"Aw, come on, baby. Aren't you going to wish me—?"

Click. I hung up that phone.

Within a few months after our divorce was final, Mr. Playboy married Natasha, the "home-wrecker." *They deserve each other. I hope they have a wonderful life.*

I wallowed in self-pity. Before long, bitterness ate at me, so much so that I had stopped attending church altogether. I even tried therapy. *Twice.* But for whatever reason, stopped. Yet I will never forget the counselor's comments to me. First, he said I had a resiliency that got me through everything I had ever gone through. I could accept that theory. Second, he said I was a diamond in the rough. That idea was more difficult to embrace; I saw myself as anything but. Perhaps the *brilliancy* of the dazzle blinded me.

It was like a dagger to my heart to know that the one I loved rejected me. No counselor had to tell me about my low self-worth. I tried to overcome. Still, the coat of rejection wasn't an easy cast off. I still carried the hurts. When I took the kids to see Disney's *Beauty and the Beast*, I cried like a baby—over a cartoon, for goodness' sake! I wept when *Belle* knelt by her *Beast*, thinking he was gone forever, and when she pleaded, "Don't leave me."

Yeah, right. They always leave, I thought, glad we were sitting in the dark and no one could see my tears.

During my workdays, my co-workers insisted that it was time to meet someone new and to quit moping over Donny. "There's a whole world out there," they'd chime.

Certain that I was through with men, I found it tough to think about starting new with someone else. Anyone else! I became gun-shy about dating, filled with fresh waves of insecurities, doubts and fears. Meeting someone else meant being vulnerable, possibly opening up to more pain and hurt. Who needed that? Besides, I had my children to think about—one with special needs.

Six Months Later

I agreed to go out with the girls after work. They hauled me through the swinging doors of a popular country-and-western joint called *In Cahoots*. There I started to laugh again, regain self-awareness, and even learned the two-step. But it wasn't until we entered *The Yellow Rose of Texas* that I was caught by the alluring smile of an Irishman from California.

The crowded room pulsed with loud country-and-western music. Couples waltzed and spun across the square wood floor. I tried to follow their moves, but the onlookers at the rail bunched together and blocked my view. Then I noticed that someone slid to the side a couple of inches, enough for me to squeeze in and have a better look. I took my cue.

He leaned over. "Having fun yet?" His voice, pleasant, deep and low, made me feel at ease.

"Not yet," I volunteered.

His laughter lit up my shadows. We exchanged names and, before long, he asked me if I wanted to go for a spin.

"I'm not very good at this," I confessed.

"That makes two of us." His eyes were trusting, his voice soothing. He took my hand and led the way. His gentle touch sent shivers up my spine.

Mark had a rugged but kind, short-bearded face with laughing brown eyes and charm that wouldn't quit. He stood at my same height, wearing cowboy boots, blue jeans, and a western shirt that hugged ironing-board abs. He was two years older than me.

We began dating regularly and talked easily about everything and anything. We came from similar marital backgrounds. We each knew what it was like to be in an abusive relationship, encumbered with alcoholic spouses, broken promises, and betrayal. We both shared the same desires, placing honesty and trust at the top of the list.

When Mark asked one day what my goals in life were, I couldn't answer, turning my face as the tears fell. Consumed with daily matters clouded my vision for the tomorrows. For the first time in a long time, I thought about a future and possibly having one with Mark.

After Mama met Mark, she said to me in private, "You're a lucky woman. He's crazy about you, Mary."

I smiled and felt my heart swell. "I pray he never changes."

There may not have been plenty of money floating around, but in my eyes, Mark proved himself worthy. He waltzed away all reservations in my heart. I felt he could be trusted. He treated me with respect. He took my breath away, loving me for me: tenderly, passionately, completely. He even—as they say in the movies—"made my toes curl." Moreover, as much as he loved me, he loved my children. They loved him in return. We didn't have to compete with any of his friends for his attention. When his buddies told him that other fish were in the ocean (fish that didn't come with four small guppies), Mark boasted, "Not like this one."

The real test came when he had to go out of town. But my fears soon turned to joy as I opened his handwritten letter to me:

Mary A. Pérez

April 19, 1991

My Dearest Mary,

  I've only been gone one day and I find myself thinking of you and the kids and missing y'all. Pretty bad, huh? You're a fine woman that any man would count himself lucky to be seen with. I really enjoy our quiet times together – how you hold my hand, the way you snuggle up under my arm, our talks, your voice, your smile.
  It's these little things that mean the most to me, and I find myself missing them tonight. I don't know where we're going, but I'm sure having fun getting there.

While it may have been true we didn't know where we were going, we remembered where we started. And that was enough.

For three years, Mark and I remained inseparable. I loved his adventurous spirit for the outdoors, and watching him with my gang. He took us on weekend outings and summer vacations, which included dove hunting with Daniel, camp-outs in tents, air shows, the circus, barbecues at the parks, and a vacation to Disney World. Though raised in Miami, I had never been to Disney World and was as excited as the kids were to finally experience it. We stopped by my dad's, and he and Gloria traveled with us—all paid for by Mark.

But my all-time favorite excursion: A ten-day road trip to Mark's hometown in beautiful California. We stopped in San Diego where we spent the entire day at the zoo, the largest and grandest I had ever strolled through. Our second day was spent in Los Angeles. I anticipated bumping into Hollywood glitter in the form of Tom Cruise or Mel Gibson. To my shock, I indeed spotted a celebrity in the crowd at Universal Studios. Tiny Tim! I kept hearing his song *Tiptoe Through the Tulips* in my head. In Monterey, we cruised past greenery, plush golf courses, Clint Eastwood's home, and the infamous Lone Cypress tree I've seen in photos. In San Francisco, we hung out at Golden Gate Park and toured the Museum of National History before visiting Mark's sister. We stopped in Salinas and visited his aunt, and finally his brother and sister-in-law in Modesto. We spent the night in their home. My kids happily camped out in their backyard in a tent under a full moon. Out of respect for Mark's Jehovah's Witness family, I slept on their couch while Mark spread out nearby on the floor.

The most memorable time spent was at Yosemite National Park. As far as the eye could see, the view was breathtaking, beautiful and serene. We enjoyed a picnic and watched a spectacular waterfall close by. Then we went exploring.

Wherever Mark led, the children followed. I never cared much for heights, so I stayed on "lower" ground, taking pictures. The kids trailed Mark, fearlessly climbing one rock after another. When he wanted to venture farther along where the river ran, he instructed them to wait for him while he climbed higher. But when time to descend, Mark found himself in a tight spot. From where he stood, the drop was too far down to hop off. After some scheming, he threw his wallet and keys to the children and then bravely jumped into the cold river and swam until he could gain better footing and get back on track. Before returning, he and the kids continued with their hiking, surveying their surroundings. Just as I started to get worried, they raced down the trail with Mark in tow.

"Mommy! Mommy!" they cried in unison.

"Where'd you guys go?" I asked.

"You should have seen Mark," they said, trying to talk at once.

As Mark drew closer, I noticed he was soaking wet. Amidst the ranting of what had occurred, I teased him by saying he had fallen into the river (instead of voluntarily jumping in).

In the Still of the Night

One evening, I lay in my man's arms while we talked in the dark.

"You've grown quiet on me," Mark whispered, kissing the top of my head.

I felt heaviness in my heart but didn't know how to explain it.

"What are you thinking?" Mark persisted.

"'Bout stuff."

"I'm all ears."

"Mark, I need for you to understand something. As much as I love you, I feel miserable inside."

"Okay, now you're beginning to worry me."

"Listen, babe. You know how I feel about you. Yet, what's troubling me won't go away. I know the difference between 'playing' church and in being in true fellowship with the Lord. At one point in my life, I felt so close to God. But after Donny . . . well, I grew bitter, cold, and drifted away from my faith."

Mark caressed my hand for reassurance but remained silent, allowing me to speak. I knew it was now or never and continued.

"Sometime after Donny left, I dated a couple of guys and acted a fool, as if I was a reckless teenager again. Except this time in front of my own children, the way my mom had done with me. Yet I knew better, and I feel as if I've frustrated the grace of God. His Word says that if we honor Him, He will honor us. I need His forgiveness. I need to repent."

Tears rolled down my face as I waited for Mark to speak. I feared that, by sharing something so personal with him, he'd label me a kook, a Jesus freak, and write me off. Still, I had to try to make him understand my heart. We promised that we'd never keep anything from the other. Mark reached for his can of Mountain Dew without responding. His silence was killing me. Most likely, I was taking the risk of throwing away what I'd searched for my whole life. Why couldn't I be satisfied with what I had? Did I have to push my Christian beliefs on the man I loved, maybe pushing him away for good in the process? What was wrong with me? As great as Mark was, I ached with a void in me that I knew no man could truly fill.

I'd seen that pattern amplified in my own mother's floundering relationships throughout the years. If any man showered my mama with attention, she threw herself at him. Yet no man met all her needs or made her whole. After my daddy, no matter how far she searched, she never found "the one." While I believed Mama's behavior created the wrong example for me, in time I repeated similar patterns.

After my separation, I knew I couldn't stay at home. I had to find a job to earn income. But my being away left the children's safety net to unravel. She tried, but since Mama wasn't the world's greatest babysitter—even though she was present—the kids fended mostly for themselves.

I felt guilt-ridden a long time afterward. A complete failure.

Children watch. Learn. Imitate.

Tired of pretending I had everything together, deep down I knew God had always been the glue in my life. I knew what was right, what was true. But would living that truth now make Mark leave?

What if I'm abandoned? Again. Forever?

Incomplete individuals usually search for fulfillment and happiness in others instead of finding their sense of well-being and self-worth from within. But I had learned that my completeness didn't come from having faith in any man, but in a perfect God who loved me unconditionally, like no other.

I loved Mark, wanted him by my side and even believed that God had brought us together. But it wasn't enough. My heart threatened to pound right out of my chest; his silence was eating away at me.

Gently, my man took his thumb, wiped my tears, and spoke four words I will never forget:

"Let's find God together."

New Beginnings

Days later, Gwen, a dear friend from church, shared something with me. She suggested that, instead of waiting for the perfect timing to marry, that we move forward in becoming husband and wife at the courthouse. The formal wedding plans could wait for a later date. She reminded me that Easter was around the corner, and there was no better time for a new beginning.

"Dresses of the Beast?"

Mama and I sat at Olive Garden poring over the menu. Once we ordered, I leaned forward, anxious to share some news with her.

"Mama . . ." I said slowly, "Mark and I have decided . . ." I paused for the effect.

"Yes?"

"To go to the Justice of Peace," I gladly finished.

Silence. A blank, stoic stare.

"What? What's wrong?" I demanded.

"Dresses . . . of the . . . beast?"

"Say what?"

"Mary," Mama gushed. "You said, 'dresses of the beast,' I don't under—"

"*I* said—? You're kidding, right?"

"But Mary, that's what I heard you say—"

"Mama, I can assure you, I said no such thing!"

Five minutes went by as we bickered over what she thought she heard what I said to what I actually had said, sounding more ridiculous by the minute. Once the real news of my engagement finally hit her, she started smiling, then giggling. *¡Por fin!* I saw the joy I'd hoped my original announcement would create. At that point, we both started snickering until we burst out laughing with tears in our eyes, like those times when she would tell me quirky stories as a kid.

I loved my mother. I had come to terms with the fact that we walked different paths and, most times, didn't even speak the same language. Right or wrong, it was far better for me to see her as a friend to share jokes with than for me to seek her out as a source of motherly advice. I had to accept this about her and forgive her (multiple times), while I sought healing for the pain that stemmed from my childhood with her. I heard it said: A mother-and-daughter relationship can be complicated. It'll tear you apart if you let it.

A minister once said, "Love them, bless them and set them free. People must find their own path. We may give them help, wish the best for them, but ultimately allow them the freedom to choose their own way."

While my lunch date with Mama was an unusual one, I would always remember the moment when something serious turned out comical. "*La vida loca,*" as they say.

"I Do"

On April 6, 1994 — three years after meeting my soul mate and best friend — we joined hands and hearts, locked eyes and announced, "I do" at the Justice of Peace, with Mama present.

Mark and I promised to love, honor, respect each other and remain committed in our marriage, no matter what. We also agreed that if we ever disagreed or became upset with one another, the word "divorce" would never come up. Seven months later, we flew to Miami to have my dream wedding. I wore a tea-length, off-white dress, and walked down the aisle with Daddy. At last, Mark and I repeated our vows before God, a minister, family and friends.

Twelve-year-old Daniel was the best man and gave a heartwarming speech. I was so proud of my son. There wasn't a dried eye present. The girls looked stunning in their mauve dresses. We took photos, cut the wedding cake, and sipped

Running in Heels: A Memoir of Grit and Grace

Our Wedding Day - a match made in Heaven!

on champagne. Just as we did when we first met, we gazed into each other's eyes and danced. Our theme songs—we had two—*The Dance*, by Garth Brooks, and *All My Life*, by Linda Ronstadt.

After the reception, we checked into our suite on the fifteenth floor of the Marriott. Come morning, Mark nudged me awake and said that breakfast was on the way. While I went into the bathroom to get ready, Mark let in the bellhop who arrived carrying a covered silver tray.

"Babe," Mark soon called. "Come on out; the food's ready."

Finished with my makeup and hair, I was more than ready for some coffee.

"Mark, *where's* breakfast?" I asked, fearing the answer.

"Right out here, my love." He smiled and reached for me.

"Mark, no. I can't." My eyes shot out on to the balcony. A cloth-covered table topped with a vase of yellow roses held breakfast, a pot of coffee, and a pitcher of orange juice—fifteen floors up. And me so skittish about heights! Uncertain whether it was the fear of falling or the fear of heights that freaked me out, I tended to get vertigo.

"Come on, babe," Mark pleaded. "It'll be fun. You can do this."

Wanting to be a good sport and not ruin the *fun*, I inched my way out and tried to remember to breathe. The process took a minute or two, while Mark patiently continued to coax me, holding my trembling arm.

Several minutes later, finally seated, we enjoyed our cheese omelets, patty sausages, flaky croissants and fruit salad. When we finished, Mark leaned over the balcony to enjoy the view below. I nearly passed out.

After our meal, we went on a mini day-cruise. Under the sun's rays, we sipped on Piña Coladas while Caribbean music played. A couple of hours later, we stood at the far end of the boat deck to join in with others skeet shooting across the blue ocean.

Back on land, we strolled along Bayside, munching on *empanadas* (fried meat pies) and sipping on coconut drinks. Live bands played Spanish music as couples danced *Merengue* and *Salsa* until late into the evening.

I couldn't get over how downtown had changed since I was a kid.

"You know, Mark, this whole area used to be called Bayfront Park, and once a week I came here with my grandparents."

"So, you did the Latino moves as a youngster?"

That image alone made me chuckled. "Oh, no." I laughed. "None of this outdoor festivity took place here back then. Besides, my grandparents would never have approved of such nonsense."

I thought back to those weekly outings as a child with my grandparents, which always filled me with a sense of love, security, and adventure. It was fitting that the same warmth of well being flooded my heart, returning here as an adult with the love of my life.

CHAPTER 43: FULL CIRCLE

BY 2001, I HAD worked two years for a reputable high-end carpet-cleaning company. I started out as a receptionist, and then promoted to inside sales. I sported around in a Jeep Grand Cherokee and I'd been married for seven wonderful years. Mark had become a devoted Christian, and we attended church as a close-knit family. In April, we purchased our home southwest of Houston in Fort Bend County. Five months later, while driving to work, my tranquil life was interrupted by distress and unexpected terror.

On September 11th, around 7:50 in the morning, I heard on the radio that a plane had crashed into the World Trade Center in New York. As soon as I arrived at the office, I flicked on the TV to see the live broadcast of a massive hole in one tower caused by the plane's impact. Co-workers gathered around and we couldn't peel our eyes away from the screen. Black smoke billowed out the building, soon engulfed by flames.

We heard what we didn't want to hear and continued to see unbelievable images that will forever be etched in our minds. My heart plummeted as I saw a second plane hit the other tower. Buildings collapsed minutes later and we all gasped in horror knowing that hundreds—thousands—lost their lives.

That night, President Bush spoke powerful words: "Freedom itself was attacked this morning by a faceless coward, and freedom will be defended."

Freedom isn't free, I thought, *and freedom is worth any cost.*

For the first time I truly felt free. Free from the clutches of loneliness. Free from wondering where the next meal was coming from. Free from being a prisoner in my own mind, my marriage, my home. I also knew that, in a split second, a life could be gone. I experienced that harsh truth the day I lost my baby sister by a hit-and-run driver. I lived through that stark reality from nearly drowning twice as a youngster. I relived that nightmare every time my former husband abused me and, again, on the day he shot at me.

A couple of months later, we enjoyed our first holiday in our new home and all the festivities by the fireplace while sipping hot chocolate and eggnog, taking pictures and exchanging gifts. Everything felt warm and cozy with a household surrounded by love, a great contrast to my upbringing. My lovely family that morning included my husband, son, daughters, son-in-law, and Mama.

As I gazed around and counted my blessings for each new beginning, I never imagined what else fate had in store for me.

"I'm in a bit of a pickle," Donny said over the phone. "I don't have anyone else to turn to."

"What's the matter, Donny? What's wrong?"

"You know . . . this is hard. I wouldn't ask you if I didn't need . . . ," his voice trailed off.

"I know that, Donny." He had always been a self-sufficient man to a fault. I knew that this phone call had required him to swallow — perhaps choked on — his pride.

"I'm behind on my truck payments; I can't lose my truck. I need new prescription glasses before I can renew my license."

I asked him how much. After he gave me a figure, I told him I needed to talk with Mark and would get back with him later.

That evening, I discussed the call with my husband. "What do you think we should do?" he asked.

"Well, Donny would never call us if he wasn't in a jam," I suggested.

"No, he wouldn't."

"I read 1 John 3:17 and think we can't 'shut up our bowels of compassion' as the Bible teaches. Mark, if nothing else, this will speak to Donny in a huge way. Or at least it should."

"Well, I can't disagree."

"Babe, let's go ahead and wire him the money."

Mark reached out for my hand. "Whether he pays us back or not?"

"Whether he pays us back or not," I said, sensing a peace about our decision. Then we said a prayer and committed the results to God.

"Okay," Mark agreed. "Let's do it."

A couple of nights after Christmas, I got another call from Donny. I peered at the clock. It read well after ten. He said he had taken care of his affairs and temporarily left his truck behind. He wanted to know if we'd pick him up at the Greyhound station.

"You're *back* in Houston?" I asked.

"I couldn't find work. Can my son come and get me?"

Always quick and to the point. "Of course, Donny. Just stay put."

I knocked on Daniel's bedroom door. "Your father's in town."

With only my son left living at home, Mark and I were semi-empty-nesters. My instruction to Daniel was to bring his dad straight home. "Don't go anywhere else," I said. "It's late, and he can crash in the spare room."

With a grin and an air of determination, Daniel said, "Don't worry, Momma, he won't get past me." At the age of nineteen, and just a hair over six feet, my boy towered over his dad.

I waved as Daniel drove off, and then went to wake Mark to tell him of our soon-to-arrive guest.

"Er, excuse me?" Mark asked, blinking, sleep still in his eyes.

I cautiously told him what was about to transpire. "Soooo Mark. Whatcha think?" I squeaked, hoping to make light of the subject.

Mark slowly sat up, processing what I had said.

Needles of anticipation pricked as I waited—half-expecting what his answer might be—knowing what any other husband would say.

"First . . . ," Mark began, squinting in my direction. "I'm not overly happy about this. Second, I do trust you, and third—"

"Yes . . . ?" I spoke out.

"This *is* the Christian thing to do."

A sigh of relief escaped from my lips. "Oh, Mark, I knew—"

"And fourth," he continued, "I need to finish waking up. Any coffee?"

I gave my sweet husband a smooch and bounced away toward the kitchen.

An hour later, Daniel returned with a solemn Donny. He stood at the doorway haggard, not the self-assured man we were used to seeing. He wore a faded jacket covering a wrinkled, cotton shirt. His hair, streaked with gray, hadn't been touched up with Grecian formula. Dark shadows circled his eyes. Stubble covered his unshaven face. His shoulders slumped.

Mark offered him a handshake. "You look as if you've been to hell and back, guy."

Donny sighed. "Yeah, buddy." He scratched his head and put his cap back on. "You can say that all right," he chuckled, pumping Mark's hand.

"Well, come in and sit. Mary's in the kitchen warming a plate for you."

"Oh, now, don't go to any trouble. I don't need anything."

While Donny ate my homemade lasagna, he told us about his ordeal trying to start his own construction business. He'd landed a remodeling contract, and used most of the retainer to purchase materials. Then the homeowner decided to go on vacation, putting the project on hold, and left him entirely out-of-pocket.

"You turned out to be a good cook," Donny commented, yawning.

"Yeah, imagine that," I said, remembering all the times he had given me grief because I couldn't boil water.

The time well past midnight, Mark and I tried to convince Donny to sleep in the guest bedroom.

"Thank you, but I'll be fine," he said, leaning back the recliner. "I don't want to be any more trouble. I'll just get a little shut-eye right here." One night turned into two, two into three. Eventually, Donny relented and began sleeping in the guestroom.

My Mark never ceased to amaze me. For him to allow my ex-husband into our home to live with us was a remarkable show of his trust. Mark showed true Christianity in action, which spoke volumes to all who knew us.

Sunday morning, the church band played and the music leader set the tone to praise and worship in the congregation. Pastor's lesson on the "God of Second Chances" and "New Beginnings" was timely. We stood in awe, covered in an aura of harmony. We sensed God and basked in His presence.

I knew what it was to lose hope, to wonder if there might ever be a day of reckoning for me; to wonder if my burdens would ever lift. Only when I truly learned to let go and trust in the "Burden Bearer" did the pain from past hurts ease. I learned many lessons—none overnight. Then I discovered inner healing.

First, I had to forgive myself. I had my own flaws and knew I'd failed miserably and made tons of mistakes as a daughter, wife, and mother along the way. Second, I had to forgive those who had hurt me deeply. That included my mother and, of course, my former husband Donny. While I didn't believe I'd forget, I came to the place where I could remember without the pain—a huge breakthrough for me.

The stirrings of my heart in church that morning had me praying for two people: the one sitting on my right, that he'd always speak words of wisdom and that his heart would be forever one of understanding. For the one on my left, I prayed that he would learn to forgive himself and accept the Peace Maker.

On my right sat my husband Mark, the most gentle, patient, and forgiving man I knew. To my left sat Donny, now fifty-eight, still the most prideful and self-reliant man I had ever known. Daniel, a spitting image of him, sat on his left. There I sat on the pew, smack dab between the two men who had affected half of my life.

While Donny was at our home, I watched him demonstrate true humility coupled with forgiveness. Home was where he and Mark exchanged handshakes, shared opinions about world events and work-related matters. Home was where Donny grew closer with our son, while offering a listening ear and an open heart.

A few days later, we gathered, clicked champagne glasses with friends and shot fireworks to welcome in the New Year. I felt confident and positive about the future, certain that all the pieces of the puzzles of unresolved issues were reconciled. I never imagined that a year later, my faith would be unsettled yet again.

Running in Heels: A Memoir of Grit and Grace

CHAPTER 44: A LEAF IN THE WIND

"To everything there is a season, and a time to every purpose under the heaven: A time to be born and a time to die . . ."
Ecclesiastes 3:1-2

OUR DEAR FRIEND, Ronnie, had become gravely ill. Months later, we were shocked and heartbroken to learn of his passing away. The news shook Donny to the core. When he asked if I would accompany him to a men's clothing store and help him choose a black suit to wear for Ronnie's funeral, I said yes. While there, he wanted to purchase a new one for Mark too, and wouldn't take no for an answer.

Donny stayed in our home for nearly six months without touching one drop of liquor. He made amends with his boss and buddy, Chuck, and had begun working for him, as if he never left. They shared a great kinship and understanding. More than employer and employee, they were more like brothers. Once again, Donny put in long hours, often too worn out to eat a full meal when he came home. He usually went straight to bed after a bite and a shower.

Mark and Donny liked to share jokes between themselves by calling each other "husband-in-laws." They welcomed the mornings over coffee and Fox News before heading off for work. Weekends consisted of house chores, and Donny went out of his way to do whatever he felt needed to repay the loan. He had already repaid the money we'd wired him, yet he still couldn't do enough for us. He replaced our cedar fence with new boards and had a repair crew work on the brick wall outside our home. He even talked about getting some of his men to re-do the driveway and to landscape around our house.

By June 2002 — before his fifty-ninth birthday — he said it was time for him to move on. He left, on good terms, to reside at a rental property where he supervised a remodeling project.

Six months later — six days before Christmas and ten days before our first grandchild was born, I received a shocking call from Donny's roommate. She said she'd been unable to rouse him that morning and immediately called 911. They rushed him to the hospital. But on the way there, Donny had passed away.

He was gone.

The news hit me like a freight train. I recalled then how he had always said he never wanted to live past sixty. They say hypertension contributed to his demise, but I couldn't help wonder if his end was from that or something else.

In a daze, I called Mark at work. Somehow, I told him to come home. I don't recall all I said to him. Within half an hour, he and Daniel arrived together, running in. Like a statue, I still sat on the floor by the phone, too stunned to move. I tried to speak in a controlled voice but blubbered out, "Donny's . . . dead!"

While I may not remember every detail, I would never forget the shock and the pain that traveled my son's face before he looked away and curled on the floor in a fetal position. In three short months, my boy would turn twenty-one years old. And now his father was gone.

After some time, we agreed that we needed to go to the hospital and say our goodbyes.

Farewell

If I didn't know better, I would have thought he was peacefully napping.

Time froze as I gazed down at the man who had fought his demons. Vivid memories rose to the surface of my mind: his dimpled smile, lilting voice, broad shoulders, bow-legged stance, and the shuffling of his feet when he walked. Recurring thoughts of the what-ifs raced through my mind. At that moment, I remembered the good and not the bad, his strengths instead of his weaknesses, his triumphs instead of his failures. Nothing else mattered.

Anna Marie barged into the room, rushing to his side as if to wake him from sleeping. "Dad! Dad!" she shouted, shaking him. "Dad!"

"Anna," I spoke sharply and held her hand still. I softened my tone, "He's gone."

"But why, Mom? Why...?"

"Anna, I don't know. It was his time; he was ready to go. He never wanted to grow old, become a burden." My voice trailed off. I recalled what he had said, how he wouldn't live past sixty, as if sixty was old, too old, and he never wanted to get "like that." How soon the years pass.

"No, Mom!" Anna Marie shook her head in disbelief, red-face. "Not yet!" she sobbed.

I held her tight and cried with her.

Soon the others arrived. We gathered around. My baby girl, Angela, was nine months pregnant with her first child,

and I was concerned for her well-being. But when she gently placed Donny's immobile hand over her swollen belly, I broke down.

As always, Mark's arms were there to comfort me.

Only God knows the future; we humans don't know from one second to the next. I learned a long time ago that my attempt at controlling anything was futile.

"Did he make it? Did he make it?" I found myself asking that nagging question. In the end, Carolyn and I shared a common belief that Donny not only made it to glory, but that his brother in the Lord, Ronnie, ushered him in.

Summer 2006

It's hard to breathe while sobbing at the same time. I never imagined, after so many years, *how much my heart would still hurt.*

With Mark's encouragement, I had agreed to revisit the baby sister I'd lost four decades before. While vacationing in Florida and visiting my brother, that time had come. One morning, Ruben drove me to her gravesite forty-five minutes from his home to show me where she lay.

The area was a lowly, plain grass-field devoid of even a tombstone for my sister. No headrest. No name written. Or flowers anywhere. Just hard soil. And plenty of weeds. I crumbled to my knees and sobbed.

I needed to share my thoughts and release the heaviness of my heart:

Anna, I'm sorry. Sorry I couldn't do better. Sorry I failed you. I promised, "for always," yet fell so short. If I could hold you now, I would.

Closer.

Tighter.

Never let you go.

If only I'd done more, fought more, loved more. I see myself holding you. Holding you so tight, that time stands still. Darkness cannot swallow us. Pain cannot touch us. Death cannot rip you from my arms. Sorrow cannot engulf us.

God, it still hurts . . . bring healing.

Before I left the cemetery, I purchased a tombstone and had it engraved. Months later, Ruben would send me half the cost.

"*Por fin,*" I imagined my grandma saying.

"Yes, Grandma," I whispered. "At last and long overdue."

Running in Heels: A Memoir of Grit and Grace

Mary A. Pérez

CHAPTER 45: THE BEST FOR LAST

WHILE IT TOOK a while for me to trust again, despite my confusion, I believe God stepped in and brought Mark and me together. When anyone asks where we met, my response, "Perhaps we met at the wrong place at the right time."

As I fixate on my husband's face—his eyes weathered by deep trenches of experience, his hair and beard more gray than brown—a sense of contentment warms me. Mark's gaze still carries the familiar twinkle, the one that speaks of tenderness, honesty and devotion. His eyes say I am a star in his galaxy, and that he will remain by my side through thick and thin. They confirm that together we are one. Moreover, those eyes proclaim that, with God, we can weather any storm.

I hadn't always known gentleness and steadfastness in a mate. But this one was my second chance at love and happiness, assuring me that my mate and best friend accepts me unconditionally and without reservation. He loves me on my worst days. He loves me on my best days. I don't feel alone even when he's away.

My loving husband continues to be my solid *Cerro de Punta*. We recently celebrated our nineteenth wedding anniversary. Together we have faced scores of satisfactions and disappointments, victories and losses, accomplishments and failures, heartaches and joys. Some we understand, some we don't. God gives us peace that exceeds our comprehension.

Mark looked at me tenderly, "You know what, Mary?"

"What?"

"The first time I saw you in those white jeans, I knew you were mine." Mark winked. "For what it's worth," his voice grew serious, "in knowing what you've been through, it's all the more remarkable. You're a fine *Latina* woman, a wonderful mother, and a fun and loving wife."

As I think about God's grace, I am merely an imperfect woman trying to serve a perfect God. With faith in the Heavenly Father, I've journeyed a lifetime of healing in my mind and in my heart. Through the process, God replaced my pain with peace. Furthermore, He has brought me a fine-looking, gentle and kind man to be my helpmate, one easy to love, who believed in me before I believed in myself.

"And," Mark continued, placing a yellow rose in my hand, a reminder of where we had met, "I'm glad that the good Lord upstairs saved the best for last for me."

As his eyes held mine, warmth flooded my heart. "For *always*?"

"For always, forever, and for true."

Our journey together has only begun.

La Familia: From left to right - Li'l Brother Ben, Maggie, me, Big Brother Ruben, Gloria and Daddy.

EPILOGUE

I MISS MY grandparents. They instilled values and stability in me.

In their home, it is where I basked in tranquility, a distinct contrast to the anarchy of the rest of my childhood. I firmly believe that their prayers, without which I would have withered long ago, helped to make me the person I am today. Because their actions demonstrated Christ-likeness, their examples drew me toward my own faith in God. I stayed with them for almost three wonderful years, but even after leaving, I'd always reflect back to that moment in time.

Mama, in her late seventies, lives alone. I have come to the place where I am able to let go and let her live her own life. She enjoys a contented life. She loves playing Bingo and the group outings on the Metro-Lift with Charles, her traveling companion. She has a provider who cleans, cooks, and provides assistance. While Mama has learned not to rely upon me as heavily as before, she knows I will be there whenever needed.

Initially, when I shared with Mama that I was writing my memoirs she laughed and squealed, "Mary, what kind of book is that going to be?"

I chuckled, answering, "Stranger than fiction, of course."

Later, with a more serious tone, Mama asked, "So . . . you're going to blame me for everything that happened?"

While our relationship and communication continue to require work, I assured her that I don't blame her for all the bad. Let me be clear: I do not hate Mama. I NEVER hated Mama. I hated her behavior. I resented everything and everyone that took her away from me as a child! Though my mind may still remember the neglect, I realize that nothing I did or did not do could have changed her then. Or now. I can only change myself, choose to be better and not bitter.

In the dynamic of things, I felt Mama did her best.

As we all try to do.

A few years ago, someone recommended *Irregular People*, by Joyce Landorf, which helped me tremendously. Nearly everyone has a difficult or an "irregular" person in his or her life. They can be emotionally tone deaf and not really hear you. They may be emotionally blind and not see you. They may even have a speech impediment and not say the right thing to you. You cannot please that person; you cannot change them no matter how much you wish to.

I can be at peace and know that the way Mama chooses to live her life isn't a reflection of me.

Daddy recently turned eighty. He retired from working in the produce department at Publix Market, moved to Orlando for ten years, and then back to Miami. He and Gloria remain happily married, sharing the joys of grand-parenting, gardening and their *cafésito* after a hearty home-cooked Puerto Rican meal prepared by none other than Gloria. She is still (now according to Mark) the best cook in town. Both of their children are fine people, married wisely and have added to *la familia* with their own gorgeous children.

My three beautiful daughters each hold different personality traits and talents. To date, Anna Marie hasn't married and for the present—until "the one" comes along—appears quite content and self-sufficient. But her eyes and heart remain open for the right man someday.

After Donny left, I finally received the proper help caring for Diana's demanding and special needs. After much testing and evaluation from the state, she became a resident in a state school for mentally challenged adults that provide the special care she needs around the clock.

I have come to terms with the fact that she is as perfect as God requires her to be. Even so, lingering thoughts remain: *Did I do my best for her? Was my best good enough?*

My youngest, Angela, is married and has given us two

adorable grandchildren, whom we cherish. Watching the way Angela loves her own children is a pure delight. She has much more patience than I ever did.

Daniel's work allows him to travel. For a while he even worked alongside Chuck. Life has many twists and turns; watching them work together, it seemed like it came full circle.

My strapping, handsome son has not married yet. Daniel is a spitting image of Donny, but I thank God he is a remarkable individual in his own right, a young man of integrity and sound wisdom. He'll be a fine "catch" for that special woman one day.

As far as the children and their father's relationship: he and Anna acted more like best buds, and she easily befriended all his conquests after he and I split. Sadly, however, Angela never connected emotionally with her father. She didn't feel comfortable having heart-to-heart talks with him. She remained guarded, always closer to me. Father and son spent many summers working together. One statement that Donny repeatedly made to Daniel was, "Don't be like me; be better than me." While they grew close in those times, our son never felt close enough.

Donny's death was heartrending.

Chuck — for whom Donny worked and whom he loved like a brother — rushed on over when we called him with the devastating news about Donny's sudden death. Chuck generously offered his help by gifting a burial plot and making the necessary funeral arrangements. Together he and Daniel selected a majestic wooden casket, ornate and hand-carved, a beautiful floral spray arrangement, a headstone, and even the pallbearers. Donny would lay to rest under a large, shady oak tree.

Ironically, Donny's final ensemble was the black suit that he had purchased to wear to Ronnie's funeral nine months prior.

On the day of the funeral service, Dorrie drove hours from out of town to give her respects to the family. She had met Donny during the time he and Natasha had split up. Dorrie was the only girlfriend that Donny ever hooked up with that I took a liking to. But he had betrayed her as well. Dorrie, quick on her feet, would have none of it. She didn't stick around for any of his shenanigans. And she and I became close friends—enough to call each other "wife-in-laws."

On the second day of the funeral service, one long distance phone call to the funeral home turned the tide of events. A woman over the phone insisted that she was Donny's wife, and that she was *not* in agreement with any proceedings taking place. It was *she*. Natasha. She threatened to sue the funeral parlor if the ceremony wasn't stopped. (All along, we believed they had gotten a divorce—Donny had said as much—but we never dreamed their divorce hadn't been finalized.) She said she had papers to prove that she was his wife. Her demands: if the family acknowledged her as the wife, only then would she allow the burial to proceed.

There would be no need of the pallbearers' services. Donny's casket couldn't be moved from the building, let alone carried to the plot for burial. Even so, because Donny had fought in Vietnam, some veterans in uniform performed a moving memorial service on his behalf. After they folded the flag and presented it to Daniel, several volleys of shots fired in the sky in Donny's honor. After the guests (many of whom I'd never met before) paid their final respects, we couldn't do much else but leave.

Weeks later, we learned that Donny's remains were placed on ice and "she" didn't come to claim him until three months afterward. Then she had him cremated. The funeral home even tried to bill us for services rendered. Natasha wasn't anywhere to be found.

Earlier at the wake, I had the pleasure of finally meeting one of Donny's daughters from his youth. Dona lived in California and was five years younger than I was! Our eyes met, the tears flowed, our hearts connected. Time stood still as we embraced at length. Afterward, we kept in contact and my children have become well acquainted with their elder sister.

Donny's legacy was a difficult one to grasp. Most of his life he talked a good talk. His internal scars remained deeper than his external ones. Known for running away from responsibilities, he never thought about the hurt he caused others. He never got his affairs in order. He had no insurance, no will, and left no inheritance for his children. Perhaps he thought he had more time. Maybe he figured he'd beat the system. Or fate. Even though his funeral was a bleak day, we gathered to pay our final respects and to remember his strengths and uniqueness.

Overall, Donny remained an enigma. He couldn't be read easily. We never knew what to expect. Even so, he never hesitated to help others. He'd come alive when discussing something pertaining to work or fishing or talking about some accomplishment. I knew he was proud of our kids. In the end, his demeanor mellowed, and those of us who knew him loved him best.

Alcohol abuse destroys lives and families. Alcoholism is the number one drug problem in America, with over 12 million addicted. Through trial and error, my adult children have developed a healthy fear of its dangers, understanding that no one is above the subtle clutches of addiction.

My children continue to live out their own lives and salvation. At the crossroads of life, my prayer for each is that they discover their own dependence upon God. While their father may not have been an ideal role model, I vacillated in that department too. As much as I desired to shield them from patterns of abuse, wrong choices and pain I, just like my mama, remained preoccupied while trying to sort out my own problems. In their adulthood, my kids have experienced their own share of defeats and disappointments, thrills and triumphs, while I could only watch and pray. Scripture says in Luke 12:48, "To whom much is given, much is required." With maturity comes responsibility. I'm glad to add, we have all embraced changes for the better.

The day I located my friend Liz on FaceBook and contacted her, joy flooded my heart. She lives out of town and drove through after attending a conference; we reunited at a local diner. We played catch-up over a glass of iced tea. We talked about the present, and before long, reminisced about the past, some thirty plus years ago.

"I never expected anyone to come to my apartment to try to sell me some Avon, let alone talk about Jesus."

"Mary Ann, I had to come over," Liz said, her eyes growing misty. "I used to hear you and Donny argue. Every time you two fought, I heard everything. I even used to hear him hit you . . . then to hear you crying."

"I didn't know that." I glanced away, and watched droplets of water slide silently down my glass, like my tears so long ago.

"Whenever I heard the fights," Liz continued, "I would lay my hands on the walls and pray for you, until my husband would tell me to get away from there and to mind my own business."

I studied my friend from long ago. "Well, I'm so glad you made me your business. When I needed a friend, *you* were there."

My oldest brother Ruben married late in life and quickly started his own clan. He, his beautiful wife and their three robust boys live in Ft. Lauderdale. During this writing, two of our half-brothers, Willie and Jesse, sadly remain incarcerated for different offenses. One claims his innocence and blames the whole world, our entire family, his lack of education, and not having a father around for all the injustices in his life. The other takes his lumps, is doing his time and blames no one, even though he's been incarcerated the longest. Alas, he appears more comfortable behind prison bars than in the outside world.

There, but for the grace of God, go I.

I read a quote: "Life becomes easier when you learn to accept an apology you never got."

Forgiveness is a choice. I chose to forgive to gain freedom.

I had to pray for the ability to forgive, and God gave me the grace needed to apply that forgiveness. I may still remember, but I no longer carry the pain.

In closing: Sometimes we don't have all the answers to why things happen. I am determined not to allow unanswered questions to derail my faith. Man can't explain God. It is an act of faith to put your trust in Him. Though faith may be a crutch to some, I believe it is also a stepping-stone for something greater.

Today I work for an outstanding customer service company owned by a phenomenal Christian and motivational speaker. Howard has a genuine passion for reaching out and helping others grow in their potential. He saw something in me and has always encouraged me to stretch myself. We appreciate both him and his wife.

Regardless of how I look, what I own, or whose family I come from, it takes a made-up mind to want to do better in *any* situation and to strive to remain teachable. One thing I know is that God loves me. He is for me. He has made me brand new. I am no longer that hungry, insecure little girl anymore. While I've managed to subdue my past, I believe my past hasn't spoiled me, but has prepared me for the future. I may not be perfect but, whenever I stumble, I can wipe the crud off and walk on.

Life is precious. Life is worth living. As I choose to walk in forgiveness, to become better and not bitter . . . I am whole. I am significant.

I am free at last. *¡Wepa!*

About the Author

Although born in the Bronx, I grew up in Miami in a broken home with a mother who found solace with men who loved booze and who never quite understood what to do with children once they weren't babies anymore. Despite the strong example of faith and love set by my grandparents, I followed in Mama's footsteps. After a stint in Juvy, I thought I had found myself a knight in shining armor and allowed him to whisk me away, becoming a teenage bride to a sweet-talking, hard-hitting man twice my age. It would be years of trials and four precious children later, before I found the courage to stand on my own two feet and the faith to forgive.

After starting a new chapter in life with my second husband, Mark, I gained some distance from the pain in my past and discovered a passion for writing. I write because I know I have a story to tell. As a kid, eventually I discovered we were dirt poor. In my teens looking back, I realized that I was neglected and forced to grow up too fast. I was ashamed of my childhood and bitter that I was my mama's mother. As I "matured", settled down, married and had children of my own, along the way I found I was a stronger person because of some of the things that I endured as a child. Once I embraced the God of my grandparents, I became a much better person, too. Not that I have it all together; I still have a few things to learn. But I've learned that it is much better to let go of the bitterness and to forgive, than to hold onto the junk. That was my freedom — still is — and God has called us to liberty, not to be in prison or in bondage. I share my story that I might help someone else understand this; and if I have done that, then I have done a good thing.

I now reside in Houston, Texas, where I am blessed to be the mother of four grown children, "Mimi" to a couple of gorgeous grandchildren, and happily married (the second time around) to a phenomenal man for twenty years.

To date, I am proud to be affiliated with a local women's shelter as a certified advocate for domestic violence and abuse. The more I hear of others' stories of survival, the more I feel their voices need to be heard. My next project will be a compilation of such stories. I am of Puerto Rican descent; however, this is not a Latino problem. This is a universal problem. My vision is that our testimonies, experiences, and life lessons will serve to truly help and inspire anyone who may still be in an abusive state. To let them know that they are not alone and hopefully will see that they, too, can eventually let go of that mindset and lifestyle and come out a better person in spite of what they've been through.

Together we can make a difference!

Running in Heels: A Memoir of Grit and Grace

Dear Reader,

I hope you enjoyed *Running in Heels: A Memoir of Grit and Grace*. I have to tell you that writing a couple of characters was truly an emotional undertaking—namely, Mama and Donny. Although Mary is the heroine of this story, trying to figure out how to escape the poverty and tragedy that life throws her way, she is not without flaws. The reverse is true for the antagonists in her life, all of whom have redeeming qualities, and for whom God offers abounding grace.

After I began writing and joined a writer's critique group, I received so much encouragement to complete my memoirs, and I was challenged to dig deeper. Eventually I started honing in on the social media side of things and became a blogger. There my community continued to grow and I was humbled to receive positive feedback. As an author, I love feedback.

Here's where you come in. Tell me what you liked, what you loved, even what you hated. To whom and what could you relate? I'd love to hear from you. You can send letters to my P.O. Box: Mary A. Pérez, 5300 N. Braeswood, Houston, TX 77096, or via email at maryaperez827@gmail.com. Also, please visit my weekly blog on WordPress, *Reflections From the Heart,* at www.maryaperez.com.

Finally, I need to ask a favor. If you're so inclined, I'd love to have you leave a review of *Running in Heels* on Amazon. It doesn't need to be long, and it doesn't need to be five stars. But you, the reader, have the power now to make or break a book.

Thank you so much for reading *Running in Heels* and for spending time with me.

Much gratitude,

Mary A. Pérez

Mary A. Pérez

QUESTIONS AND TOPICS FOR DISCUSSION

1. What is the story behind the title, "Running in Heels"? Why do you think the author came up with that title?

2. Mary was transparent in showing us some raw and painful moments that she experienced. Can you relate to the author of being a victim and if so, how did you recover?

3. Did you find it helpful to relate to topics in history such as President Kennedy, Vietnam, etc.?

4. Mother and daughter's relationship was a strained one. What do you feel was Mary's compelling force in forgiving her mother repeatedly?

5. In your opinion, why do you think Mary didn't just leave Donny?

6. How important is it for small children to be surrounded by love and acceptance?

7. Name some of Mary's obstacles she had to face and overcome.

8. What do you think Mary's greatest strengths were? What would you say is the main antagonist's greatest strength?

9. Compare this author's style to another. Name a comparative title.

10. Name some of Mark's greatest attributes.

11. What were some happier highlights in this story? What were some of the saddest?

12. Mary claims she loved Donny. Years later, it is obvious she found a second chance at love and happiness with Mark. Compare the two loves of her life.

13. Love lost? Or love gain?

14. In what way does the topic of faith shape the memoir overall?

15. If life was good with her dad and grandparents, why did Mary go back and live with her negligent mother?

16. Can a person love someone to a fault, perhaps enabling them to become co-dependent? Why or why not?

17. "Running in Heels" is synonymous with childhood difficulties. Discuss how Mary's young life evokes images of a child running in heels, shoes too big for her feet, amidst the problems she encounters.

18. Mary's internal strength sustained her from youth to adulthood. Do you think her ability to laugh at herself and her situation was essential for her survival, and how has laughter in the face of stress helped you?

19. Mary's faith was a driving force in her redemption. How did that faith allow her to forgive not only herself, but her ex-husband and mother?

20. How does your life compare with Mary's, and how has her story informed your perceptions of childhood neglect and struggle?

21. Do you think the Child Welfare system failed Mary and her siblings? If so, visualize Mary's life if the system worked the way it should.

22. Are you tempted to value the people in your life based on performance or perfection?

23. How do you define success in the lives of those you love?

24. Have you ever experienced a loss that made you doubt God or feel angry towards Him?

25. In Chapter 13 the term "Damaged Goods" is mentioned. What does that mean to you?

26. Is domestic abuse a Hispanic problem or a universal one? What can we do to make a difference?

www.ingramcontent.com/pod-product-compliance
Lightning Source LLC
Chambersburg PA
CBHW071554080526
44588CB00010B/902